TOWARD CONTINUOUS MISSION

Strategizing for the Evangelization of Bolivia

by W. Douglas Smith, Jr.

William Carey Library

533 HERMOSA STREET • SOUTH PASADENA, CALIF. 91030

Copyright © 1978 by W. Douglas Smith, Jr.

All rights reserved.

No part of this book may be used or reproduced in any manner whatsoever without written permission, except in the case of brief quotations embodied in critical articles and reviews.

In accord with some of the most recent thinking in the academic press, the William Carey Library is pleased to present this scholarly book which has been prepared from an author-edited and author-prepared camera-ready manuscript.

Library of Congress Cataloging in Publication Data

```
Smith, W       Douglas, 1932-
   Toward continuous mission.

   Bibliography: p.
   Includes index.
   1. Missions--Bolivia.  2. Missions--Theory.
I. Title.
BV2853.B4S54      266'.00984        77-21490
ISBN 0-87808-321-9
```

Published by the William Carey Library
533 Hermosa Street
South Pasadena, Calif. 91030

PRINTED IN THE UNITED STATES OF AMERICA

To my Wife

AUDREY,

My Family

Doug, Kirsten, Alysan, Leith and Amy

and

My Colleagues in World Mission

Contents

Figures vi
Tables viii
Foreword ix
Biblical Preface xi
Preface xii
Acknowledgments xiv
Introduction:
 Three Moments in the Missiological Process xvii

PART ONE: TRENDS *(Ethnohistory)*
Significant for the Expanding Bolivian Church and Population, 1900-1980

  1. Clearing Informational Smog   3

  2. Picturing Growth Rates   14

  3. Clarifying the Facts by Upstreaming   29

  4. Looking Ahead to the Unfinished Task:
     Bolivia 1980   51

  Summary   62

PART TWO: PRIORITIZING *(Ethnotheology)*
Biblical Goals toward Continuous Mission

  5. Creation, Conscience and the Church in Mission   65

  6. The Church in Continuous Mission   75

  Summary   92

Contents

PART THREE: STRATEGIZING *(Ethnostrategy)*
Ethnic Participation in Continuous Mission

   7. Rural Mission   97

   8. Urban Mission   116

   Summary   136

CONCLUSION   138

APPENDIX

   A. Statistical Data   143

   B. Target Area Maps   161

BIBLIOGRAPHY   167

INDEX   184

Figures

Figure		Page
1.	1530 Quechua-Aymara Speaking Area	6
2.	1960 Quechua-Aymara Speaking Area	6
3.	Bolivian Age and Sex Population Distribution: 1950	11
4.	Four Types of Church Growth; Four Types of Evangelism	12
5.	AAGR Time Graph	21
6.	ECU 1930-1976 Rates of Growth	26
7.	ECU 1903-1976 Absolute Membership Growth	27
8.	Five Classes of Leaders	28
9.	Map of Nine Bolivian Departments and Capitals with Population Density	32
10.	Principal Components of Ethclass Identity - USA	36
11.	Bolivian Ethnic Group Trends	37
12.	Bolivian Ethnolinguistic Population Distribution	38
13.	ECU Adult Attendance/Membership Compared to Bolivian Population Growth	40
14.	ECU Ethnic Group Trends: 1950-1980	42
15.	1973 Bolivia Map of ECU/AEM/EUSA 271 Active Churches	43
16.	1967 Population Concentrations	44
17.	Bolivian Ethnolinguistic Divisions: 1967	44
18.	AEM/ECU Workers and Active Churches Superimposed on Adult Attendance Graph: 1910-1980	49
19.	Summary Graph	53
20.	Bolivian Ethnolinguistic-Religious Population Distribution - Protestants: 1980	54
21.	Bolivian Ethnolinguistic-Religious Population Distribution - Totals: 1980	55
22.	The Bolivian People: 1980	57
23.	God, Culture and Man	66

Figures vii

Figure	Page

24.	The Decision Making Process	72
25.	Full-Circle Evangelism Process	78
26.	Spiral Model of Continuous Supracultural, Biblical Principles vs. Discontinuous Covenantal Cultural Forms	79
27.	Continuous Mission Process: Making Disciples	83
28.	Continuous Decision Making Process	85
29.	Continuous Mission Process: Building Commitment	87
30.	Composite of the Continuous Mission Process	89
31.	Continuous Workload Transfer	91
32.	Quechua Absorption of Aymaras	102
33.	Bolivian Population Density	103
34.	Bolivian Composite	104
35.	Profile of 100,000 Aymara-Quechuas in Bolivia, 1976	106
36.	Continuous Mission Composite with Mission-Church Overlap	107
37.	ECU in Bolivia: Aymara-Quechua Harvest among 100,000 Compared	113
38.	Bolivian Ethnolinguistic-Religious Population Distribution with Ruibal's 1973 Crusade and Palau's 1974 Crusade	127
39.	Eighteen Responsibility Areas for Cochabamba Churches	128
40.	Continuous Mission Decision Making Process Scale for Urban *Mestizos*	131

APPENDIX A

1.	La Paz Department and Capital City Trends	146
2.	Cochabamba Department and Capital City Trends	147
3.	Oruro Department and Capital City Trends	148
4.	Potosi Department and Capital City Trends	149
5.	Chuquisaca Department and Capital City Trends	150
6.	Tarija Department and Capital City Trends	151
7.	Trinidad Department and Capital City Trends	152
8.	Cobija Department and Capital City Trends	153
9.	Santa Cruz Department and Capital City Trends	154
10.	Guarani Membership in the ECU: 1937-1980	156
11.	Urban and Rural *Mestizo* Membership: 1930-1980	157
12.	Quechua Membership in the ECU: 1920-1980	158
13.	Aymara-Quechua Membership in the ECU: 1930-1980	159
14.	Aymara Membership in the ECU: 1950-1980	160

APPENDIX B

1.	Challapata, 1st Subdirectorate	162
2.	Pocoata, 2nd Subdirectorate	163
3.	Cochabamba, 6th Subdirectorate	164
4.	Oruro, 7th Subdirectorate	165
5.	Potosi, 12th Subdirectorate	166

Tables

Table		Page
I.	Single Year Growth	15
II.	AAGR and Decadal Percent Increase Comparison and Rank	23
III.	Decadal Percent Increase and the AAGR for Three Bolivian Denominations, 1966-1976	24
IV.	ECU Ethnic Groups Ranked by Growth	41
V.	Summary - Resistance Receptivity Factors for the Bolivian Population Based upon Latest Growth Rates 1950-1980	46
VI.	Andes Evangelical Mission - 1976 Analysis of Field Personnel Deployment	47
VII.	Andes Evangelical Mission 1976-1977 Personnel Needs	48
VIII.	Workload Transfer from Mission to Church	76
IX.	Possible Faith Projections 1975-1985	114
X.	Moralistic Bipolar Rural-Urban Model	118
XI.	Forty-Two Participating Cochabamba Churches in Palau 1974 Crusade	129

APPENDIX A

I.	Nine Bolivian Departments and Capitals - 1950	143
II.	Growth of Nine Bolivian Departments - 1900-1980	144
III.	Growth of Nine Capital Cities - 1900-1980	145
IV.	Bolivian Ethnic Group Trends - 1910-1980	155

APPENDIX B

I.	New ECU Aymara-Quechua Congregations	161

Foreword

This book is one of a kind.

Hopefully, it is not the last of its kind. Here is the most extensive attempt I am aware of to combine the best theoretical insights of modern missiology with a practical, grass-roots application to a specific field situation. Douglas Smith's overriding burden is to evangelize the unreached peoples of Bolivia. His book is a bold attempt to provide a combination of inspirational and motivational material, theoretical principles, empirical data, and practical suggestions for implementation that will furnish a base for the completion of the task.

Who should read this book?

First, it is a book that anyone seriously involved in world evangelization should read. They may not want to spend much time concentrating on the demographics of the Bolivian situation, but they will undoubtedly want to consider it as a model for what can be produced for any mission field. They will also be deeply interested in the missiological sections that Smith includes. Such generally useful concepts as "continuous mission" or the Engel scale, or the relationship of the cultural and the supracultural in divine revelation, or the calculation of average annual growth rates, or the five classes of leaders will be of great value to any who wish to upgrade their own missionary strategy.

Secondly, Christian workers at home or on the field who are directly engaged in God's work in Bolivia will find here a gold mine of information about their field. Rarely have the careful studies of the growth and/or decline of churches been so helpfully combined with demographic data. The analyses contained in this book are of the sort that commercial companies pay thousands of dollars to gather. Douglas Smith's background in civil engineering has served him well in the development of these sections.

Thirdly, and most specifically, those involved in the work of the Andes Evangelical Mission, and the Evangelical Christian Union now have available a challenging handbook from which to plan an effective evangelistic strategy for the future. One is grateful to God for the more than 10,000 Bolivian people who are rejoicing in the Lord in Evangelical Christian Union churches. Yet, one is forced by this book to ask why it is that the E.C.U. is growing at 83% per decade when the Friends are growing at 287% and the Assemblies of God at 379%? Can the Evangelical Christian Union reach 25,000 by 1980? Smith contends that it is possible if sound principles of church growth are put into effect.

None of this happens automatically, however. God's work requires prayer, wisdom, hard work and sacrifice. It is not comfortable to disturb the status quo. There is a price to pay for stepping out and conquering new frontiers. Not all will be willing to pay it.

But some will. And it is my prayer that those who accept the challenge will find this book a useful instrument for helping to fulfill the vision that God has for those millions of people in Bolivia who yet need to "turn from idols to serve the living and true God."

C. Peter Wagner
Fuller Theological Seminary
Pasadena, California

Biblical Preface

The good man's reward lasts forever.*

After a long time their master returned from his trip and called them to him to account for his money. The man to whom he had entrusted the $5,000 brought him $10,000. His master praised him for good work. 'You have been faithful in handling this small amount', he told him, 'so now I will give you many more responsibilities. Begin the joyous tasks I have assigned to you.'

For we must all stand before Christ to be judged and have our lives laid bare before Him. Each of us will receive whatever he deserves for the good or bad things he has done in his earthly body.

I have fought long and hard for my Lord, and through it all I have kept true to him. And now the time has come for me to stop fighting and rest. In heaven a crown is waiting for me which the Lord, the righteous Judge, will give me on that great day of His return. And not just to me, but to all those whose lives show that they are eagerly looking forward to His coming back again.

Look, I am coming soon! Hold tightly to the little strength you have - so that no one will take away your crown. As for the one who conquers, I will make him a pillar in the temple of my God; he will be secure, and will go out no more; and I will write my God's name on him, and he will be a citizen in the city of my God - the New Jerusalem, coming down from heaven from my God; and he will have my new name inscribed upon him.

Let all who can hear, listen to what the Spirit is saying to the churches.

* March 27 reading from *Daily Light* (*Living Bible*)
   Prov. 11:18, Matt. 25:19-21, II Cor. 5:10, II Tim. 4:7,8, Rev. 3:11-13.

Preface

Success is measured in terms of how much remains to be done. After eight decades since the 1900 sowing of Protestant missions in Bolivia, both Protestants and Roman Catholics have yet to penetrate meaningfully sixty-five percent of the population. This group remains culturally and linguistically outside the reach of Bolivia's national Church and of most missions. Is there something new that can be done to narrow this gap?

This study defines the scope of the unfinished Bolivian task from the perspective of the Evangelical Christian Union and the Andes Evangelical Mission (ECU and AEM). I have worked with these groups since 1962. Field data has been regularly researched and tested since 1971. This has led to comparisons with some other groups also working in Bolivia. We must better synchronize our efforts in bringing in the enormous Bolivian harvest. Experience shows world-wide that once we see more objectively from where we have come and where we are going, we can significantly improve our present performance. It is possible to more than double our growth as we prepare under the direction of the Holy Spirit to take in fuller armloads of the harvest over the next five years.

At the present time, the total Bolivian Protestant movement is reproducing itself at 12% per annum. A few of the reapers are doing much better while the others are not doing so well. The ECU and the AEM are among those generally not doing as well as the national average. However, the potential is present for again surpassing the national average of 12% per annum by a closer matching of ECU and AEM workers with their harvests. The mission has lost seasoned workers among the Aymaras and Quechuas. We have yet to improve our ability to recruit, train and field a sizeable force able to cross several cultures to effectively share Christ among the unreached sixty-five percent.

Preface

It is my hope that this study will catalyze national churches and Bolivian missions to more concerted action in fuller reaping among the unreached sixty-five percent. Specific strategies will be required for reaching out to each homogeneous segment of the five million Bolivian population. A homogeneous church should be produced among each different kind of people. A church that meaningfully meets the needs of each group is imperative. Good shepherding requires good accounting. "Be diligent to know the state of your flocks" (Prov. 27:23).

The Lord of the harvest calls all of us to more clearly demonstrate our love for Him by more seriously caring for His lambs (John 21:15-17). Do you know how many lambs you are responsible for? What are the trends in your area? What are your biblical priorities? What is your strategy? That's what this Bolivian rural-urban strategy study is all about. Trusting God, let's answer these questions for the doubling of the Church in Bolivia within the next five years and to contribute toward improving church growth world-wide.

God is moving His continuous mission into a new phase with the rise of third world missions. How are we responding? As we focus on the prophetic handwriting over our times (Dan. 5:22-28), many see the demise of the West. The incoming cast of rising third world nations are overshadowing the declining West. God is directing these third world mission protagonists in playing out the final scenes as they reach to the very ends of the earth. Since ours is the first generation to see all the biblical prophecies regarding Israel being fulfilled, I believe the Lord is speaking strongly to us in the West. We must humble ourselves to voluntarily sacrifice in giving our rising third world Christian brethren the help they need to generate as many New Testament apostolic bands as possible. Paul did this at his own expense. We also should move ahead strongly before impending crisis surprises us. If we do not harmonize in moving out voluntarily with God toward a simpler life style, we may well lose out even as participants in a supporting role.

The Church, both as an inclusive Christian community and as an exclusive voluntary fellowship defined by commitment to mission, must learn to improve its coordination in completing the Great Commission during this generation. As each of us is caught up in God's continuous mission, we will become more keenly aware of our interdependent roles and functions. We can move with greater accountability to one another, especially to our brethren in third world emerging missions. We can look forward to hastening the return of the Lord of the harvest (II Pet. 3:12-15).

Acknowledgments

Where can I begin to thank all who have so liberally helped to make this study possible? First, I acknowledge God as superintending the mosaic of my life. I was born into a warm Christian family with five brothers. My parents were active in serving the Lord. God's goodness and mercy continues to pursue me and my family as we lose ourselves in His world mission. God is surpassing our fondest dreams as we are learning to discern the difference between what is eternal and temporal. My pilgrimmage of wrestling with this tension started with my upbringing in a small, newly-planted home church. Without apology, my bias is that of an evangelical Christian concerned for world mission. I write from this perspective.

Second, I acknowledge the Body of Christ as discipling, disciplining and directing me in greater obedience to the Lord Jesus in world mission. Without my wife and children supporting and encouraging me, this pilgrimmage would have been impossible.

After our first term of service in Bolivia, I received a greater appreciation for God's Word at Trinity Evangelical Divinity School. Now, after our third term, the School of World Mission (SWM) at Fuller Theological Seminary has answered my search for a clearer understanding of the tension between cultural forms and the supracultural Word of God. My 1969 M.A. thesis discusses this tension under the title, *Grace and Law from Adam to Moses in Pauline Thought*. My Latin American colleagues encouraged me to work through a contemporary application of this question. I hope that this strategy document shows the way to develop some possible solutions to this dilemma in Bolivia.

In attempting to do so, I acknowledge the significant role of

Acknowledgments

the SWM, founded by Dr. Donald A. McGavran, still the inspiring Dean Emeritus at seventy-nine years. Dr. McGavran and his dedicated staff have pledged themselves to discovering and teaching the truth about how churches spread world-wide. I am indebted to each of the following faculty members for helpfully interacting with various parts of this study. Each has spurred me on to a greater appreciation for the following areas: the biblical basis and theory of world-wide Church and missions, Drs. Arthur Glasser and Donald McGavran; the dynamic of the historical development of the Christian movement and of the training of the ministry, Dr. Ralph Winter and Professor Fred Holland; the relation of man to his environment and the indigenous Church, Drs. Allan Tippett, Charles Kraft and Paul Hiebert; the dynamic of the Holy Spirit in awakenings, renewal and evangelism, Dr. J. Edwin Orr; the principles of church growth, strategy and sociology, Dr. C. Peter Wagner and Professor Ed Dayton, and finally, the relationship of the concept *"elements of the world"* with culture, Drs. Arthur Glasser, Charles Kraft and Everett Harrison. Dr. Wagner deserves special credit for working with me as chairman of my dissertation committee and as first reader. Doctors Kraft and Harrison offered invaluable insights as second and third readers. All of the faculty have been most gracious to me and inspiring in their love for Jesus Christ.

The Andes Evangelical Mission, of which I am a member, granted me a two-year study furlough, making possible the research that forms the basis for this study. I am grateful for this privilege and for the inspiration of pioneering Director Emeritus, Verne D. Roberts, retired on the field, and Ex-General Director, Joseph S. McCullough, now representing the AEM in the U.S.A. I am grateful to my mission colleagues, new General Director, Ron Wiebe, and Quechua Evangelism Director, John Lloyd, with whom I shared my early ideas. They have encouraged me with suggestions and data. Above all, continuing to work with my Ex-Associate General Director, Peter Wagner, as his teaching assistant has been invaluable.

Third, I acknowledge the need to test all of this teaching in Christ's work applied to the real world through His Body. I thank Pastor Ray Ortlund of our Lake Avenue Congregational Church during this study furlough for the balance in his three-priority emphasis. I thank John Wimber, Director of the Department of Church Growth at the Fuller Evangelistic Association (FEA) for part-time employment, challenging me to creatively apply church growth principles and theory to the North American scene. This, coupled with teaching workshops and sharing my findings with SWM volunteers, Roger Bosch, Dennis Griggs, Bucky Sydnor and others has been excellent preparation for returning to Latin America to teach faithful men, who will be able to teach others also (II Tim. 2:2).

In conclusion, the document that follows represents not only my work but that of many others, not the least of whom is my dear wife, Audrey. Without her devoted effort this book would still be a dream. She has typed and retyped the manuscript, corrected, and criticized the material. She typed it into final form.

"Go up to the mountain . . . bring wood . . . build the house; and I will take pleasure in it, and I will be glorified, saith the Lord" (Haggai 1:8).

May 16, 1977   W. Douglas Smith, Jr.
Pasadena, California

Introduction

Increasing concern for the unreached coupled with rising third world missiologists like Orlando Costas cause some third-term missionaries like myself to pursue more answers to the riddles of mission. Apart from several years of working in Spain, we as a family had little cross-cultural preparation for beginning our ministry in Bolivia in 1962. Dr. Donald McGavran had not yet become so well known, nor was the School of World Mission at Fuller a reality. This study describes my searching out of some causes and cures for the unfinished Bolivian task as we approach 1980.

We thank God for being part of the biblical theology movement that has been rediscovering the centrality of mission. Costas describes this in Chapter One of his recent book, *Theology of the Crossroads in Contemporary Latin America* (1976:7). The Church is both a product and an instrument of mission. Christ calls us out of darkness into His marvellous light to declare His wonderful redemption to the ends of the earth with the power of His Spirit upon us (Acts 1:8; I Pet. 2:9).

Three Moments in the Missiological Process

The Church was born through mission at Pentecost. It continues to be born through mission. To be a biblical Church it must spawn missions which give birth to more churches. The Lord of the harvest intends that this process continue until He comes at the end of this age (Matt. 28:19,20). This is the reason for the title of this study. It is designed to stimulate the continuous mission process world-wide, not only in Bolivia, which merely provides the background for this study.

Unfortunately, the Church has not always fulfilled its calling to continuous mission. This accentuates the need for missiology.

It helps the Church in her multiple expressions in the world to critically analyze her performance, question her motives and outlook, and more clearly project new ventures. Missiology is the servant of mission. But mission is not always missiological. It only becomes so when mission is accompanied by what Costas calls three moments in the missiological process (1976:23,24). I have adapted these three moments, especially the third, where Costas appears to repeat moment one by taking another, more comprehensive, analytical look at what has already come into being. Rather, I prefer to convert his third moment into strategizing what should come into being. I have redefined his three missiological moment process as a:

1. Critical reflection on contemporary trends.
   Part One defines this as ethnohistory.

2. Systematical theologizing of biblical priorities for continuous mission within each ethnic group.
   Part Two defines this as ethnotheology.

3. Strategizing for ethnic participation in continuous mission.
   Part Three defines this as ethnostrategy.

This three-fold combination offers a new way to approach the Bolivian harvest.

Missiology: Origin and Definition

Missiology has been considered a discipline since the days of Gustav Warneck, the founder of modern missiology (Holsten 1971: 643ff). Angel Santos Hernandez, a Spanish Jesuit missiologist, defined missiology as an historical-theological discipline (Costas 1976:13). For Dutch Reformed missiologist Johannes Verkuyl, missiology is a scholarly and critical examination of the presuppositions, motives, methods, structures, relationships and policies of these *missiones ecclesiarum* and the *missio hominum* . . . in the contemporary world (Costas 1976:14,15). One of the tasks of missiology is to train and equip participants and volunteers. South African David Bosch agrees with this, seeing missiology as a specialized form of theological reflection (1975:11ff).

Australian Alan R. Tippett represents the School of World Mission view, which is similar to the previously mentioned views above. All agree on the traditional concept of missiology as an academic discipline relating theology, history and the social sciences. Tippett's definition differs from the others in seeing missiology as a discipline which is historical, yet not history; anthropological, yet not anthropology and theological, but not theology (1974:27). Tippett defines missiology as the:

academic discipline or science which researches, records
and applies data relating to the biblical origin, the
history (including the use of documentary materials),
the anthropological principles and techniques and the
theological base of the Christian mission. The theory,
methodology and data bank are particularly directed
towards:

1. the processes by which the Christian message is communicated,
2. the encounters brought about by its proclamation to non-Christians,
3. the planting of the Church and organization of congregations, and the growth and relevance of their structures and fellowship, internally to maturity, externally in outreach as the Body of Christ in local situations and beyond, in a variety of culture patterns.

Immediately it will be apparent that such research requires some familiarity with the tools and techniques of anthropology, theology and history. Yet even this is not all. The missiologist may find himself calling on the resources of . . . linguistics or psychology. Nevertheless, missiology is a discipline in its own right. It is not a mere borrower from other fields, for these dimensions are related to each other in a unique manner. They interact, influence, modify each other. Missiology is dynamic, not static. It is not like a physical mixture but is more like a field of chemical interaction, combination and recombination, producing new substances by what I believe is called 'the transmutation of elements', or in biology, the coming together of germ cells to form some completely new organism. Missiology is a new thing with its own autonomous entity (1974:27,28).

With this background on the origin and definition of missiology, we are now prepared to launch into the three missiological moments, which follow in Parts One, Two and Three. This study is an attempt to apply the theory of missiology to a practical problem we face in Bolivia. The influential Swiss thinker on intellectual development, Jean Piaget, affirms that the application of theory must always run ahead of that theory. The School of World Mission is never merely the practical outcome of church growth theory. It sees itself primarily as an open-ended, creative educational experience where theory and practice merge in a simbiotic relationship (Furth and Wachs 1975:30).

Nearly two years ago I came to the School of World Mission with a burden for improving our denomination's slackening growth rate in Bolivia. The national Protestant average rate of growth was 12% per annum while we were dropping off to 3.8% per annum. I came expectantly with only the minimal field statistics requested of our denomination. Moreover, inspired by Green Lake '71, I had done a field survey of our 271 churches in 1973. Little did I dream of the fountain of facts that would bubble forth from this data. Now, thanks to founder, Dr. Donald McGavran, and the vision God has given to him and to his dedicated, capable team at the School of World Mission, this analysis describes my pilgrimmage to search out the causes and the cures for our situation. As a first attempt, it remains to be field tested upon our return to Bolivia later this year. Hopefully, others interested in more clearly defining and prioritizing their harvest may be equally stimulated to follow a similar process when only minimal data is available.

To reach the objective of doubling the present growth of any church desiring to do so, will require passing through the three steps outlined in this work. By conducting regional church growth workshops, each church and denomination desiring to participate in growth may determine its own:

1. Past trends.

2. Present biblical priorities.

3. Projected short-range and long-range faith goals.

The fruit of such joint accountability could be the inauguration of a Bolivian Cross-Cultural Research and Training Center for measuring church growth progress and for providing in-service training to speed completion of the unfinished task.

Part One: Trends

Significant for the
Expanding Bolivian Church and
Population, 1900 - 1980

1

Clearing Informational Smog

Smog is caused by man contaminating the atmosphere. We are responsible for clearing up the sources. The same mandate applies to missions today. We must clean up the pollutants that cloud a clear view of missions.

To do so, this study analyzes the geographical, ethnic and religious population trends among five million Bolivian people yet to be discipled. These trends become the basis for prioritizing the receptivity of each ethnic group. A biblical strategy follows God's initiative as He ripens each group for harvest. The Bolivian population is surveyed through the eyes of the national Church, known as the Evangelical Christian Union (ECU).

Today, the Andes Evangelical Mission (AEM) and the Evangelical Union of South America (EUSA) cooperate with this national Church. The ECU became autonomous in 1966. The AEM began in 1907 as the Bolivian Indian Mission to aggressively evangelize the many Quechua speaking people of this country (Wagner 1970:73). The EUSA sent its first missionaries to Bolivia in 1937. They opened work in Aripalka in the department of Potosi to evangelize the Quechua Indians, with the consent of the Plymouth Brethren already there (Grubb 1938:12). Their primary ministry has been evangelism and church planting in the departments of Sucre and Santa Cruz, especially among the seventeen thousand Guarani of the Camiri area.

We anticipate returning to Bolivia to begin sharing and field testing the process put forth in this document. Workshops are planned for each of the five homogeneous groups related to the ECU. Hopefully, this will result in better harvesting among all segments of our population. We have received church growth eyes.

The Lord Jesus described church growth eyes as he encouraged His perplexed disciples in Samaria along side Jacob's well. They stood gaping as the recently converted adulteress hurried back to the city. She went to call her men friends to see the man who told her all she ever really wanted to know in life - acceptance, forgiveness and hope. This is what the Lord of the harvest said and still says today as He puts in His sickle for souls:

> Do you think the work of harvesting will not begin until the summer ends four months from now? Look around you! Vast fields of human souls are ripening all around us and are ready now for reaping *(Living Letters, John 4:35)*.

Informational smog causes frustration and confusion in attempting to define the Bolivian harvest. The still life portrayals describing the Bolivian scene as given by other authors are brought together here, forming an integrated, moving pattern over the past seven decades. This still life sequence emphasizes that each statistic has two basic properties, size and change. The dynamism of change may be expressed as a trend or rate similar to compound interest paid on an investment. Hopefully, the outcome of this study could become a model for measuring the vitality of the growth trends for any changing population, whether secular or ecclesiastical. Finally, the continually changing Bolivian harvest is prioritized and compared with the corresponding deployment of missionary and national personnel. The validity of this deployment is reviewed. Some readjustments are recommended for better reaping.

The following anecdote illustrates the growing need to close the gap between reality and some of the wonderful impressions created by missionary promotion. January, 1977. A Christian folk group from Bolivia returned to the States for a third tour since their first 1970 visit. Once again churches and schools across the country thrilled to their singing and challenge. "Thank you for what you have done. Please continue to help us bring in the abundant harvest."

The group leader enthusiastically reported the phenomenal growth from forty congregations with 625 believers at the 1950 organization of the national Church to over 300 congregations with 12,000 believers attending services each Sunday. The last official head count in 1973 was 10,077 with 271 active churches and congregations. Tremendous growth!

An impressed listener remarked, "Anybody could be happy with those statistics".

"That is, unless you know something about the receptivity and resources available for the harvest", responded an ex-missionary standing nearby. "It should have been twice that amount!"

"Well then, how can we possibly judge good growth?", the listener retorted. "What standard rule of thumb could become an acceptable yardstick so that we could universally measure all church growth against one lowest common denominator for any time period?"

FIVE CAUSES OF INFORMATIONAL SMOG

1. Unintentional Omissions

Responses to the May 1976 Forum of the Association of Church Missions Committees (ACMC) show the rising concern of most of their related churches to upgrade missions' stewardship. Evaluation is absolutely necessary. The present frustrating, complex evaluatory process must be streamlined (Hamilton 1976:2). More and more churches are requiring that the missionary have specific goals. He and his agency must be willing to be evaluated on how well they are reaching these goals. Reports must be more concise, readable and objective. How can this possibly be done when even the field personnel are as equally frustrated?

McGavran says that as one contemplates the amazing consistency with which mission writings omit any reliable and meaningful picture of church growth, one must not imagine there has been a conspiracy of silence. Simple fog is not only a kindlier but a more correct explanation. Omission of this vital information is curious and disastrous, but it is strictly unintentional (1970:71).

2. Educated Guesswork

A key Quechua worker in Bolivia, John Lloyd, describes his frustration in attempting to work with the educated estimates of other workers.

> For the year 1967 Wagner gives the absolute membership of the Evangelical Christian Union as 9,229 (1970:185). Read gives the figure for the same year as 7,000 (1969:109). Wagner gives the Assemblies of God as 4,255 while Read reports them as 1,431. . . . This is not to discredit either author, but the fact is, both are educated guess work and nothing more (1973:9).

3. Fuzzy Definitions

Read describes his frustration in attempting to arrive at the correct number of members for the ECU. He recognizes that the Union has always had a large number of unbaptized believers (1969:112).

4. Lack of Specific Mapping

Keith Hamilton graphically demonstrates how the AEM, like other missions, baptizes with great caution. Interestingly, he gives a table describing people movements in three areas within the receding Aymara speaking region, gradually becoming Quechua speaking (1962:34). But he fails to specify where his three target areas appear on his maps, Figures 1 and 2.

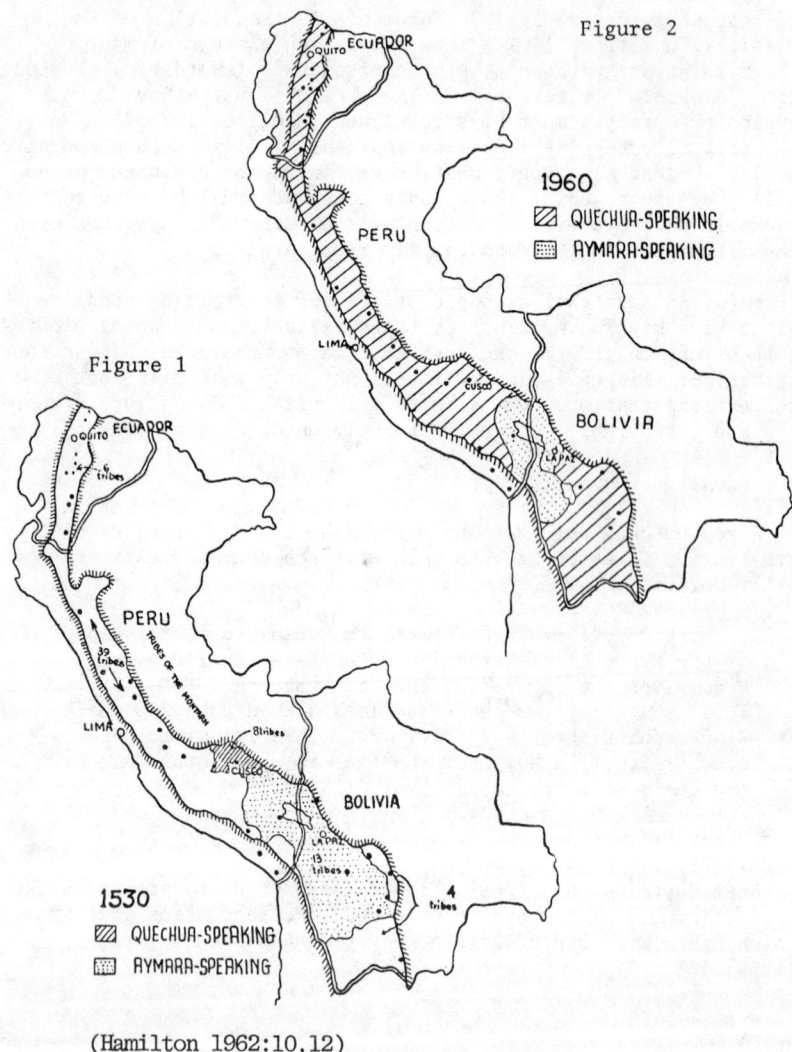

(Hamilton 1962:10,12)

5. Imprecise Census Data

At the beginning of February, I checked into the irregular Bolivian statistics reported by the Population Reference Bureau over the last five years. I was advised that the recent Bolivian census drops one million people, resulting in the following corrections (Myers 1977).

   a. The mid 1977 population is 4.81 million and not 5.95 as projected.

   b. The pivotal mid 1950 population of 3.019 million was too high and should have been only 2.704 million.

   c. The resulting population Average Annual Growth Rate (AAGR) is 2.156% instead of the previously widely used 2.5%.

These five cases of informational man-made smog show the need to isolate the contaminants and clear up the source. The following are some likely pollutants, according to Dr. McGavran (1970: 71-80).

1. Statistical: haphazard, inaccurate membership accounting blurs reality. Omissions distort. Inconsistent definitions mislead.

2. Administrational: egalitarian distribution of human and financial resources, without measuring outcome; promotes the attitude that faithful work is all that matters.

3. Cultural Overhang: veils church growth because evangelism is done according to the missionary's cultural frame of reference. To some, evangelism is preaching, distributing tracts, broadcasting, teaching the Bible and doing good works. It is sowing the seed and hoping that church growth happens.

4. Semantical Vagaries: like work, witness, church, friendly interest, response, outreach, encounter. All cover many activities without telling much about actual congregational increase.

5. Psychological Rationalizations: those growing slowly are not interested in "numerolatry" or quick, easy ways to conversions. They aim at something higher like quality of Christian character.

6. Promotional Communication: aims at favorably impressing donors. Dry statistics cannot compete with human interest stories. Overemphasis of the good clouds reality. What is

promoted is assumed to be exactly what should be done to carry out the Great Commission. Critical evaluation is risky.

However, every missionary should be both a promoter and a diagnostician. He is a steward giving an exact account of the total picture. He should distinguish carefully among aims, hopes and outcomes.

7. Theological Shifts: cause uncertainty about mission goals and results. The reinterpretation of mission and the attempted capture of this 400 billion dollar enterprise deserve a book. But, let three illustrations suffice.

    a. Some leaders say the Church is purely instrumental for creating a better world. God loves the world (John 3:16). He spreads His kingdom of justice, peace and righteousness among all, whether they call themselves Christians or not. To the degree that churches are alive with social action, humanizing society, they are in line with God's purposes.

    b. Others, freed from biblical authority, say God has revealed much in other religions. This leads to an attitude of learning together in dialogue. Church planting is outmoded.

    c. Finally, a third group says service is a sufficient witness. *Diakonia* has increasingly become the chief business of organized missions. Most agree that wealthy nations owe help to their less fortunate brethren overseas. But is this a total or a partial witness? Most say both service and church planting must go on simultaneously. But a vocal minority downgrade the importance of increasing the number of baptized believers.

In summary, these seven pollutants combine to form a smog which sweeps in, making it difficult to clearly appreciate the scene. Now that we have isolated some contaminants, we should go back to quantify and qualify the source.

All growth is both quantitative and qualitative. A numerical approach is essential to understanding church growth. In the parable of the stewards, the Lord Jesus commends or condemns faithfulness according to the return received on His investment of gifts and talents (Luke 19:12-26). We will be evaluated at Christ's tribunal by the way in which we have been investing, either in the right place at the right time or in a less promising place when we should be elsewhere (I Cor. 3:9-23; II Cor. 5:10-11). Since we belong to Christ, should we not examine how we have been doing during the last seven decades in Bolivia? This should help us to more clearly define what we should be doing during the next decade, should Christ tarry.

Since the days of the New Testament, evangelistic effectiveness has been a quality measured quantitatively. All growth is either seen as an increase or as a decrease in size, rate and location.

Tippett classically refers to three kinds of growth:

1. Quantitative membership size of a church or community (1970:7).

2. Qualitative spiritual maturity as measured in Solomon Island Christian piety (1967:308-18).

3. Organic development of organizational structure (Acts 2:46-7).

All three can be measured and be expressed in absolute numbers - never as an end in themselves, but as a source of clues (1970:17).

Size can be measured by a myriad of direct and indirect scales of different kinds, such as average attendance at a certain kind of meeting, at an annual conference, the number of congregations, pastors, hymn books, and space utilized. But none of these measurements made singly at any point in time as a snap shot can tell anything about the vitality of the change in size. To do so, the same type of snaps shots must be made at two different points in time. The rate of change is demonstrated by the slope of the line connecting two points in time, introducing the concept of growth rate.

Nothing alive is static. Any population is continually experiencing an influx or outflow of people. This results in either a change of size expressed positively or in a change of size expressed negatively. There are three kinds of change that add to membership and three that subtract:

1. Positive components of membership growth by those coming in through:

   a. birth, defined as biological growth.

   b. conversion, defined as conversion growth.

   c. transfer, defined as transfer growth.

2. Negative components of membership growth result through:

   a. death, defined as negative biological growth.

   b. reverting to the world, defined as negative conversion growth.

   c. transfer out, defined as negative transfer growth.

Thus, the net biological, net conversion and net transfer growth is the difference between each corresponding pair.

Since any one of these factors changes the membership totals extensively, it is folly to put too much confidence in any one or two factors without the others. It is even more incorrect, though common, to suppose that the overall net growth (the algebraic sum of all six factors) is assumed to be the result of one factor like conversion.

In Bolivia, the ECU has been growing from 2 people to 13,118 members in seventy years. It will be shown later that biological factors alone account for much of this. Subtracting the expected amount of net biological growth from the overall net growth gives the sum of net conversion and net transfer. Often this is no longer so impressive, especially if it is well known that many members of a certain church grew up in other churches. This occurs in Bolivia through the upward social climb from Pentecostals to the ECU to the Baptists and finally to the Methodists.

Growth also takes place at a specific location. Usually the overall, global growth of a denomination is a result of the uneven growth among regions, age groups and congregations. The poor growth of one area is often disguised by lumping it together with the good growth elsewhere. Area lumping is dangerous, giving a false impression of vitality. The lumping of statistics for a congregation may obscure which age group is or is not growing. The good overall growth of the congregation may be derived mainly from those coming from the youth belt on the age/sex pyramid shown in Figure 3, especially in Bolivia.

We should differentiate among various types of growth - single congregational growth, denominational growth and cross-cultural congregational growth. The following distinctives can help clarify church growth, pictorially described in Figure 4. E_o represents internal evangelism and nurture because it transforms mere members of the church community into communicant members, crossing no cultural barriers. E_1 represents expansion evangelism, crossing the cultural barrier between the church and the world, adding near neighbors as members of the local congregation.

Figure 3

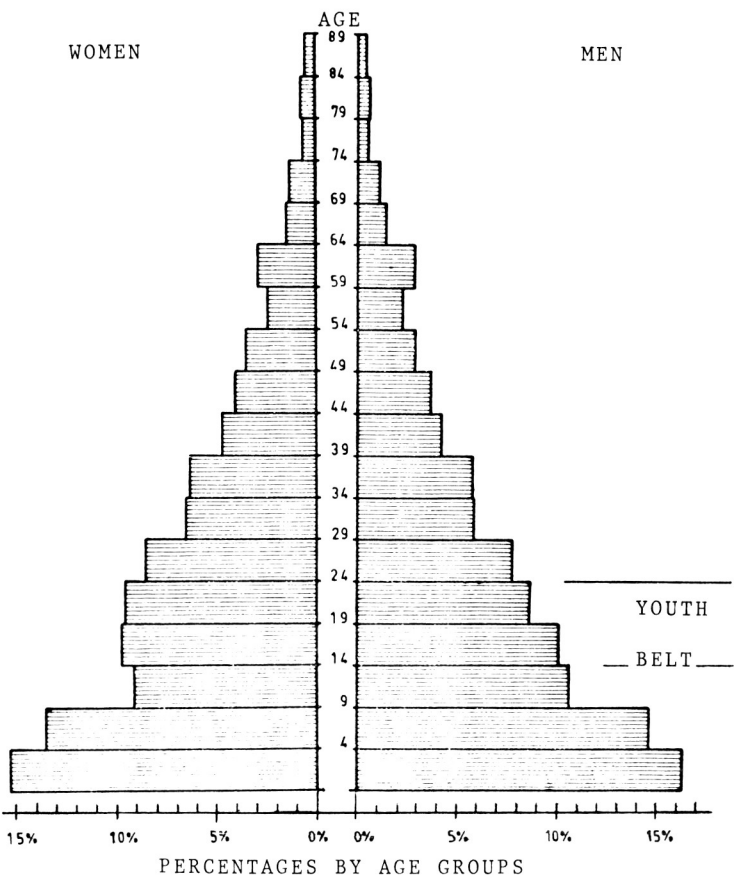

(Alonso 1961:163)
Cf. Mesarovic and Pestel 1974:182.

FIGURE 4

FOUR TYPES OF "CHURCH GROWTH"

I	II	III	IV
INTERNAL GROWTH	EXPANSION GROWTH	EXTENSION GROWTH	BRIDGING GROWTH
"CHRISTIAN NURTURE"	"EVANGELISM"	"CHURCH PLANTING"	"MISSIONS"

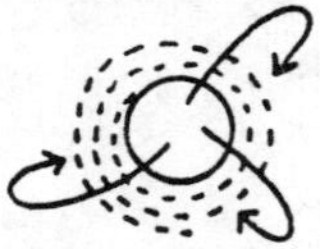

"CHRISTIAN NURTURE"
1. Quantitative E_0 Conversion
2. Qualitative   Spiritual Maturity
3. Organic Development   Organizational Structure

"EVANGELISM"
1. E_1 Conversion
2. Transfer in
3. Biological Growth

"CHURCH PLANTING"
• Church Planting by Transfer of Growth to New Location.

"MISSIONS"
• Cross-Cultural

FOUR TYPES OF EVANGELISM

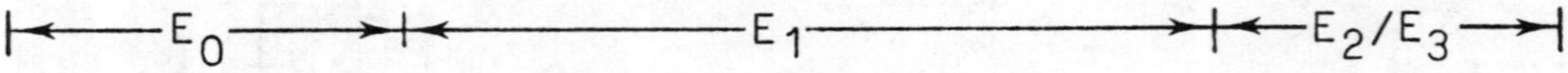

|—— E_0 ——|—— E_1 ——|—— E_2/E_3 ——|

Adapted from Winter 1974a:19

E_1 also represents extension growth by planting new churches among the same kind of people. E_2 represents bridging growth when congregations are planted in new, similar cultures while E_3 represents bridging growth of congregations in distinctively different cultures (Winter 1974a:19).

As the congregation expands through E_1 evangelism in its own community, the internal structure must become more elaborate to absorb these new people. Large groups cannot minister as effectively as smaller groups. Meeting this need is the most crucial, unsolved mystery in the Church today. Wagner speaks of the proper balance among cell, congregation and celebration in a well-integrated church life (1976a:97-109). Tippett calls this organic growth since it is a problem of developing an adequate structure to meet the needs of the new people.

The same problems are compounded when congregations multiply within a pluralistic society. Relationships cannot remain the same. Most church movements in one way or another must change their structure to meet new needs. Structurally, the ECU developed into sixteen regional directorate boards reflecting each geographical area. Could some way be found to better relate the five ethnic groupings within the present sixteen regional directorates?

One way to better reach each ethnic group might be through the formation of voluntary, second commitment sodalities within congregations or within the denomination. These include women's societies, young people's groups, and within a church movement, mission societies, student work, etc. These sodalities represent organic growth and are now being better understood (Winter 1974b: 121-39).

The least tangible side of growth is the spiritual dimension. Some will continue to use quality as the designation for this. Actually, all growth involves various qualities simultaneously. The size of membership is a quality. All measurements of any quality inevitably are both qualitative and quantitative. Winter has proved this in his interesting article in *Crucial Issues* (1972:175-187).

Since all growth is both quantitative and qualitative, we are now ready to look at a process for clearing contamination at the source by picturing growth rates.

2

Picturing Growth Rates

Facts obtained from population statistics, questionnaires, and interviews should be visualized pictorially. This makes the facts stand out in such a way that interpretation and evaluation are sharpened. Good analysis depends upon graphs showing growth of membership at various points in time. McGavran observes that columns of figures giving the membership of any given church and its homogeneous units contain locked up knowledge. By careful study, the figures can be forced to reveal their secrets, but the process is tedious. When, however, each set of figures is transformed into a graph of growth, the secrets leap out at the reader. He who would understand church growth should construct line graphs showing at a glance what has transpired. He can then ask why it happened (1970:108).

Several of us at SWM have worked through church growth calculations. Some of these have been published in Ebbie Smith's *Manual for Church Growth Surveys*. Part of the sequence that follows is derived from this source (1976:56-65).

Graphs show trends when constructed for each region or type of work. One graph should be made for each province, district and for all homogeneous units* within the area as well as for each type of work being carried out there. Regional graphs should be constructed on the same scale to facilitate comparison. Later this year when church growth workshops begin to be offered in Bolivia, graphs for local congregations will be constructed. These also will be done to the same scale to facilitate comparisons. For more striking results, several churches may be plotted on the same paper.
*Defined later on pages 34 to 36.

Picturing Growth Rates

The phenomenon of growth is related to time. The horizontal axis measures time usually in years. The vertical axis will usually measure membership, attendance, number of baptisms or conversions from the world.

Both growth and non-growth can be pictured on a simple line graph. But many times this alone may cloud as much as it reveals. As a church increases, the membership base increases. Then it becomes misleading to compare the yearly increase in a later period with that of an earlier period when the comparison is simply based on the number of new members added. A fifty member jump on the graph in an early period when the church only had one hundred members is much more significant than when the same church later has a thousand members and grows only by fifty. Yet, the line on a simple graph only moves up by the same amount in both cases. This is why simple line graphs of membership appear to get steeper at the same rate depicted by a straight line as the years pass. However, the real growth per hundred members actually becomes smaller. This is what often occurs when congregations and denominations become older and larger. Thus, the most revealing question to ask when comparing growth rates is, "How many new members have come into the church over a given time period for every hundred who were already members?" Or, "How many new members have been baptized per hundred former members?"

Raw data does not come in nice round numbers. The following cases from Ebbie Smith's manual showing growth for a single year are more common (1976:59).

Table I
Single Year Growth

	A Beginning Membership N_o	B Ending Membership N_t	C Net Increase (N_t-N_o)	D Beginning Members ÷ 100 $N_o/100$	E Calculation: $\frac{(N_t-N_o)100}{N_o} =$	F Answer: New members per 100 = % increase
1.	400	440	40	4.00	40 ÷ 4.00	10.0%
2.	420	483	63	4.20	63 ÷ 4.20	15.0%
3.	285	410	125	2.85	125 ÷ 2.85	43.8%
4.	1,260	1,640	380	12.60	380 ÷ 12.60	30.2%
5.	30,400	32,500	2,100	304.00	2,100 ÷ 304.00	6.9%

Notice how the fastest growing church added nearly forty-four new people for every hundred. This is 43.8%. Just by looking at the first two columns, it would be difficult to guess that church number three had the highest percent increase. This observation proves the importance of the additional steps of calculating the *rate* at which the church is growing.

In Table I it was assumed that all of the samples grew from size A to size B during the same time period. The resulting percentage increase would not have been comparable had the periods of time been of different lengths. Thus, growing by 43.8% is *not* faster than 20% if the 20% took place in one year and the 43.8% took place over two years.

Two observations may be made.

1. The average yearly increase cannot be computed by simply dividing the total increase by the number of years between samples. For example, notice what happens to a church with a 10% growth per year over a four-year period. Each one hundred members grows as follows:

   ```
   100
    10  plus ten more, or adding 10% of 100
   110  at the end of the first year.
    11  plus eleven more, or adding 10% of 110
   121  at the end of the second year.
    12  plus twelve more, or adding 10% of 121
   133  at the end of the third year.
    13  plus thirteen more, or adding 10% or 133
   146  at the end of the fourth year, or
   ```
   a total of forty-six more per hundred in four years is a growth of 46% per four years. This is the result of adding 10% each year, *not* 46÷4=11.5%.

2. For the same reason, the average yearly percentage increase called the average annual growth rate (AAGR), cannot be calculated by dividing the increase per hundred members by the length of time between samples.

The Average Annual Growth Rate (AAGR)

The AAGR is so meaningful because population growth rates measuring the biological growth rate of a nationa are reported in these terms. Knowing the AAGR of a church or of a denomination allows comparison with the population growth of the nation. We can see whether growth is simply at a biological rate, beyond or below.

Biological growth rates vary from near zero in developed countries to 3% or more in developing nations. The latest Population Reference Bureau Chart shows the following AAGRs:

Japan	1.2%	Bolivia	2.156%
Germany	.2%	Nigeria	2.7 %
United Kingdom	.1%	Colombia	3.2 %
USA	.8%	India	2.0 %

If a church in a developing nation like Colombia grows only 3.2% per year, it is not growing any faster than its surrounding biologically active community. Although the ECU went from 200 to 13,118 during the last fifty years at an 8.73% AAGR, it has levelled off to 3.8% during the last decade, slightly more than the average annual population growth rate for Bolivia at this time.

Knowing the AAGR provides meaningful comparison for:

1. The growth of a church over two differing time periods.

2. The growth of various churches over two differing time periods.

3. The biological growth of a church compared to that of its surrounding community.

Properly done statistical analyses can demonstrate that conclusions based upon crude analyses are completely false. A shepherd should know his sheep, whether they are a day old or fifty days old, according to Proverbs 27:23. Several statistical problems are encountered in any given situation:

1. Sample size: A 100% increase per year starting with 10 is different from a 100% increase starting with 1000 members. Let n determine this level of significance.

2. Probability: This also plays a role, particularly when only yearly measurements are recorded. For example, if one flips a coin 10 times and seven turn out heads, that would not be considered significant. If, however, one flipped a coin a thousand times and 700 were heads, that would be significant.

3. Frequency of observation: The more frequent the observations, the more accurate the interpolations or extrapolations from the data. Decadal projections from only a few data points are subject to great errors.

4. Exponential growth of populations: Growth or decline of a church is the summation of several continuing factors. Each factor may be modeled in a simple manner by someone familiar with statistics and a portable slide rule computer. Growth is expressed by an exponential series of equations, according to the formula:

$$N_t = N_0 \, e^{nt} \qquad \text{where:}$$

N_t = the number of members at the end of the time period t.

N_o = the initial number of members.

n = the boundary ratio constant expressing the rate of net biological, transfer and conversion growth.

These can then be compared to the area and national population growth. Such analyses can be done weekly, monthly or annually, if the shepherd knows his sheep.

Another equivalent exponential series is used by bankers and population growth experts, since money and population grow in similar fashion (Mesarovic and Pestel 1974:8,73; Ehrlich 1970:6,7). The compound interest/population formula is expressed by the relationship:

$$N_t = N_o (1 + r)^t \text{ where:}$$

N_t = the number of members at the end of the time period t.

N_o = the initial number of members.

t = the time period elapsed between samples.

r = the net rate of growth expressed as a decimal. This is not the AAGR, which is expressed by the decimal rate r multiplied by 100, or percent.

Perhaps the best way to describe the growth rate is in terms of "doubling time". For example, the time required for the population to go from 5 million in 8,000 B.C. to 500 million in 1650 was nearly seven "doublings" over a 9,000 year period, representing a 100% increase. On an average the population doubled every 1,500 years. The next doubling, from 500 million to a billion, took 200 years. The doubling from a billion to 2 billion took only 80 years until 1930. World population reached 4 billion in 1975, having doubled in 45 years. At the present growth rate, it will double again in about 35 years, by 2010 (Ehrlich 1970:6,7).

The mathematical rationale for calculating the AAGR and the steps involved in punching and reading the calculator are explained on the following page.

Picturing Growth Rates   19

The Mathematical Rationale

If net church growth is from:

explains it, since 4.1% $\underset{550}{N_o}$ to $\underset{700}{N_t}$ in $\underset{6}{t}$ years, you can see how 4.1% means 1.041 more each year.

So, 550 × (1.041)(1.041)(1.041)(1.041)(1.041)(1.041) = 700
or, 550 (1.041)^6 = 700 , to use shorthand.

But, suppose we did not know that 4.1% would do it. We could experiment with different values, multiplying them out -- like (1.04)(1.04)(1.04) . . . etc.
or (1.039)(1.039) . . . .
or (1.042)(1.042)
until we hit it right.

<u>OR</u> , "<u>let 'r' be the net rate of growth</u>" (as a <u>decimal</u>, not %, which is the AAGR).

Then 550 $(1 + r)^6$ = 700

Now, to solve for r, we can do this two different, equivalent ways:

a) $N_0 (1 + r)^t = N_t$ b) $N_0 (1 + r)^t = N_t$

   550 $(1 + r)^6$ = 700   550 $(1 + r)^6$ = 700

   $(1 + r)^6$ = 700 ÷ 550 $(1 + r)^6$ = 700 ÷ 550

   $1 + r = \sqrt[6]{700 \div 550}$ 6 ln(1 + r) = ln(700 ÷ 550)

(as decimal) $r = \sqrt[6]{700 \div 550} - 1$ $\ln(1 + r) = \frac{\ln(700 \div 550)}{6}$

   <u>OR</u>   AAGR = 100 $\sqrt[6]{700 \div 550}$ - 100 $1 + r = e^{\left[\frac{\ln(700 \div 550)}{6}\right]}$

   as a % = $100 \left[\sqrt[t]{N_t \div N_0} - 1 \right]$ $r = e^{[\ ]} - 1$

Average Annual Growth Rate % = $100 \left[e^{\left[\frac{\ln(700 \div 550)}{6}\right]} - 1 \right]$

OR, BY CALCULATOR:			OR, BY CALCULATOR:		
	<u>PUNCH</u>	<u>READ</u>		<u>PUNCH</u>	<u>READ</u>
1.	700	700	1.	700	700
2.	÷	700	2.	÷	700
3.	550	550	3.	550	550
4.	=	1.272727273	4.	=	1.272727273
5.	y^x	1.272727273	5.	ln x	0.241162056
6.	6	6	6.	÷	0.241162056
7.	1/x	1.6666666	7.	6	6
8.	=	1.0410	8.	=	0.040193676
9.	×	1.0410	9.	e^x	1.041012374
10.	100	104.10	10.	-	1.041012374
11.	=	104.10	11.	1	1
12.	-	104.10	12.	=	0.041012374
13.	100	100	13.	×	0.041012374
14.	=	4.10	14.	100	100
			15.	=	4.10123739

Read as 4.10% Average Annual Growth Rate (AAGR)

Perhaps you wonder why it is not possible to divide an eight-year percentage increase like 204% by eight years to arrive at the AAGR. In doing so, 204% ÷ 8 = 25.5%, which is not the correct 15% AAGR. This quotient of 25.5% is actually the answer to a different question, "How many new members per hundred original members have been brought into the church annually?" This would mean that the new members since incorporation have had no part in sharing their faith. Only the original people were active in causing growth. This is unrealistic. The more meaningful question is answered by the AAGR, "How many people have new and old members brought in annually?" This question can only be answered by using the mathematical rationale explained on page 19, the AAGR Time Graph in Figure 5, or the exponential table offered by Ebbie Smith's Appendix A (1976:117), or any other similar method where the proper calculations have been made.

As any movement gets larger and older its very success tends to isolate its second and third generation members from evangelistic contacts with non-Christians. Thus the annual number of additional members per 100 existing members tends to decrease. Thus, the AAGR becomes smaller with time and growth, even though the popularity of a large church tends to increase its overall membership. Knowing the AAGR makes compatible comparisons possible with:

1. Known biological growth for the general population.

2. Other churches and denominations.

In concluding this section, we can say that the AAGR is the best single growth rate measure over any time period. Trends given by the AAGR are clues to general church health just as temperature and blood pressure are indicators of physical health (Winter 1972:181).

To underscore the importance of these clues, a ten percent membership increase annually may not prove the presence of all the fruits and gifts of the Spirit in a given church. However, the absence of any growth, or a constant loss of membership often is a vital clue to the absence of certain fruits and gifts of the Spirit. This is especially so in non-western countries where membership is mainly composed of first generation converts with an enormous population yet to be discipled. Something must be wrong if 75% of the Bolivian population professes to be under the Roman Catholic banner with less than 5% actively participating in a meaningful fellowship where their spiritual needs can be met by growth in grace and in the knowledge of the truth in Jesus Christ. Meanwhile, thousands of Bolivians are surging into the capital cities and lowland resettlements, ripe for harvest.

Figure 5

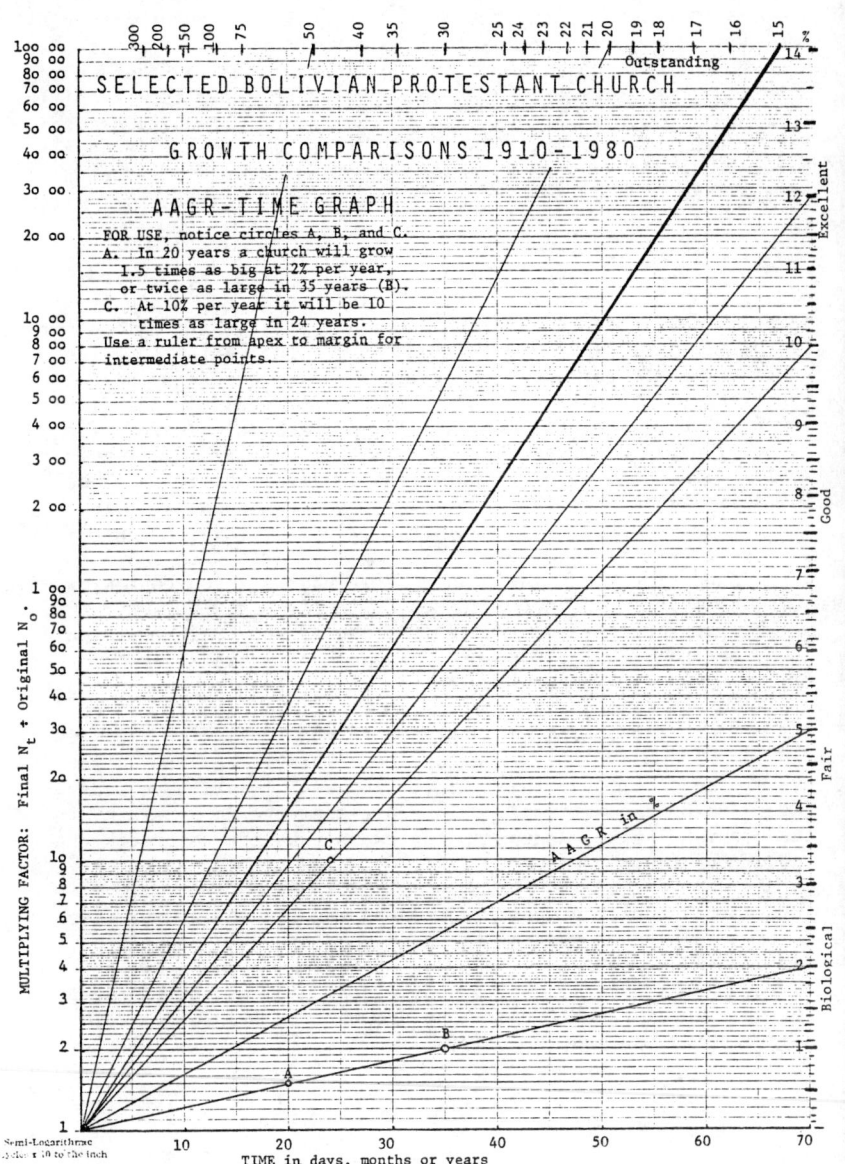

Adapted from R. D. Winter in Martin 1974:421.

Graphing and Comparing Growth Rates

Drawing graphs that show growth rate trends as clues is easier and much more rapid than making calculations outlined in the previous section. Graphing trends is easier because of the special tool utilized called semi-logarithmic graph paper. This is used because the vertical scale increases in the same way that churches actually grow. The uniqueness of this graph paper is its ability to show a constant, steady rate of church and community biological growth as a straight line. This same, constant rate on a simple graph is seen as a rapidly steeping curve. The steepness of the line on semi-logarithmic paper is proportional to the rate of growth.

Semi-logarithmic paper is much easier to use than it is to explain. But for those interested in its qualities, the only difference between standard graph paper and semi-logarithmic paper is the vertical scale. Both kinds have a horizontal axis representing years. For both, the vertical axis represents size - of membership, attendance, baptisms, or anything else. The simple graph measures vertically with a linear, absolute scale. The semi-log paper measures vertically with a special logarithmic scale. Since only one of the scales is logarithmic, this paper is called *semi*-logarithmic. This scale could also be called digital because each cycle or major division increases by one digit as a power of 10. Thus, the first cycle starts with *one*, not zero, since $10^0 = 1$. The second cycle adds a zero, beginning with 10. The third adds another zero, beginning with 100, etc. Or, if the first cycle begins with 100, the second cycle must add a zero, beginning with 1000, etc. The cycles increase exponentially. Since our number system is in the Base 10, we increase each cycle by the power of 10: $10^0 = 1$, $10^1 = 10$, $10^2 = 100$, $10^3 = 1,000$, etc. The exponent "3" in the expression "10^3" is the logarithm of 1000 to the Base 10. This is the reason for the use of the term logarithmic in titling semi-logarithmic paper. Each move up the vertical scale represents the same percentage of the previous value, squeezing the numbers as they approach the end of the cycle.

Before actually graphing and comparing growth rates, it is helpful to have an idea of the possible straight line slopes of various AAGRs plotted on semi-log paper, shown in Figure 5. Based upon C. Peter Wagner's wide experience, he shares the following rule of thumb for ranking growth rates (1976b:4). The same ranking applies in Bolivia.

Table II

AAGR and	Decadal Percent Increase		Comparison and Rank
2.256% =	25% per decade	–	biological growth only: POOR
4.137% =	50% per decade	–	FAIR for North America
7.177% =	100% per decade	–	GOOD for North America
11.612% =	200% per decade	–	EXCELLENT
14.869% =	300% per decade	–	OUTSTANDING
19.623% =	500% per decade	–	INCREDIBLE

Whenever possible, one should evaluate a church or denomination on the basis of its average annual growth rate. The corresponding decadal percent increase or five-year increase are incompatible quantities like apples and oranges. They cannot be compared directly to each other nor to the varying population growth rates. It seems that these latter forms of measurement will gradually fall into disuse as the greater versatility and usefulness of the AAGR is appreciated for making comparisons over any time period.

Steepness of a curved line at any point on semi-logarithmic paper is in proportion to the rate of growth at that point. As the angle becomes flatter in a concave, down direction, the rate becomes slower. This phenomenon is demonstrated in the graph of the ECU portrayed in Figure 6, based upon Table III and the ECU Ethnic Groups Table appearing later in this analysis. It is difficult to appreciate the meaning of data in tables until it is pictured in meaningful graphs.

The Apostle John recognized in Revelation 2 and 3 a tendency for second generation churches of Asia Minor to peak after about thirty years. Peter Wagner has popularized this cooling off of a church's ardor for Christ in evangelism as St. John's Syndrome. Figure 6 demonstrates this phenomenon near the end of the forties and seventies.

Figure 6 is drawn on two cycle semi-logarithmic paper. Yearly and decadal changes in the AAGR for the three denominations are indicated by the changing slope of the various lines. It is easy to see that the ECU is growing little more than the biological growth rate since 1977. This is apparent by comparing its growth to the 2.2% biological growth starting in 1977. The straight line in Figure 6 shows the biological growth intersecting the ECU growth at approximately the year 1977. During this present decade notice how the AAGR is further decreasing to 3.8%.

Table III

Decadal Percent Increase and the AAGR

for Three Bolivian Denominations, 1966 to 1976

	N_o	N_t	$(N_t - N_o)100 / N_o$	Decadal % Increase	t	AAGR
	1966	1976				
ECU	6,168	11,283	5,115÷61.68 =	82.9%	10 yrs.	6.2%
INELA	4,700	18,200	13,500÷47 =	287.0%	10 yrs.	14.5%
ASSEMBLIES of GOD	3,800	18,200	14,400÷38 =	379.0%	10 yrs.	16.96%

Here is a surprise. Figure 7 shows the ECU as a growing community, although growing less than INELA and the Assemblies of God. As a simple arithmetic plot, Figure 7 may easily mislead the observer. Thus, the contrast between the measurable clues demonstrated in the semi-log graph of Figure 6 compared to the hidden information in Figure 7 is elegant proof of the superiority of the former. This should amply illustrate the value of the little extra effort required of the church diagnostician to utilize and interpret semi-log graphs showing rates of growth as well as simple yearly membership graphs.

In the present period, the actual membership curve is approaching biological growth. Comparisons such as these reveal much about the vitality of the church. This raises serious questions for serious study and strategizing for correcting the causes. Notice especially that all these comparisons may be made by plotting directly on semi-logarithmic paper with a minimal number of calculations beyond a few AAGRs marking distinctive segments bounded by hinges of change.

The semi-logarithmic graph is a powerful tool for anticipating trends at least five years or more before they happen. This phenomenon may be readily seen by comparing the marked difference in the slope changes of the semi-log graph in Figure 6 with the same data shown in the simple graph of the ECU in Figure 7.

Another important principle to apply in graphing was observed by Aristotle (Problems XVI:10). Naturally grown objects are always beautifully and symetrically rounded. Man's imperfection causes sharp corners or abrupt changes. Population or church growth is smooth and should be graphed accordingly. Any sharp changes are caused by incorrect over or under reporting.

Eventually, these inconsistencies require a purge of the membership rolls that should actually be averaged out over the entire period. The same principle applies to sharp changes in personnel, either missionary or national, or to the total number of churches reported. Each should be averaged out with a smooth curve to assess the overall impact of each component on the others in the entire process.

Percentages, Ratios and Distributions

Factual material uncovered by a survey can be objectified simply by calculating percentages. The fact that 42% of the membership of a certain church was "transfer growth" led to a new strategy. When another church learned that 81% of its members lived within two kilometers, the church recognized the need to multiply the number of congregations. When 23% of the missionaries in one survey reported that they had not won anyone to Christ in a year, the group was shocked into action. A great soul-winning field was revealed by a survey that showed that 68% of the church members were from non-Christian homes (E. Smith 1976:70).

The way percentages are presented can bias interpretation. One may say that 15% of the membership is a result of transfer growth, or one may say that 85% of the members have never been incorporated in any other church. A different feeling is produced by each statement.

Ratios are helpful. Knowing a given church movement has grown to 13,118 is further illuminated by asking the ratio of total members to those regularly worshipping each Sunday. In one case the answer might be 38 per congregation for the ECU in Bolivia in contrast to a 24,000 single congregation in Chile. Information demonstrating such a large contrast may very well signal that a different definition of a worshipping unit is being used. Another valuable ratio is the number of worshippers per ordained or trained pastor. This may expose a training gap, an ordination lag, or both. It is also valuable to learn the ratio of full members to trained pastors. How can a church be healthy and stable if there are many more than 50 to 100 full members per trained leader, as is occuring in the ECU? McGavran points out five kinds of leaders and the crucial relationship between the ratios of each of these groups of people within an ongoing congregation and denomination (McGavran with Arn 1973:89-97). Figure 8 demonstrates the importance of a proper ratio of class two and class four workers.

Some factual material is not adequately objectified by percentages and ratios alone. To know that sixty percent of the members are under twenty-five years of age is helpful. To know that the average age of members is twenty-one can be still more helpful.

A frequency distribution curve presents factual material such as ages, educational background, and other material more clearly than simple percentage figures.

Figure 6

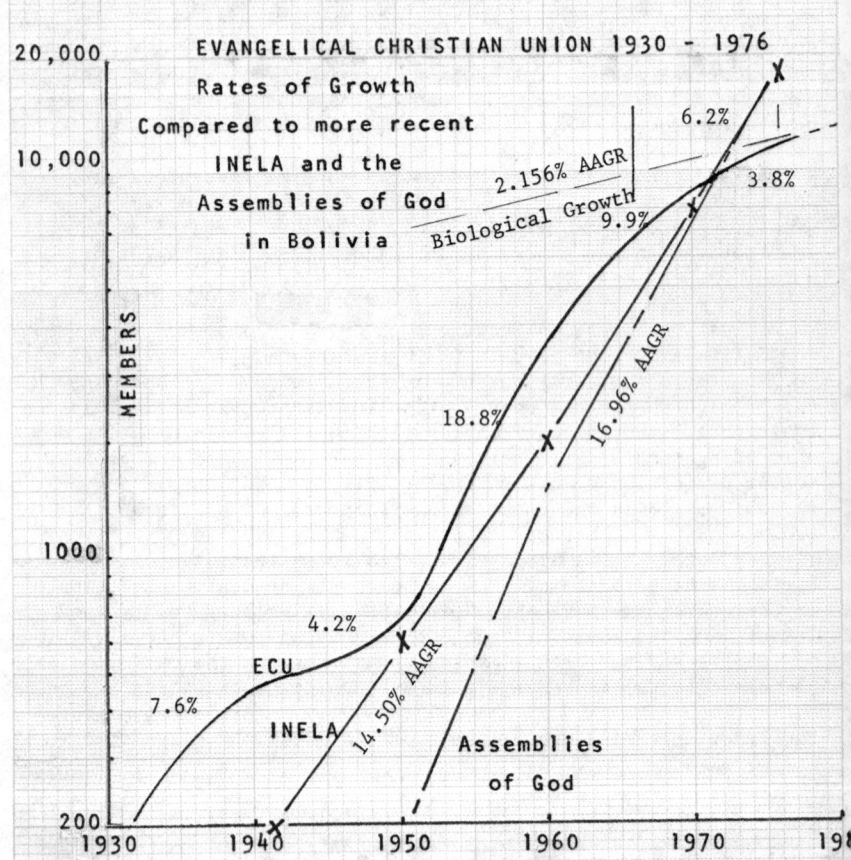

Figure 7

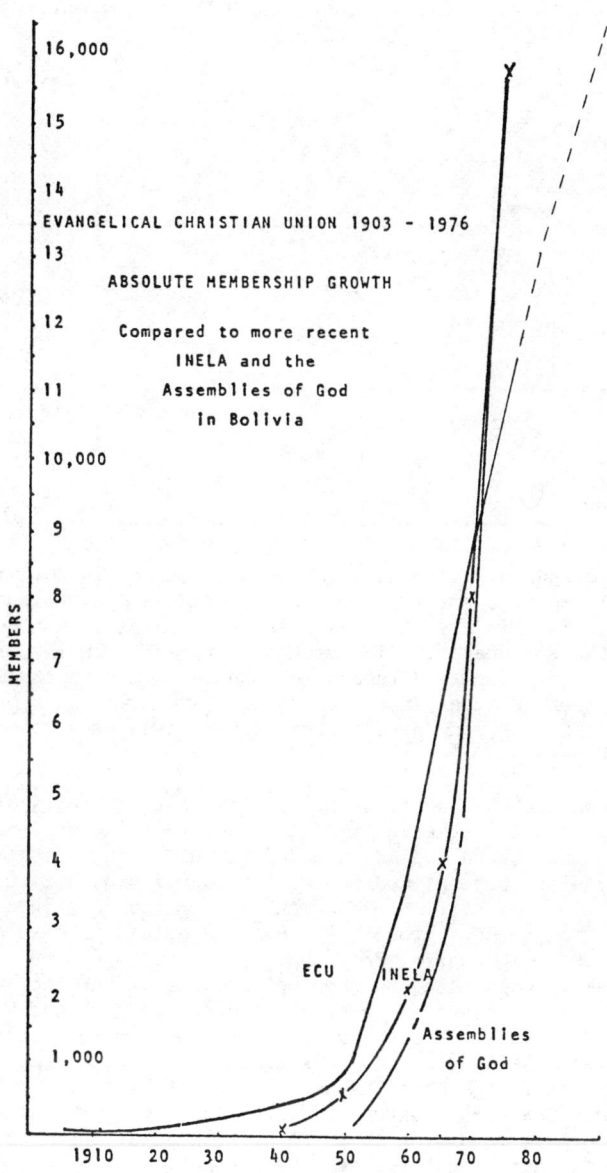

Figure 8
Five Classes of Leaders

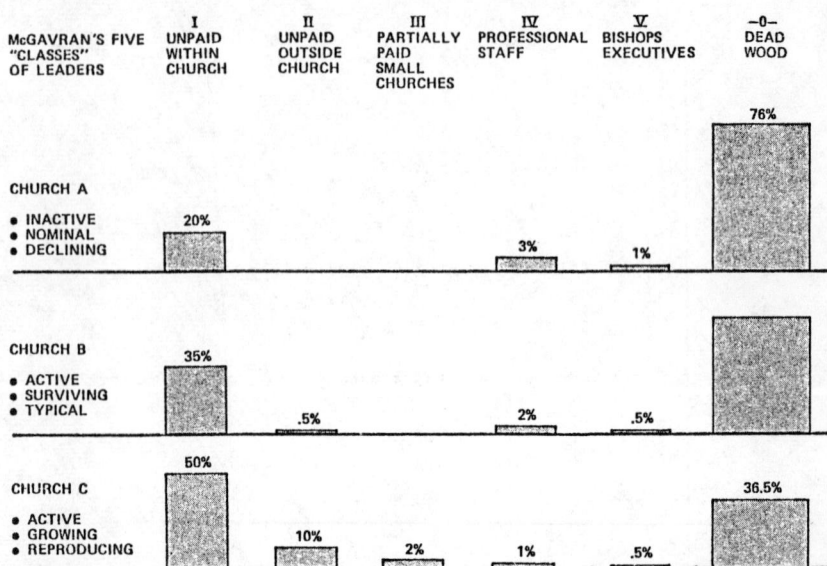

The age span of potential members of a church in Bolivia can be visualized by observing the age/sex frequency distribution in Figure 3. In this case the possible membership is most numerous through the age span from 14 through 39 years. Usually, it is helpful to make separate tables for men and women in the local church. When these are put back to back and drawn as a bar chart, the result is the common "Christmas tree" that demographers draw, seen in Figure 3.

To summarize this section, we can say that the facts of growth, though diligently gathered, may still not tell the whole story. The facts must be coaxed and prodded through the tools of graphs, frequency distributions and the evaluation of growth rates. The facts must be objectified. They must be broken down into distinctive, homogeneous groupings. Each denomination must determine its own components. Only then do the facts expose themselves to analysis. Only then can the implications of the facts be grasped. It is essential to plot all data first, before arriving at the conclusions. Picturing growth rates is more important to analysis than selling conclusions to others. Selling conclusions is a valuable fringe benefit when the objective analysis has been well done. The next chapter clarifies the facts by upstreaming to the source - returning to the ECU/AEM headwaters to better understand the historical flow to the present.

3

Clarifying the Facts by Upstreaming

There are five areas in which the frustrating missions informational smog must be cleared for better goal setting. Only then can we more adequately meet our responsibility to the Lord of the harvest for this, our generation. Here are five suggested areas needing further attention:

1. More readable, concise, objective missionary reporting to supporting churches. What concrete steps are being taken toward the completion of definable goals?

2. More reliable field demographic data.

3. More responsible accounting of annual membership, both denominational and local. Decrease the excessive ratio of unbaptized to baptized believers in the national Church.

4. More specific pinpointing of the geographic location and density of each basic homogeneous group.

5. More precise population data by country, state (department) and capital cities.

Smog, by definition, is a mixture of man-made contaminants with fog, which by itself is a natural phenomenon. What we must do is reduce our part in the contamination.

The clarifying process, "upstreaming", is an ethnohistorical research tool (Dark 1957:231-278; Fenton 1962:1-23; Sturtevant 1966:1-51). Fenton originated this concept in 1949. It means researching history in reverse, going from the known present to the unknown past. Imagine yourself standing at the mouth of a river and working upstream to the source. Thus, starting with the present and working back to the 1907 beginnings of the AEM/ECU pilgrimmage through time is the essence of this diachronic process. By going back through time, the field researcher and the reader avoid projecting their prejudice and learn beyond the mere data. Dramatically, the dynamic ingredients for the successful communication of the Gospel, conversion, church planting, indigeneity and meaningful incorporation stand out in bold relief. What may have been previously overlooked as being insignificant becomes significant as the researcher answers the question *why* from history.

Some of the past smog has been caused by scorn for maintaining church statistics. Those opposed look for biblical support, citing God's displeasure with King David's census (II Sam. 24:1-10). They overlook many instances in Numbers where God commands a diligent accounting for all Israel and every tribal component (Num. 1:2,3). Moreover, Luke's reporting of numerical increase in the book of Acts cannot be overlooked. A. R. Tippett affirms from Scripture that the motive for numbering determines God's approval or disapproval (1965 *CGB* I:3).

No one has been saved by statistics or cured by a thermometer. X-rays never knit a broken bone. Yet, the skilled physician uses these means to help him realize curative goals. Equally, growth facts will not bring anyone to Christ. But they can stimulate any church willing to awake to the facts, to maximize its impact for Christ in its community.

What factors are needed for an objective analysis of the changing Bolivian population seen through the eyes of any of the forty Protestant groups now discipling? As an example to other denominations in Bolivia, the remainder of this essay will go through the diachronic process as seen through the eyes of the ECU/AEM. Six areas are discussed.

1. Population totals and trends from 1900 to 1980.

2. Ethnic group sub-totals and trends.

3. Resistance and receptivity trends.

4. Trends in the deployment of national and missionary resources, both human and financial.

5. Trends in the percent of each homogeneous unit professing to be Protestant by 1980.

6. Priorities for the remaining challenge.

Clarifying the Facts by Upstreaming

This process represents a significant shift in church growth methodology. Emphasis is given here to the two properties of every statistic: both size and change must be reported simultaneously for any realistic analysis and for proper goal-setting. Integrating the still life "synchronic" portrayals of other authors describing the Bolivian scene into a single, closed system, is done here by forming a moving, graphic pattern over the last seven decades. This is done for all segments of the population. Nothing is lost or unaccounted for among the five million. These trends are reported as average annual growth rates observed over each decade. Each ten year mark acts as a minor hinge, indicating an up or down change in direction. Once the AAGR is determined for each decade, it is easy to calculate the annual steps between the decadal boundaries.

Population Totals and Trends from 1900 to 1980

The nine Bolivian departments (states) and corresponding capitals are depicted in Figure 9 with the associated population density. In countries where minimal demographic data is available, secure the most reliable census data as given in a reliable source like the Encyclopedia Britannica (1959 III:818,19; 1910 IV:171).

Two-fifths of the land area to the southwest is the highland *altiplano* where three-fourths of the population live. Using a closed-system approach in constructing the population-time tables appearing in Appendix A, shows that the actual highland percentage was 86% in 1900. By 1980 it drops to 85%. This is one of the many examples where authors make still life synchronic descriptions which do not reflect the size-change dynamic.

All the large cities in settled areas lie above 8,000 feet, many going to 12,000 feet. Below 6,000 feet, Santa Cruz and Trinidad are the two largest cities. The national census of August, 1950 was 3,019,031 compared to 1,633,610 in 1900. Of this total 1950 major hinge year population, 52.9% was Indian *campesino*, 32% *mestizo* and 14.8% white. The Indian population is largely composed of civilized Aymaras and Quechuas in the Andean highlands and of lowland Indians in the eastern forests and grasslands. By 1950, 37% of the total population was urban, including 23% living in the nine capital cities. The crude birth rate was 41.9 per 1,000 population in 1950. The crude death rate was 15, and the infantile mortality was 106.5 per 1,000 live births.

The present white population descended for the most part from the early Spanish conquerors. Also, some came from the Spanish and Portuguese neighbors. This group, numbering 446,817 in 1950, completely dominates the country. Especially after the close of the Chaco War in 1935, the government induced immigrants to come from Europe and the United States. Some came from Czechoslovakia,

Germany, and other European countries to settle in the eastern territories. But total immigration has remained small. In general terms, whites are landowners and government officials. The *mestizos* are tradesmen, skilled workers and minor civil servants. The Indian *campesino* is a farmer, herdsman, commercial transporter and small scale merchant. The Indians are a class apart, suspicious of changes as being new methods of exploitation.

Figure 9

NINE BOLIVIAN DEPARTMENTS AND CAPITALS

WITH POPULATION DENSITY

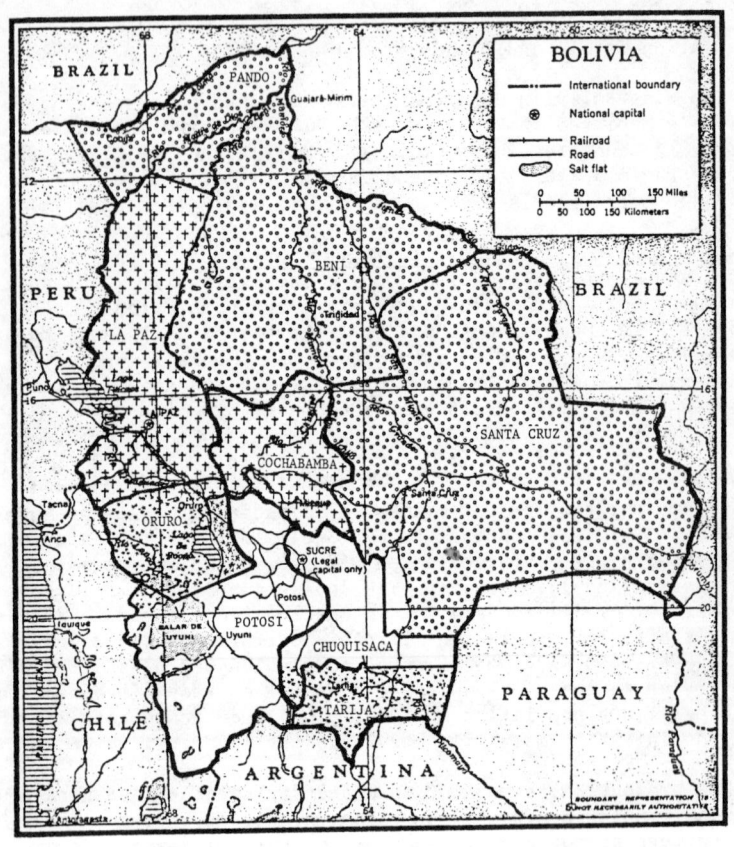

	7 - 9	persons per sq. km.	Data taken from Bolivian National Census, 1950
	4.5-5.5	" " " "	
	3 - 4	" " " "	
	less than 1	person " " "	

The nine Bolivian departments with their 1950 major hinge year populations and the 1900 and 1970 boundary year populations are shown in Table I under Appendix A. Also shown are the corresponding capital cities with their respective populations.

The data for 1900 and 1970 in Table I under Appendix A had to be corrected for territorial losses to Brazil and Chile. Furthermore, the data for 1910 and 1980 was projected from official estimates. These come from various sources besides the Britannica for 1910 and 1957 (Europa 1975:152; Brockhaus 1953:229; Walle 1914:56 and Weil 1974:61-70). With the raw data of Table I in hand, it is possible to correct each figure as it finally appears in Table II under Appendix A. This is done by applying a series of ratios formed by the relationship:

$$\frac{\text{Incorrect Subtotal}}{\text{Incorrect Total Population}} = \frac{\text{Corrected Subtotal (X)}}{\text{Correct Total Population}}$$

Solve for (X) since all the other elements are known. Tables II and III under Appendix A are the result. This process sets realistic parameters for determining each component which contributes to the overall national population. Once the corrected 1900 - 1950 - 1980 boundaries have been established, the AAGR between them may be calculated. The major "hinge" year is definitely 1950. This is well illustrated by the plotted data on semilogarithmic paper for each of the nine departments with its corresponding capital compared to national population trends over the same period, Figures 1 through 9 in Appendix A. The same size paper and scales are used throughout to facilitate comparisons.

The overall population shift favors the lowlands. This shows that the government resettlement programs are beginning to have national impact. The capital city of Santa Cruz is growing the most rapidly. Sociologically, these people are open to change. Spiritually, they are very ripe for harvest. McGavran has specified the following causes for fluctuation in receptivity: resettlement, returned travellers, crisis, rising nationalism, freedom from social control mechanisms and acculturation (1970:216-232). Building on McGavran's idea of constructing a resistance-receptivity axis, each department and its capital has been assigned a relative receptivity rating based upon its AAGR compared with its neighbors. This method eliminates the subjective guessing that had to be done in the past to locate people on the resistance-receptivity axis. It is constructed by drawing a line from A to Z so that every population may be located at the letter which corresponds to its likelihood to become Christian. At the left would be those people who solidly resist Christianity. At the right would be those who are the most responsive. In between lie all others according to their responsiveness (1970:228).

Ethnic Group Sub-totals and Trends

One of the most useful concepts to come out of the church growth movement is the homogeneous unit as a vital part in the development of the Body of Christ. This term has been used for more than a decade. It has become more and more useful. The historian uses it to unscramble many riddles throughout the historical expansion of Christianity. The anthropologist recognizes that this concept is wider and more flexible than culture. The missionary constantly uses it to evangelize the unreached. The minister and shepherd discovers that he can better serve his flock when he sees Christians in their particular socio-economic context. The theologian finds the homogeneous unit principle firmly rooted in the Bible (Wagner 1977:207-43).

The homogeneous unit concept is fighting a losing battle against public acceptance; eventually it must go. Larger and larger racial and linguistic groupings are developing. But in the meantime, homogeneous units are a reality and will likely remain so for some time, according to McGavran (1977a:10). He recommends that the Church disciple each group out to the fringes, operate within them, preserve the richness of their cultures and promote love and justice among all men. The Church working in this way with the homogeneous unit and not against it, will liberate many ethnic groups, bringing them into the glorious liberty of the children of God.

During this interim, Christian theologians and ethicists are debating the desirability of homogeneous churches. Empirically, most churches are essentially composed of similar kinds of people, while the surrounding society is heterogeneous. The opponents of homogeneity affirm that such churches deny the Christian principle of being "all one in Christ Jesus" (Gal. 3:26-28 and Wagner 1977: 105-114).

This issue is relevant to both North and South America. Both are entering a new ethnicity phase. The North is emerging from the 1960s' civil rights crisis with a new social psychology. The South is rushing toward greater internal development to catch up with the affluent North. Oil money is creating new tensions in Latin America. Over night many are becoming wealthy.

The melting pot model for understanding American society has always been a myth. Yet its idealism has fanned our imagination and influenced our decisions.

The original definition of homogeneous unit (HU) given by McGavran, is a section of society in which all members share some distinctive characteristic in common (1970:85). It might be a political or geographical unit or sub unit. The common characteristics might also be language, culture, tribe or caste (Cf. Num. 1:19-20).

Clarifying the Facts by Upstreaming

A more realistic "stew pot" model is now being suggested by Wagner. He recommends this metaphor because it emphasizes the individual distinctiveness of the ingredients (i.e., different homogeneous units) brought together in such a way that each is flavored by the other while yet maintaining its own identity and integrity (1977:73-80).

Figure 10, Wagner's Ethclass Model, is a tool to more accurately identify homogeneous units. The model weighs together the principal components of ethnic group and social class. The ethnic group is further divided into the sub groups of race, religion, national origin, and assimilation factors. Social class subdivisions are: economic status, vocation and formal schooling. Regional identity and the rural-urban orientation are interrelated with all the foregoing factors.

Based upon Wagner's refined definition, for the purpose of this analysis of the five million Bolivian people through the eyes of the ECU, we may divide the Bolivian population into nine broad ethnic groupings as shown in Table IV under Appendix A. Again, the AAGR trends have been calculated with 1950 serving as the major hinge between 1910 and 1980. The percent breakdowns of the respective populations in 1910, 1950 and 1970, projected to 1980, were determined from the previously mentioned sources and plotted on Figure 11 as a check to be sure that all components were accounted for. Again, the receptivity rating has been recorded in the right hand column of Table IV under Appendix A as a relative ranking of the trend of each ethnic group. The respective AAGR indicates the dynamism or degree of change occurring within each unit. This may be considered to be an indication of the people's openness to new ideas, as possibly presented by an advocate of the eternal Gospel.

Figure 12 is a snapshot of the Bolivian population projected to 5,128,075 by 1980 at a 2.156% AAGR. This type of ethnolinguistic grid originated with Dr. Ralph Winter for Missions Advanced Research and Communication Center (MARC) in preparing the unreached peoples surveys for the International Congress on World Evangelization in Lausanne, July, 1974. Since preparing the 1973 Bolivian Profile (Smith 1974:1) for MARC, I have been continually upgrading the methodology for using this tool. It helps the researcher to maintain a realistic relationship among the homogeneous ingredients within the "stew pot". Because this is a closed system, all parts must be accounted for. All the parts are interrelated. Once the percentage of the population is determined for any given moment in time, then the ethnic mosaic may be determined at that same period of time.

Once this process is accomplished for a denomination like the ECU by upstreaming to the data source, pinpointing when work

Figure 10

PRINCIPAL COMPONENTS
OF ETHCLASS IDENTITY - U.S.A.

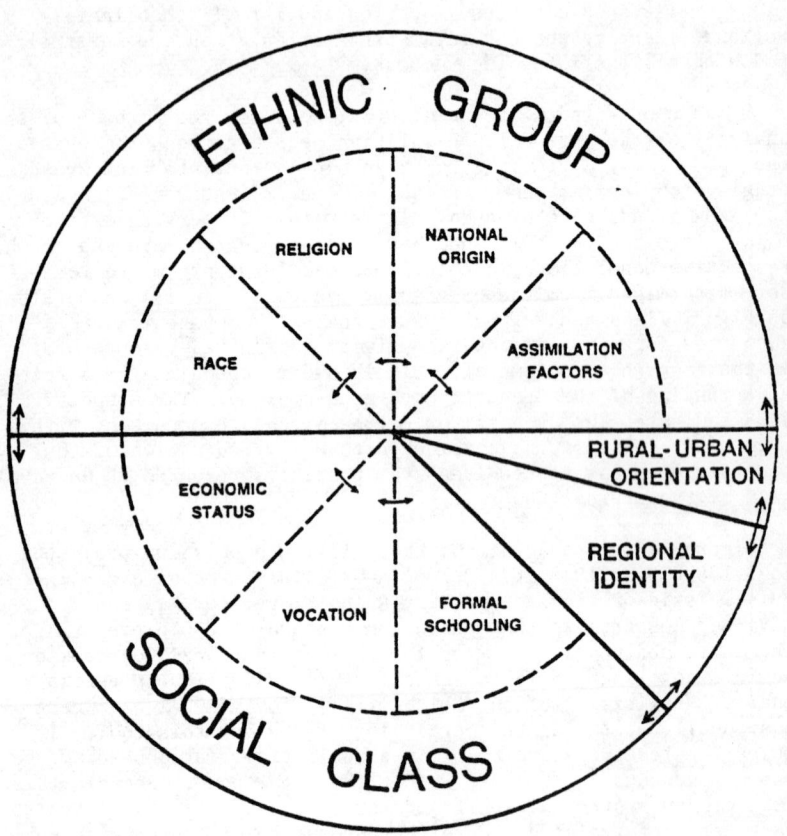

(Wagner 1977:124)

Figure 11

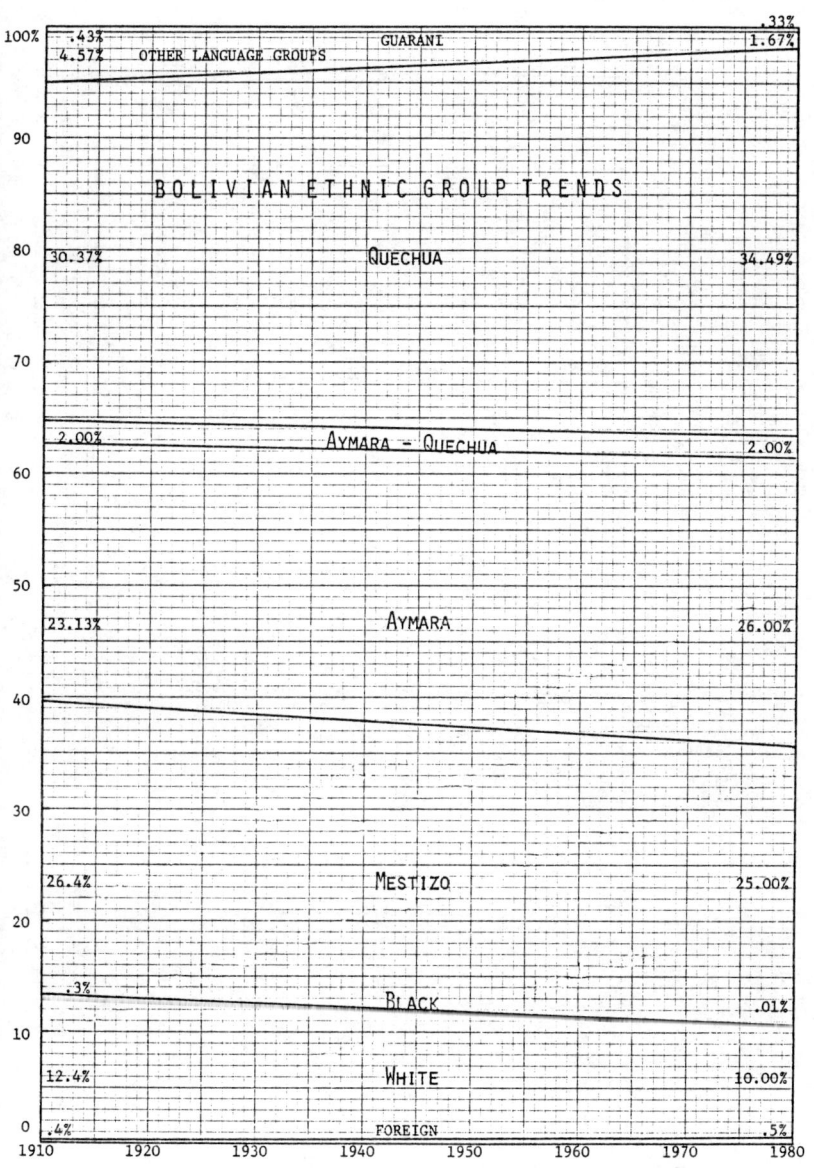

Figure 12

Figure 12

BOLIVIAN ETHNO LINGUISTIC POPULATION DISTRIBUTION

5,128,075 at 2.156% AAGR Projected by Mid 1980

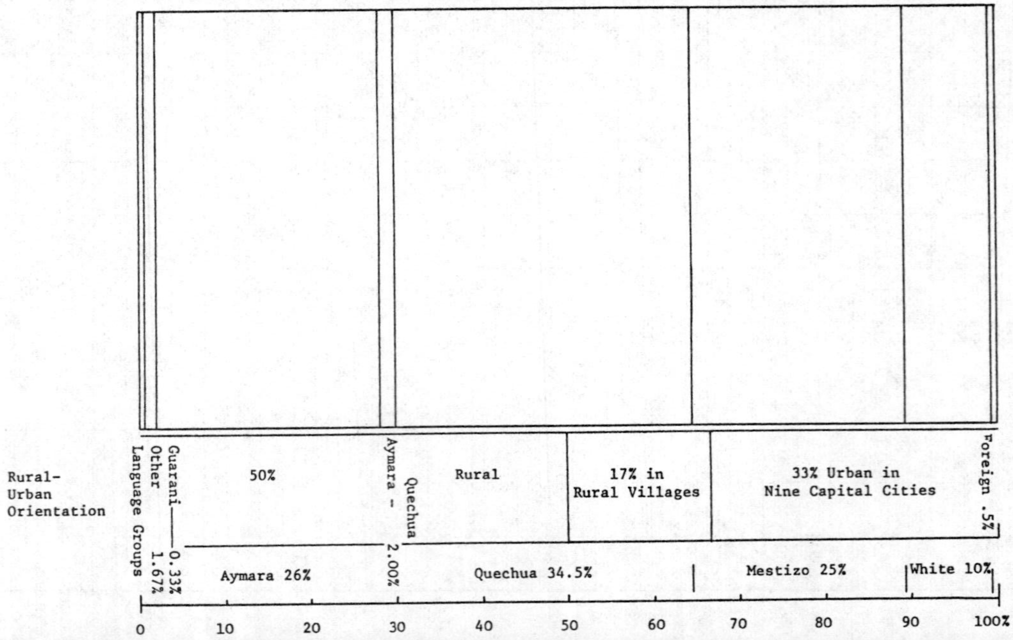

Rural-
Urban
Orientation
Guarani——0.33%
Other 1.67%
Language Groups
50%
Aymara -
Quechua
2.00%
Rural
17% in
Rural Villages
33% Urban in
Nine Capital Cities
Foreign .5%
Aymara 26%
Quechua 34.5%
Mestizo 25%
White 10%
0
10
20
30
40
50
60
70
80
90
100%

Clarifying the Facts by Upstreaming

began among each homogeneous unit, Table IV comes to life. The global data already available as plotted in Figure 13 can now be broken down into its five component parts. Table IV was derived by upstreaming from the ECU ethnic breakdown given in my 1973 field survey of the 271 ECU churches (Smith 1973:1-35). By connecting the points for 1973 with the points of origin and the respective 1950 percentages, each ethnic group trend from 1950 to 1980 unfolds in Figure 14.

Figures 10 through 14 under Appendix A are the result of plotting out the data for each of the five ECU homogeneous unit churches (HUCs). A homogeneous unit church is defined as a cluster of congregations within one denomination growing within a given homogeneous unit (McGavran 1970:87). Now armed with a graph for each HUC it will be possible to treat each one according to its distinctive needs. We can be more accountable in our work instead of lumping all the data together as has been done in the past, shown in Figure 13. Later on the HU components will be superimposed on Figure 13 to give the reader a better idea of the interrelationship among these units as compared to the trend of the Protestant movement nationally.

McGavran emphasizes the uniqueness in the growth of each HUC. Each must be treated individually and never lumped because each HU growth pattern is according to:

1. A different pattern from all others. There is no overlap.

2. A pattern distinctively its own.

3. Its own rate of growth.

4. Its own upper population limit.

5. Its own enabling sources from the outside, either weak, strong, long or short-term.

A 1973 synchronic snapshot of the geographical distribution of the ECU's 271 active churches appears in Figure 15. Compare this to the population concentrations, Figure 16, and to the Bolivian Ethnolinguistic divisions, Figure 17, to appreciate why the ECU is only concerned with the five major HU groups already noted in Figure 14, with further details in Table IV. According to several authors, all minor language groups totaled only 2.5% of the 1955 to 1960 population (Alonso 1962:101; Fifer 1972:261 and Comas 1962:13-17). This means that the entire ethnic population of the five HUs with which the ECU is working, in conjunction with some forty other mission groups in Bolivia, will total nearly 4,503,549 people, or 87.8% of the population by 1980. This represents the upper limit of the number of people for which the ECU/AEM team is committed.

Figure 13

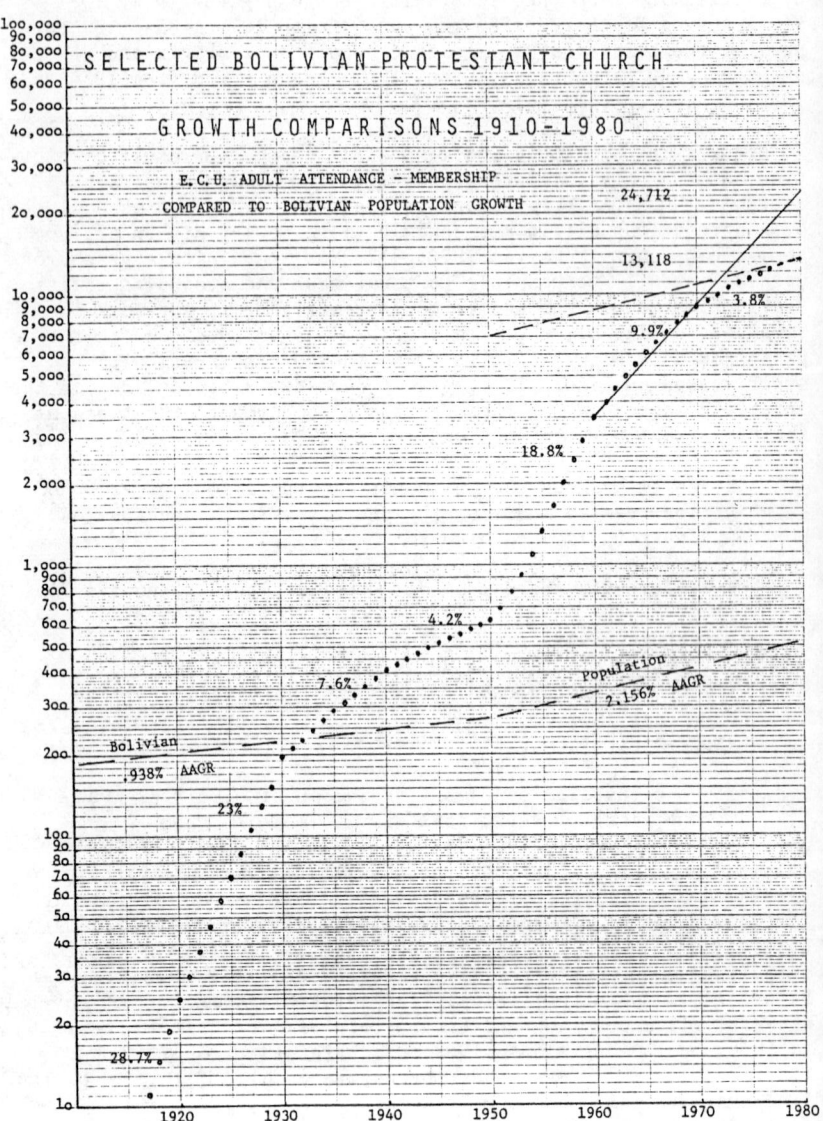

Table IV

E.C.U. ETHNIC GROUPS RANKED BY GROWTH

	GUARANI	% of ECU	QUECHUA	% of ECU	AYMARA - QUECHUA	% of ECU	AYMARA	% of ECU	MESTIZO	% of ECU	TOTALS	Biological Growth per Decade	Net Gain/Loss
1910			2	100.0%							2		
AAGR			28.7%								28.7%		
													2
1920			25	100.0%							25		23
AAGR			20.8%								23.0%		
													27 173
1930			165	82.5%	15	7.5%			20	10.0%	200		
AAGR			6.1%		12.8%				12.5%		7.6%		
													220 195
1940	50		300	72.0%	50	12.0%			65	16.0%	415		
AAGR	23.1%		2.9%		7.8%				10.7%		4.2%		-60
													685
1950	400*	35.5%	400	35.5%	106	9.5%	39	3.6%	180*	16.0%	625 AEM (500 EUSA)	1125 = 18.8%	2107
AAGR	6.8%		9.8%		17.4%		24.2%		16.7%				
												1,393	
1960	770	22.0%	1,015	29.0%	525	15.0%	350	10.0%	840	24.0%	3,500		4668
AAGR	5.0%		9.5%		10.6%		15.2%		10.8%		9.9%		
												4,332	
1970	1,260	14.0%	2,520	28.0%	1,440	16.0%	1,440	16.0%	2,340	26.0%	9,000		
AAGR	3.6%		3.9%		3.3%		4.8%		3.7%		3.8%		
(LOW)1	1,305		2,617		1,487		1,509		2,427		9,345		
2	1,351		2,718		1,536		1,582		2,517		9,704		
3	1,399	13.8%	2,823	28.0%	1,586	15.7%	1,658	16.5%	2,611	26.0%	10,077		
4	1,449		2,932		1,638		1,738		2,708		10,465		
5	1,500		3,045		1,691		1,821		2,809		10,866	11,140	1,978
6	1,553		3,162		1,747		1,909		2,913		11,284		
7	1,609		3,284		1,804		2,001		3,822		11,720		
8	1,666		3,411		1,863		2,047		3,134		12,171		
9	1,725		3,543		1,924		2,198		3,251		12,641		
1980	1,786	13.6%	3,679	28.0%	1,987	15.2%	2,304	17.6%	3,362	25.6%	13,118		
AAGR	5.0%		9.5%		10.6%		15.2%		10.8%		10.6%		
1971	1,324		2,760		1,593		1,659		2,592		9,928		
2	1,390		3,023		1,762		1,911		2,872		10,958		
3	1,461		3,310		1,949		2,201		3,182		12,103		
4	1,534		3,626		2,156		2,536		3,525		13,377		
(HIGH) 5	1,612		3,971		2,385		2,921		3,906		14,795	11,140	13,572
6	1,693		4,349		2,638		3,365		4,327		16,372		
7	1,779		4,763		2,918		3,876		4,794		18,130		
8	1,868		5,216		3,228		4,465		5,311		20,088		
9	1,963		5,713		3,571		5,143		5,884		22,274		
1980	2,062	8.3%	6,257	25.3%	3,950	16.0%	5,925	24.0%	6,518	26.4%	24,712		

POSSIBLE HIGH PERCENTAGE OF EACH ETHNIC GROUP TO BE REACHED BY THE ECU BY 1980				
12.0%	.35%	3.85%	.44%	.51%
RANK: V By Latest AAGR	IV	II	I	III

* For continuity, begin to count the EUSA components though they did not merge with the ECU until 1959.

Figure 14

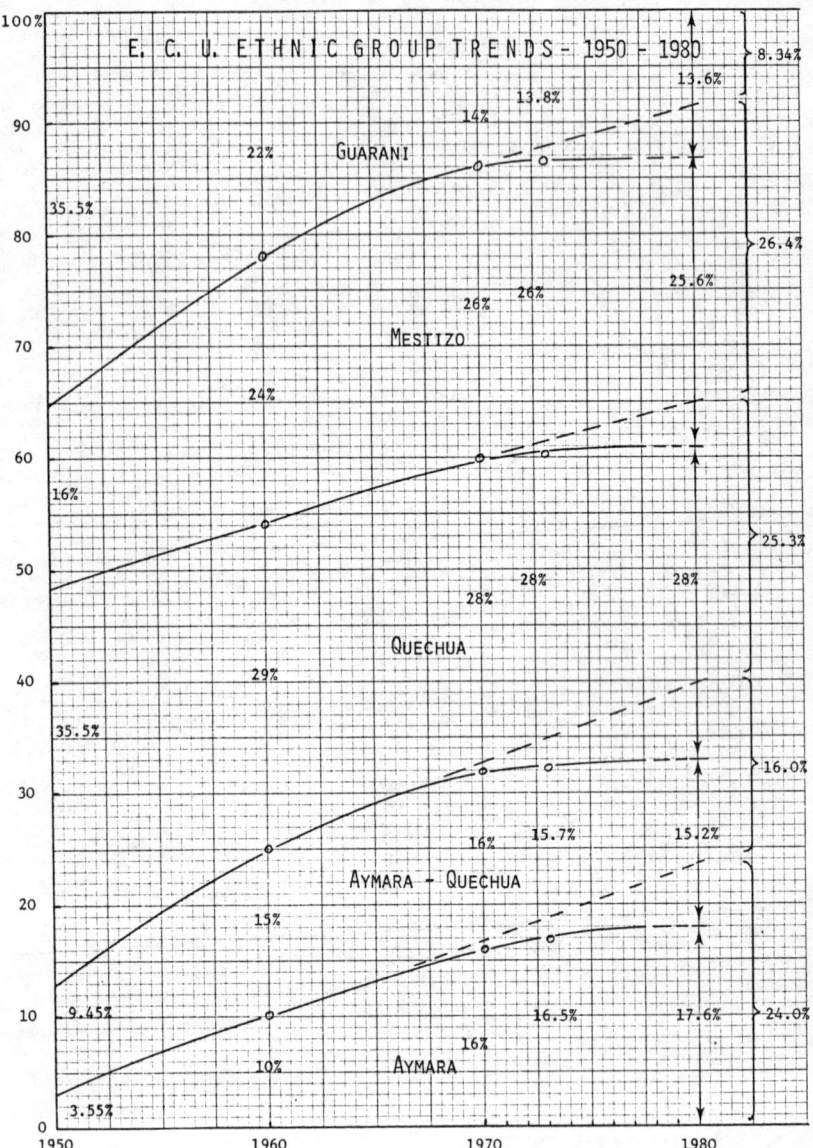

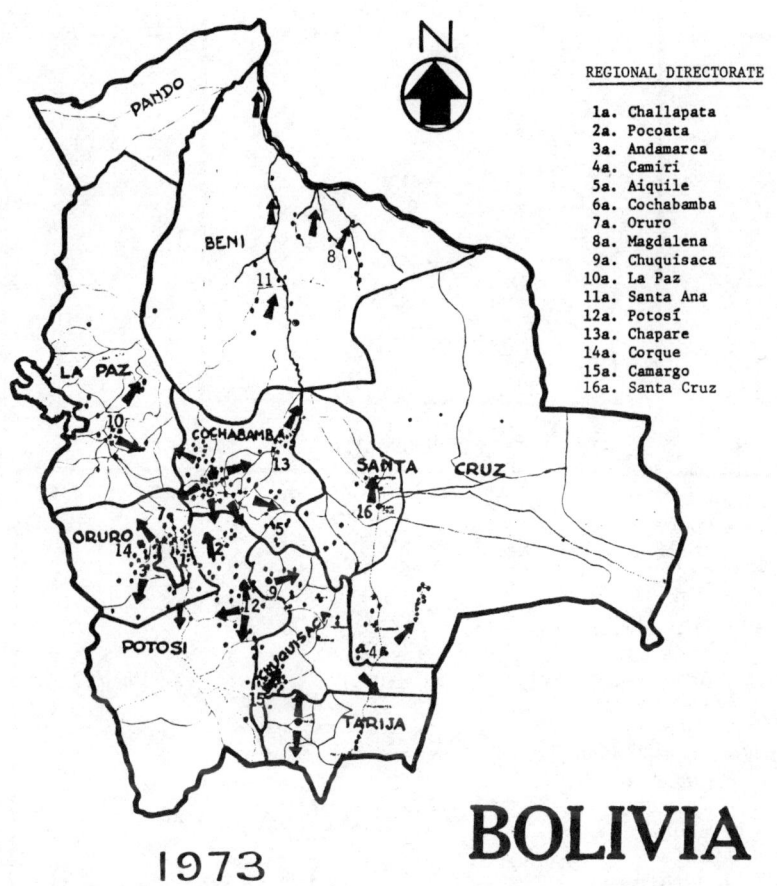

Figure 15

Figure 16: 1967 POPULATION CONCENTRATIONS

Over 50,000
Over 5,000
SOURCES:
1950 census
1967 official estimates

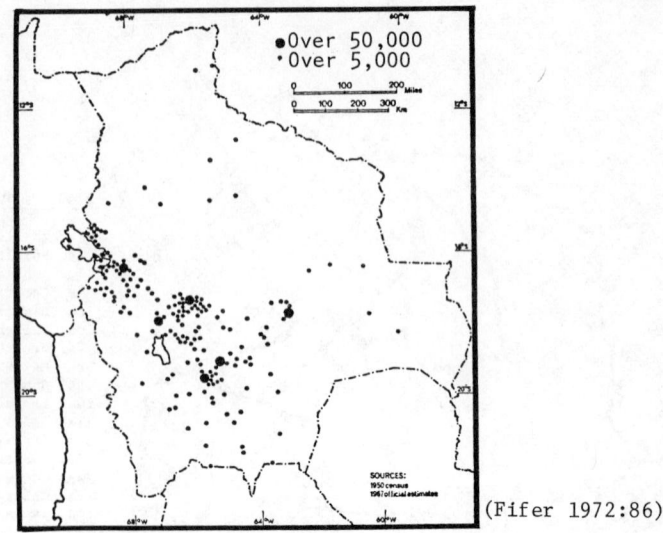

(Fifer 1972:86)

Figure 17: BOLIVIAN ETHNOLINGUISTIC DIVISIONS

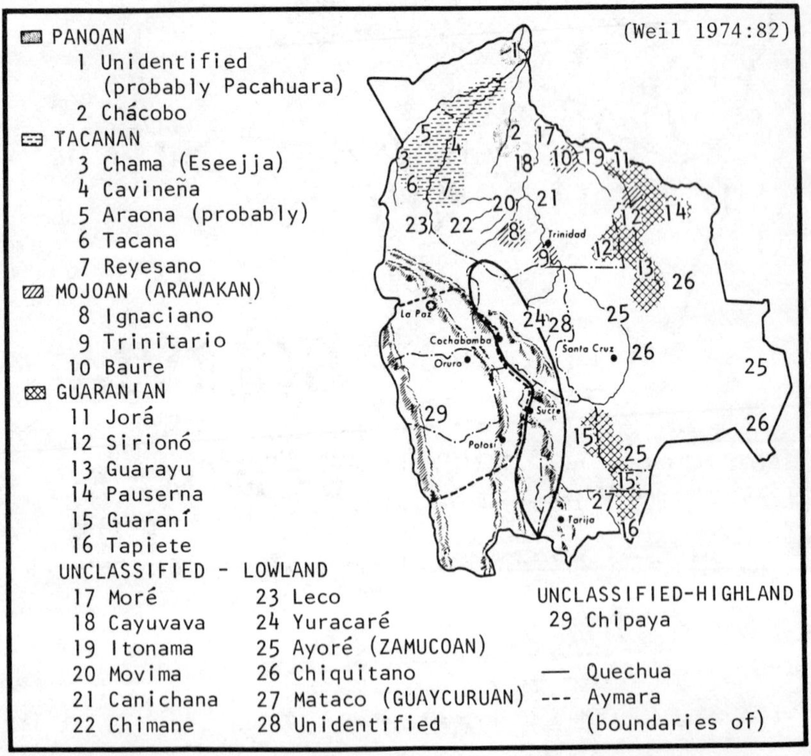

(Weil 1974:82)
PANOAN
1 Unidentified (probably Pacahuara)
2 Chácobo
TACANAN
3 Chama (Eseejja)
4 Cavineña
5 Araona (probably)
6 Tacana
7 Reyesano
MOJOAN (ARAWAKAN)
8 Ignaciano
9 Trinitario
10 Baure
GUARANIAN
11 Jorá
12 Sirionó
13 Guarayu
14 Pauserna
15 Guaraní
16 Tapiete
UNCLASSIFIED - LOWLAND
17 Moré
18 Cayuvava
19 Itonama
20 Movima
21 Canichana
22 Chimane
23 Leco
24 Yuracaré
25 Ayoré (ZAMUCOAN)
26 Chiquitano
27 Mataco (GUAYCURUAN)
28 Unidentified
UNCLASSIFIED-HIGHLAND
29 Chipaya
— Quechua
--- Aymara
(boundaries of)
Trinidad
La Paz
Cochabamba
Oruro
Santa Cruz
Sucre
Potosí
Tarija

Clarifying the Facts by Upstreaming

Resistance - Receptivity Trends

Table V is a Summary of the Resistance - Receptivity Factors noted thus far for the nine capital cities, departments and ethnic groups, all ranked in ascending AAGR order. Notice how those above the national 2.156% average are gaining while those below are losing population. Thus, the "right end" peoples experiencing greater growth and vitality through immigration are the most likely to be more responsive (Gulick 1973:998). This conclusion is eloquently demonstrated by the spiritual response of the ECU ethnic groups also ranked in ascending order by their respective AAGRs in section II of Table V.

Trends in Deployment of Resources

Section III of Summary Table V shows how the AEM and the ECU are now deploying their resources. The national Church, relying principally upon local leadership, is much more diversified. Section IV of Table V shows how far along we will be by 1980 in fulfilling our commitment in conjunction with the entire Protestant movement in Bolivia - nearly a quarter of a million Christians! Table VI analyzes the 1976 AEM personnel deployment, showing 77.1% involved in nurture and service compared to 22.9% in evangelism. Among the latter, only five men are active among the premium Aymara, Aymara-Quechua and Quechua harvest. A more ideal deployment could result from recruiting and training forty more specialists for both the Aymara and the Quechua harvests. The higher 2.26% AAGR ethnic response for the Quechuas compared to the slower 2.10% AAGR *mestizo* response leads to the conclusion that the low 1.7% Quechua portion of the population in Table V stems from insufficient workers. So far missions have generally been unsuccessful in recruiting many effective E_3 communicators for the Quechuas (Klassen 1975:166-199; McIntosh 1971:7). Besides, these specialists take time to prepare for effective cross-cultural communication. Perhaps using some specialists teaming up with more national, second commitment sodalities suggested on page 13 would be a viable solution. Each congregation could be responsible for spawning a committed band of maximum power E_1 communicators of the Gospel to their own near neighbors (Winter 1975:219). Unfortunately, this often takes an additional effort by the E_3 missionary parent to secure the extra commitment of national believers to move out in continuous mission. Later chapters discuss this further.

Table VII demonstrates how the AEM leadership is concerned about better balancing of the 77.1% in nurture and the 22.9% in evangelism. However, the proposed 1976 - 1977 distribution of newly recruited workers is still very inadequate. The rhythm of past recruitment and deployment of missionary personnel shown in Figure 18 illustrates how difficult it will be even with great effort, to recruit and field more than 100 nationals or 90

Table V

SUMMARY

RESISTANCE RECEPTIVITY FACTORS FOR THE BOLIVIAN POPULATION
BASED UPON LATEST GROWTH RATES 1950 - 1980

Most Resistant — ← | → + Most Receptive

I. PEOPLE CHANGE FACTORS

A. <u>Nine Capital Cities</u> Rated by AAGR

9	8	7	6	5	4	3	2	1
Sucre	Cobija	Tarija	Potosí	Oruro	Trinidad	Cochabamba	La Paz	Santa Cruz
1.176%	1.662%	1.671%	2.075%	2.277%	2.462%	3.395%	3.606%	7.177%

←——— Losing ———|——— Gaining ———→

B. <u>Nine Departments</u> Rated by AAGR

9	8	7	6	5	4	3	2	1
Santa Cruz	Tarija	Chuquisaca	Cochabamba	Potosí	La Paz	Pando	Oruro	Beni
1.673%	1.676%	1.822%	1.834%	1.9%	2.396%	2.438%	2.606%	3.591%

←——— Losing ———|——— Gaining ———→

C. <u>Ethnic Groups</u> Rated by AAGR

9	8	7	6	5	4	3	2	1
Blacks	Other Lang. Groups	Guarani	White	Mestizo	Aymara-Quechua	Quechua	Aymara	Foreign
-3.18%	.256%	1.784%	1.99%	2.10%	2.16%	2.26%	2.32%	2.52%

←——— Losing ———|——— Gaining ———→

II. SPIRITUAL RESPONSE OF ECU ETHNIC GROUPS RANKED BY AAGR

	5 Guarani	4 Quechua	3 Mestizo	2 Aymara-Quechua	1 Aymara	TOTAL
Possible High Membership to be Reached by Each Group by 1980:	5% 2,062	9.5% 6,257	10% 6,518	10% 3,950	15.2% 5,925	24,712

III. DEPLOYMENT OF PERSONNEL IN 1977

A. AEM: 70 (21 in support) (EUSA)	2	44	2	1		
B. ECU: 100	14	28	26	16	16	

IV. PER CENT REACHED

	Black White Foreign	Other Lang. Groups	Guarani	Quechua	Mestizo	Aymara-Quechua	Aymara	TOTAL
PER CENT REACHED	1%	5%	12%	1.7%	3.4%	3.85%	10%	4.52%
Number by 1980:	5,366	4,278	2,062	30,140	44,050	3,950	142,000	231,846
Ethnic Pop.:	538,959	85,562	17,000	1,768,673	1,282,014	102,562	1,333,300	5,128,075
% of Total:	10.5%	1.7%	.3%	34.5%	25%	2%	26%	

Upper limit of ECU outreach shared with other groups in Bolivia. ←——— 4,503,549 or 87.8% ———→

Table VI

ANDES EVANGELICAL MISSION - 1976
ANALYSIS OF FIELD PERSONNEL DEPLOYMENT

		CULTURAL DISTANCE			TOTALS
		English 1	Spanish 2	Aymara-Quechua 3	
TASK	E = Evan. Church-Planting	0	13 18.6%	3 4.3%	16 22.9%
	N = Christian Nurture	1 1.4%	31 44.3%	1 1.4%	33 47.1%
	S = Service	17 24.3%	4 5.5%	0	21 30.0%
TOTAL		18 25.7%	48 68.6%	4 5.7%	70 100 %

CULTURAL DISTANCE

| 74.3% | CROSS-CULTURAL |
| 25.7% | MONO-CULTURAL |

TASK DESCRIPTION

| 77.1% | NURTURE & SERVICE |
| 22.9% | EVANGELISM |

<u>SCALE OF PRIORITIES:</u>

$N_2 = 44.3\%$
$S_1 = 24.3\%$
$E_2 = 18.6\%$
$S_2 = 5.7\%$
$E_3 = 4.3\%$
$N_1 = 1.4\%$
$N_3 = 1.4\%$
―――――
100%

Source: AEM Field Conference Statistics May, 1976

Table VII

ANDES EVANGELICAL MISSION 1976 - 1977

PERSONNEL NEEDS

		CULTURAL DISTANCE							
		English 1		Spanish 2		Aymara-Quechua 3			TOTALS
T A S K	E = Evangel Church Planting	0		38	43%	11	12%	49	55%
	N = Christian Nurture	0		18	20%	4	5%	22	25%
	S = Service	16	18%	2	2%	0		18	20%
	TOTAL	16	18%	58	65%	15	17%	89	100%

CULTURAL DISTANCE

| 82% | CROSS-CULTURAL |
| 18% | MONO-CULTURAL |

TASK DESCRIPTION

| 45% | NURTURE & SERVICE |
| 55% | EVANGELISM |

SCALE OF PRIORITIES:

$E_2 = 43\%$
$N_2 = 20\%$
$S_1 = 18\%$
$E_3 = 12\%$
$N_3 = 5\%$
$S_2 = 2\%$
───────
100%

Source: AEM Needs Sheet 1976-77

Figure 18

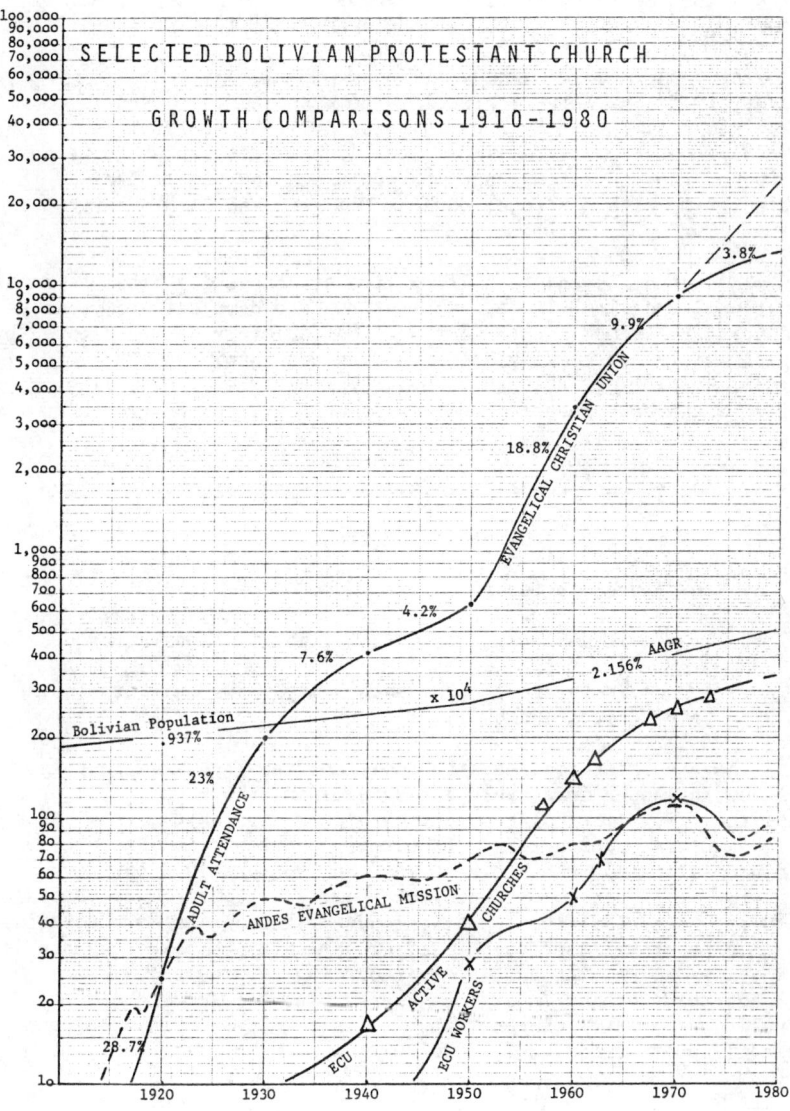

missionaries by 1980. Even if the 89 new workers were recruited, according to Table VII, their anticipated deployment would only increase the present imbalance. By all means, some new, creative steps must be taken to close the gap between the neglected, ripened harvest and the lumping of personnel in less strategic fields.

This mismatch between the whitened fields and the workers is contrary to the harvest principle demonstrated by Jesus in Matthew 10:1-15 and by Paul in Acts 17:1 (Wagner 1971:46-7). The Lord of the harvest calls us to diligently discern where He has ripened the fruit. He wants to put us in the right place at the right time with His Word, both as His seed and as His harvesters (Matt. 9:35-38; 13:23,38).

This study begins to clarify five areas causing missions informational smog in Bolivia. Parameters have been defined, complementing the somewhat nebulous and contradictory data presented by past writers describing Bolivian missions (Hamilton 1962, Hudspith 1958, Phillips 1968, Read 1969 and Wagner 1970). The following five areas have been defined for stimulating church growth in regional workshops.

1. Corrected population totals and trends from 1900 to 1980.

2. Ethnic group sub-totals and trends.

3. Reistance and receptivity trends.

4. Trends in deployment of national and missionary resources.

5. Trends in the percent of each homogeneous unit professing to be Protestant by 1980.

The ethnohistoric research tool, upstreaming, used in this study, has been invaluable for determining the boundaries for each of the five principal homogeneous groups with which our mission and national Church work. Once the correct populations are determined for the 1950 hinge year and the 1900 and 1970 boundary years, it is possible to project realistically to 1980. Hopefully, this clarification of the actual boundaries of the Bolivian harvest will spur each participant on to be more accountable in his goal setting and in his reporting of progress. We can no longer hide behind fuzzy guess work. The Lord of the harvest calls us to better shepherding. This requires improved accounting (Tippett 1965 *CGB* I; 3:28-29). Our upstreaming has just begun for Bolivia!

Now we are ready to go on to the next chapter which treats the unfinished task from 1980 on.

4

Looking Ahead to the Unfinished Task: Bolivia 1980

What creative steps can be taken to close the gap between the neglected harvest and the disproportionate distribution of reapers in less productive fields? Why should only 10% of Bolivia's nominal Christian population absorb over 90% of the the energy of national churches and missions? This is not only so in Bolivia but is sadly true of mission history world wide (McNee 1976:160). The average missionary today is no more likely to be ministering to non-Christians than are his supporters back home (Winter 1977: 11). Why is there such an imbalance?

Most of the western world being won to Christ already considers itself to be Christian. Most westerners involved in traditional foreign missions have generally evangelized nominal Christians. This is known as E_0 normal evangelism. As illustrated in Figure 4 at the end of Chapter One, E_0 represents internal evangelism and nurture because it transforms mere members of the church community into communicant members, crossing no cultural barriers. E_1 represents expansion evangelism, crossing the cultural barrier between the church and the world, adding near neighbors as members of the local congregation. E_1 also represents extension growth by planting new churches among the same kind of people. E_2 represents bridging growth when congregations are planted in new, similar cultures while E_3 represents bridging growth of congregations planted in distinctively different cultures (Winter 1974:19). Naturally, a westerner with limited experience in cross-cultural evangelism will find it more comfortable to continue ministering among nominal Christians. Even if he does succeed in discovering how to communicate Christ cross-culturally, he will have a difficult time describing to those back home how different pioneer E_2 and E_3 "missionarying" is compared to E_0 and E_1 current evangelism.

What Are the Bolivian Trends to 1980 and Beyond?

While the Bolivian population increases biologically by 2.156% per annum, the Protestant movement has been growing by more than 5.5 times that amount since 1945. Figure 19 shows the steady Protestant increase at 12% per annum, largely because of the continuous, dynamic Aymara advance since the 1920's. By 1930, Aymara Christians accounted for 66% of the Protestant response. This people movement continues to grow with only minimal foreign missionary participation. By 1940 the Aymara portion of the Protestant population dropped to 53%, though it has been gaining since that time. The Baptists, Methodists, Oregon Friends (INELA) and the Assemblies of God joined in this harvest over the last thirty years, producing a combined 13.2% AAGR along with the Seventh Day Adventists. The Adventists have the lion's share of the Aymara harvest, presently maintaining a 9% growth per annum.

At the present rate of growth, by 1980 the total Protestant membership would stand at approximately 231,846 people, or 4.52% of the population. The Aymaras would dominate 65% of this harvest. The Protestant percentage for each major ethnic group is depicted at the bottom of each column in Figure 20. This percentage is superimposed on the basic ethnolinguistic grid appearing originally in Figure 12, introduced in the previous chapter. Each ethnic group may be further refined by drawing in the boundaries of the remaining religious persuasions as shown in Figure 21. Reading this new chart from left to right, one sees that 20% are ripe animists, 75% are professing Roman Catholics, 0.48% are predominantly Asians and Jews, while the 4.52% Protestant population is depicted along the bottom, resulting in a total of 100%. Should Christ tarry and the present 12% Protestant annual growth rate continue until 1996, the conglomerate number of Protestants would approach 1,422,934, or 20% of the possible 7.2 million Bolivian population at that time. This figure reaches the 20% limit set by the Missions Advanced Research and Communications Center (MARC) for defining an unreached people. MARC considers that by the time an indigenous church reaches 20% of its population, it can then be considered mature enough to follow through on the evangelization of the remaining 80%. In the case of Bolivia, until 1996, foreign missions still have a sizeable mandate to equip the national Church for realizing continuous mission, described in Chapter Six.

Returning to Figure 19, why has the growth of the five principal ethnic groups comprising the ECU slumped to a global 3.8% per annum compared to the spurting 12% national average? Could a partial answer lie in the three following observations?

1. The impressive national Church development of the 50's led the AEM to overconfidently leave the initiative for church

Figure 19

SUMMARY GRAPH

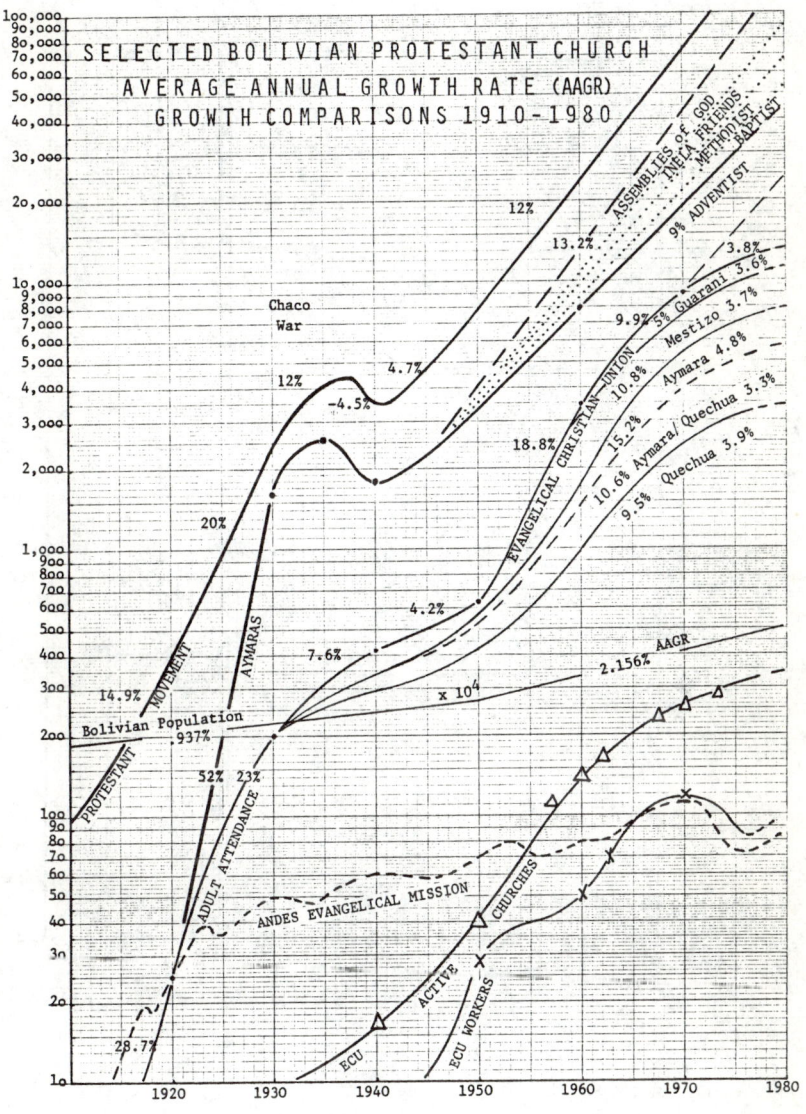

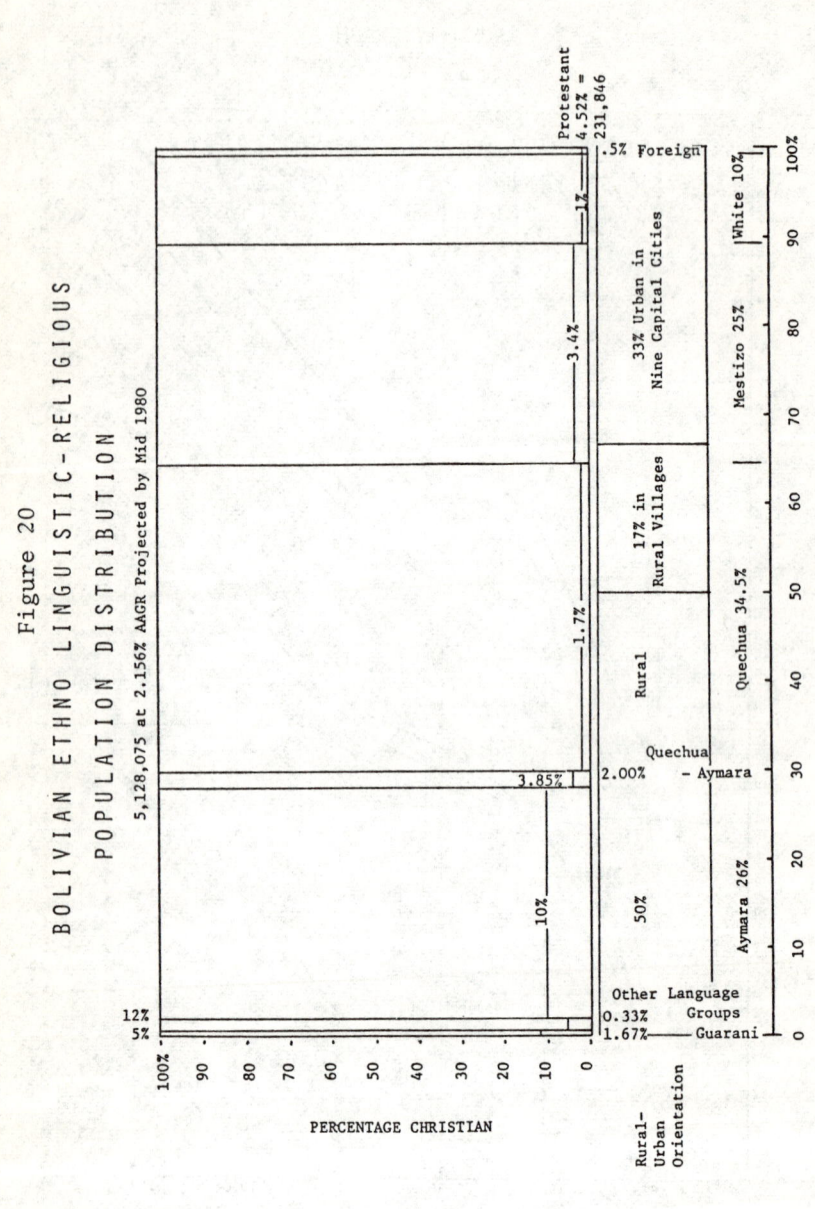

Figure 20
BOLIVIAN ETHNO LINGUISTIC-RELIGIOUS POPULATION DISTRIBUTION

Figure 21

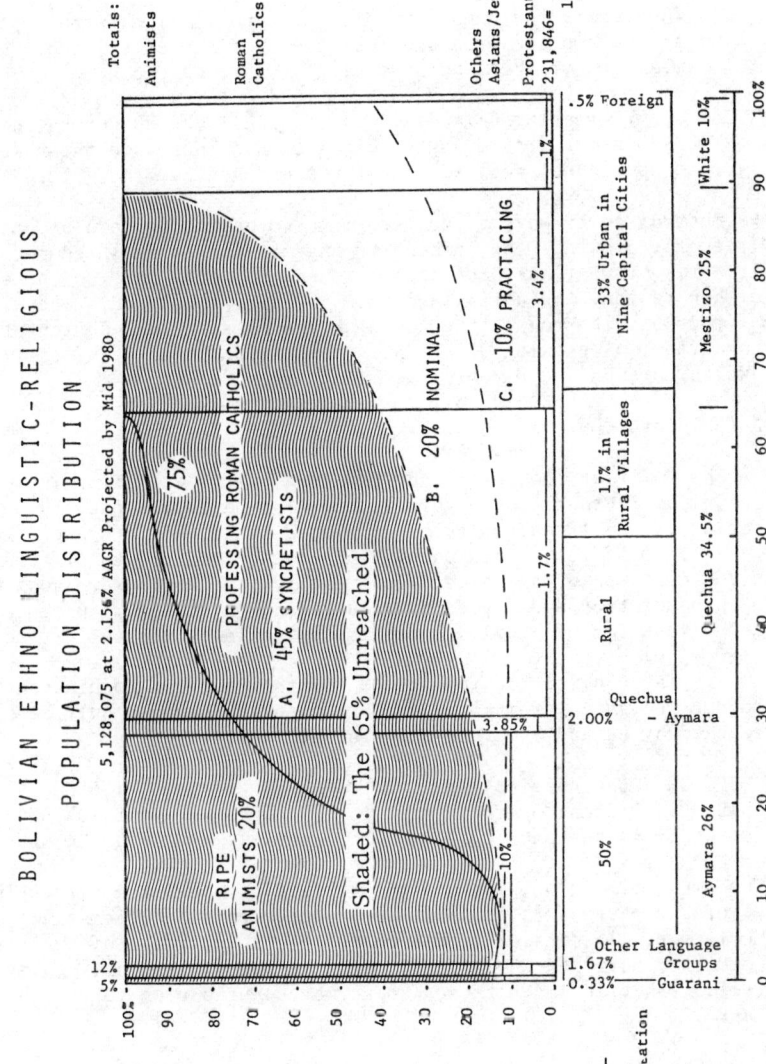

planting to the national Church. The ECU has not been able to keep pace, especially as it has lost workers because of the inability to fund national workers and the cutting off of the mission subsidy in 1963 and in 1970 (Smith 1972:5-6).

2. The decreasing number of pioneer type missionary recruits to replace the sizeable retirement of the experienced church planters of the 1950's has left a serious gap.

3. The increasing demands of the national Church during the 1960's for missionary specialists has increased the number of personnel engaged in nurture and service to 77.1%.

We must discover ways to transform these obstacles into opportunities for growth. The success of any mission is measured not only in terms of what has been accomplished, but even more so in terms of how rapidly the unfinished task is being completed. The 87.8% of the Bolivian population to which the mission and Church are committed, along with other Christian groups in Bolivia, still awaits more E_2 and E_3 Gospel communicators.

Defining the Unfinished Task: Bolivia 1980

The Bolivian people already depicted in the ethnolinguistic-religious rectangle of Figure 21 may also be represented by a series of exact scale circles developed by Dr. Ralph Winter (1977: 24-25). Different sized populations may be reduced to different sized circles to the same scale. Simply take the square root of each population and divide by a large enough number to produce a convenient set of radii. A centimeter scale is the easiest to use.

The large circle represents 65% of the Bolivian population that do not recognize themselves as Christians. They may only be reached by E_2 and E_3 cross-cultural evangelism.

20.00%	Ripe Animists	1,025,615	E_3
45.00%	Distant Syncretists	2,307,634	E_2
.48%	Asians and Jews	24,559	

The small circle outside and to the left of the large circle in Figure 22 represents the Bolivians who do consider themselves Christian. The inside circle represents an estimate of the truly committed Bolivian Christians. This is not limited only to evangelicals but includes those who may be counted upon to finish the task.

Christians:		Protestant	+	Catholic	=	Total	
4.52%	Committed	150,000		100,000		250,000	Nurture
10.00%	Nominal	81,846		412,802		494,652	E_0
		231,846		512,806		744,652	

Figure 22

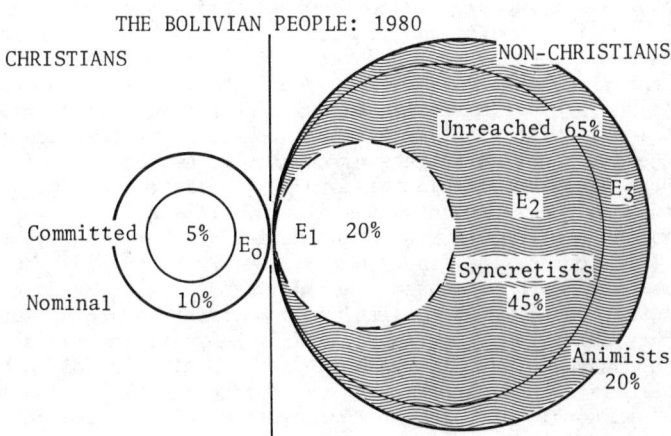

A nominal evangelical is no more likely to help in world evangelization than any other kind of nominal Christian. World wide, the number of nominal believers seems to be increasing. In Bolivia, for every committed Christian there are two who are uncommitted. This trend must be checked. Renewal and revival of the Church are crucial (Orr 1973:vii-1).

The first impression of the large circle to the right is the vast scope of the unfinished Bolivian task. But even more startling is the message communicated by the dotted circle inside. This represents the mere 20% of Bolivia's population who are non-Christians (1,025,615), approachable by ordinary E_1 evangelism. This fact explodes the myth that through ordinary evangelism, the national Church can finish the task. The shaded area represents the people who are culturally and linguistically beyond the reach of the national churches and most missionaries in Bolivia. This 65% can only be reached by a concerted E_2 and E_3 cross-cultural effort. Animists and syncretists each require a singular approach. Are we prepared to pay the price? Can we rise to the challenge put to us by the Lord of the harvest, Who has brought these two vast fields to ripeness? Yet, the existing missions apparatus is mainly concerned with Christian nurture and the winning of nominal Christians. At best we reach out among culturally similar people representing but a small 20% of the remaining task. Who will prepare and go to the 65%?

Hopefully, God will call many third world E_1 maximum communicators out of the regional work shops as well as some E_2 and E_3 pioneers from among those foreign missionaries already in Bolivia desiring to take further in-service training.

The present gap between the harvest and the disproportionate distribution of 90% of the reapers among 10% of the Bolivian population who are already nominal Christians, must be closed. In order to do so, can we accept the call from the Lord of the harvest to double our present performance within the next five years? We must make a growth commitment to realize our potential as the Body of Christ in Bolivia. Remember the parable of the talents (Matt. 25:19-21). Two stewards were rewarded for doubling their respective talents given them to invest. From the evidence presented thus far in this study, I believe that God expects us to double our present investment of gifts and talents in Bolivia for doubled growth within the next five years. Without any specific, concerted effort, our present Protestant national average is 12% growth per annum. World-wide goal setting work shops have catalyzed believers' faith and commitment to a cause around which they can rally. Statements of faith projecting goals are usually surpassed. Thus, if we could make a national commitment to raise our Protestant national growth average to 15% per annum, this would double our present levels within five years and every five years thereafter.

William Carey popularized the statement that we should attempt great things for God and expect great things from God. Schuller elaborates on this concept by saying that this does not mean we will always reach our goals. It does mean that we shall reach our maximum potential. Even if the maximum goal is not attained, the realized achievement will represent the ultimate of our abilities, under the coordination of the Holy Spirit (1967:198).

Another concern for the future is how well the national Church is progressing in overcoming discrimination and introversion to become more involved in mission to the 65% also.

Overcoming Discrimination

Most Bolivian churches are culturally homogeneous, introspective and not overly concerned about world mission. Third world theologians argue that the homogeneous principle explaining this phenomenon is morally and biblically untenable, contributing to separation, hostility and racism (Costas 1974:144). However, a new group of ethnic theologians is beginning to argue that the assimilationist, melting pot theories of American society have instead been a chief cause of social ills. Only as each ethnic group is liberated to be itself and to contextualize Christian theology and ethics in its own distinctive way, without domination by the *mestizo* culture, will reconciliation and social harmony be furthered. The following chapters expand upon this idea.

Jesus' life and ministry and that of the apostles, reflect the application of the homogeneous unit principle, which says that men like to become Christians without crossing racial, linguistic or class barriers (McGavran 1970:198). Biblical unity intends that all groups have equal access to God. All brothers and sisters in the Church universal are equal before God and before each other. There is little biblical evidence indicating a mixing of people from different homogeneous units within local congregations. But at the same time, there is a need for true Christianity to explore inter-congregational relationships with their near neighbors with growing maturity.

Integration of local congregations of the Evangelical Christian Union or of any denomination is determined by the level of integration existing within each community. In no case should barriers to worship or membership be raised to Christians of any group. On the supra-congregational level, Christians and their churches should give tangible evidence that they do relate to all other groups in love, brotherhood and interdependence. As Bolivian churches develop models which will allow each culture to safeguard its authenticity while establishing bridges of interdependence, progress will be made toward overcoming present racist discrimination (Wagner 1977:1-300).

In the mean time, building into each Bolivian congregation concrete, concerted action for reaching out to their own 65% unreached, would actually speed the maturing process, decidedly decreasing discrimination. The level of world mission commitment in any church is a reflection of its level of maturity in Christ.

This chapter concludes our searching out of the facts and trends. What can be done to further improve church growth trends within Bolivia over the next five years? How can we double our present performance? Five basic appeals come to mind.

First, I appeal to my colleagues of the Andes Evangelical Mission for improved recruiting and deployment of human and financial resources. We need better matching of the reapers with the harvest. This is in accord with our three basic mission objectives.

* The building of the Church according to scriptural principles working through churches, societies and individuals to make disciples of Jesus Christ for the fulfillment of the Great Commission.

* The training and development of leaders for the evangelical work.

* The deepening of missionary interest, vision and outreach in all churches with which we are associated in home and other fields.

Unfortunately, we appear to be approaching the solidifying fifth out of eight possible stages in the life cycle of an institution described by Towns (1972:153-5) and by Mont Smith (1976:214-16). These eight stages are: 1. Inception, 2. Initial Development, 3. Innovative Development, 4. Attainment of Program Balance, 5. Solidifying, 6. Inflexible, Steady State, 7. Slow Decline, and 8. Rapid Decline. Can we dare to recycle as in the 1950's?

Second, I appeal to my national brethren of the Evangelical Christian Union (ECU) National Church for closer accountability from each of the homogeneous unit churches within the denomination. Now that the upper and the lower growth parameters are established, we more clearly know what God expects of us now and in the future. We should forge ahead together in obedience to the Lord of the harvest to develop church growth eyes within each of the five principal groups. This will involve:

* Faith goals to double present performance over the next five years.

* Growing evaluation and accountability for each phase of the harvest at the annual national assembly.

* Baptism of the remaining one-half of the uncommitted believers attending regularly. Our goal should be 25,000 baptized believers by 1980. This goal can be realized by concerted effort being born out of regional church growth work shops. Otherwise, our present course will lead us to approximately only 13,000 by 1980.

* Discovery, development and discernment of the use of each member's spiritual gifts for edifying the Body and approaching each one's potential. Only then can we effectively reach out in Body evangelism and in church planting, especially to the 65%. Each church should attempt to plant a new church each year. Voluntary, second-commitment special evangelism task forces should be spawned with maximum power E_1 Gospel communicators among each cultural and sub-cultural group, especially focusing on the 65% yet unreached.

Third, I appeal to my colleagues among the other forty missions in Bolivia for defining a similar accountability to show where each mission is sharing in the Protestant commitment to Bolivia's continually expanding five million.

Could we possibly inaugurate a Bolivian Cross-Cultural Research and Training Center for measuring church growth progress and providing in-service training for local personnel interested in reaching the 65% who are largely animists and syncretists? This center would show where the priority needs are and spawn more E_2 and E_3 reapers.

Fourth, I appeal to my colleagues in world mission to reach some kind of agreement that would give us increased uniformity in reporting:

* Where each one is in his particular harvest, geographically and statistically, showing the percent yet unreached.

* How much longer it will take to reach that crucial 20% discipled into responsible, reproducing six-self indigenous churches (Tippett 1973:154-158). See the MARC definition for "unreached people" in their directions sheet accompanying their "Survey Questionnaire for Unevangelized and Unreached Peoples". The MARC address is: 919 W. Huntington Drive, Monrovia, California 91016.

Fifth, I appeal to our supporting churches for continued upgrading in missions stewardship.

* We missionaries need to be held more accountable for better matching of our workers with the harvest (John 4:34,35). We should be asked how much remains to be done and how long it will take.

* Local churches need to be more accountable in communicating with their missionaries and the missionaries with the churches. More than financially, we need your spiritual participation with us in the battles of Ephesians 6. And we need to participate more with you in your struggles. The earnest prayer of the righteous has great power and wonderful results (James 5:16).

As all of us focus on reaching the 65%, the Lord of the harvest will show each of us what He wants us to do about it. All of us will eventually stand before Christ's tribunal and account for what we have done. We know some of the questions that He may very well ask, like, "How many times during your life time did you double my investment in you of My gifts and talents?" It seems advisable to get ready for that final question now (II Cor. 5: 9-11).

With the trends now well in hand, we are prepared to pass on to the second missiological moment. Part Two prioritizes the biblical goals for realizing continuous mission, so crucial for doubling performance over the next five years. Each participant will be able to find himself somewhere along the road of continuous mission. Each will be able to project what should be the next short and long range, biblical goals.

SUMMARY

Part One suggests a new church growth integrative methodology where minimal, reliable data is available over an extended period. Two boundary points on either side of the 1950 hinge year were corrected and used as a basis for projecting into the 1980s. At the present rate of growth, the ninth decade will begin with a quarter of a million committed Christians mushrooming to one million by the early 1990s, should Christ delay His promised return.

Five causes of informational smog surrounding the five million Bolivian people have been cleared. Now there can be closer accountability and biblical goal setting. The ECU/AEM can have a greater share in the harvest, which God is always ripening ahead of us. Regional growth workshops are planned in order to locate the priority areas for a better balance between the reapers and the harvest. It is anticipated that experiencing the dynamic presence of the Holy Spirit in church planting will spark continuous mission long after the novelty of the goal setting experience may have been forgotten.

Since all growth is both quantitative and qualitative, numerical size, trends and location of this growth considered simultaneously, offer important clues to the health of the Church. Picturing growth rates facilitates objective comparison, analysis and goal setting by outlining the possible upper and lower growth limits before actually conducting each workshop. The quality of the data is assured by accounting for all components within a given population, treated as a closed system.

The ethnohistorical research tool of upstreaming was used to go back to the beginning of each homogeneous unit church for establishing accurate growth data. Growth trends were mobilized for objectively ranking each capital city, department and homogeneous unit on a resistance - receptivity scale. These rankings were confirmed by the spiritual response among the ECU's five homogeneous groups of growing churches.

All this is just a beginning of continuing research and cross-cultural training needed to contextualize the eternal Gospel for the unreached. Why should the 10% who are nominal Christians in Bolivia absorb 90% of the energy of the national Church and missions? This disparity can be corrected by setting and working at faith targets established in each workshop. Let us care for the flock of God until the Chief Shepherd appears (I Pet. 5:2-4). Good numbering is part of good sheperding (Prov. 27:23).

Part Two now treats the next missiological moment of prioritizing biblical goals for continuous mission.

Part Two: Prioritizing
Biblical Goals Toward Continuous Mission

5

Creation, Conscience and the Church in Mission

Priorities must be found when we are deluged with worthy causes in a world of change. Often in mission, there is little distinction among all the many good things done. It is confusing to call everything the Church does *mission*. Upon what basis should we prioritize (Dayton and Engstrom 1976:65-73)?

In retrospect, Part One demonstrated the first missiological moment by going through an ethnohistorical survey to determine Bolivian population and ethnic group trends. Trends are crucial to good goal setting. In order for these goals to be biblical, it is now necessary to go on to the second moment in the missiological process of prioritizing based upon ethnotheology. This attempts to do Christian theology from the anthropological perspective of the Bolivian people to meet their felt needs. Since the 65% of unreached Bolivians are from an animistic background, creation and conscience, largely formed through their culture, are prime formers of their world view. Effective mission begins where God begins.

As theology relates man to God, anthropology relates man to his culture. By definition, both are incomplete. Christian ethnotheology attempts to fuse both of these partial disciplines, as demonstrated by the circles that follow in Figure 22, adapted from Charles Kraft (1973:118). Man, limited in time and space, cannot embrace total reality. His vision is blurred (I Cor. 13:12). Theology alone is incomplete. Monocultural theology reduces culture to insignificance, overlooking its own limitations. By the same token, anthropology, refusing to recognize an absolute God, is distorted. We need the balanced approach of Christian ethnotheology as it speaks to each culture to avoid man's

absolutizing either his anthropological or theological views
(van Leeuwen 1964:331-33; Maslow 1964:12).

A major quest of Christian ethnotheology is to understand what
in Christianity is absolute, supracultural and valid for any
church at any time. Also, the Christian ethnotheologist must ask
what is cultural, relative and valid only for a particular culture at a given time. God is supracultural. He stands outside
culture and is not bound thereby unless He so chooses. Man, however, is immersed in culture and unable to escape its boundaries.
The Apostle Paul may very well be referring to culture in his
description of the oppressive "elements of this world", or
stoicheia in Galatians 4:3,9 and Col. 2:8,20 (Smith 1976d:12-48).
and Glasser 1977:135).

God, from the outside, reveals Himself to man meaningfully
through his culture. Some men respond to Him in repentance
while others turn away. A wide range of God's interactions with
man are recorded in the Judeo-Christian Scriptures.

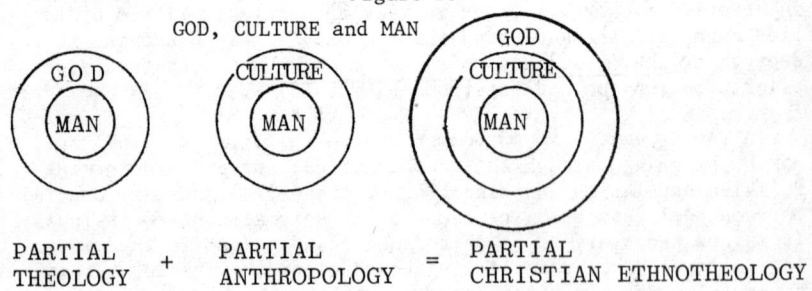

Figure 23
GOD, CULTURE and MAN

PARTIAL THEOLOGY + PARTIAL ANTHROPOLOGY = PARTIAL CHRISTIAN ETHNOTHEOLOGY

The rest of this chapter demonstrates how God chooses to meet
man where he is culturally. Scripture is the source book from
which we learn what is supracultural in the process of God communicating with man. What was supracultural for the original,
biblical participants is supracultural for us. God is willing
to start with man wherever he may be in his perception of the
Godhead and supracultural truth (Rom. 1:18-20; 2:14,15). Three
phases of God's cumulative Self-revelation are now developed.

The Role of Creation, Conscience and the Church in Mission

No truth is more overwhelming than the unyielding fact that
mankind is lost. Our minds boggle at the thought of hundreds of
generations of unevangelized heathen whose souls are already in
hell. And the vast majority of today's population will follow
shortly. We sink before the immense task of dispersing the

darkness which envelopes nearly three billion fellow human beings
(Winter 1974:228). Our feelings rebel against such a tragedy.
We know our theology contradicts those feelings, but just this
once we wish our theology were mute.

The layman can never give enough nor pray enough. The missionary, no matter how zealously he works, can feel he has stretched
himself far enough. The mission executive pensively scans his
map, mentally totaling the vast population whose spiritual destiny
may well hang on his decisions.

The colossal responsibility for the three billion weighs us
down and mocks our puny efforts. Somewhere, in some missionary
conference perhaps, someone told us that if we were truly obeying
the Holy Spirit, the world would be saturated with the Gospel.
That voice regularly reminds us how much heathen blood clings to
our hands.

Yet, less than two hundred years ago the English Church, influenced by rationalism and deism, could not have cared less. When
young William Carey in 1785 proposed to a group of ministers that
they discuss "The Obligation of Christians to Use Means for the
Conversion of the Heathens", the moderator squelched him with this
icy reply, "Young man, sit down. When God pleases to convert the
heathen, He will do it without your aid or mine" (Glover 1953:101).
In those years the Church assumed absolutely no responsibility for
the heathen.

Now the pendulum has swung to the other extreme and hung there.
The burden of world evangelization topples from heaven to earth.
Our current view nearly leaves God out of the picture. Sermons,
films, lectures, literature and even scholastic preparation for
mission service stress the human factor so heavily that mission
ceases to be regarded as a divine enterprise. To be sure, God
started the clock ticking, but according to many sincere mission
promoters, He seems to be distant, uninvolved, watching helplessly
while we botch His magnificent program of redemption. He depends
on us. We fail miserably. The unreached perish without hope.
He is bitterly grieved. We go to heaven and eventually live hap-
pily ever after.

Is God frustrated? Has He been unable to reach the pagan
world prior to the traditional date of the founding of Catholic
and Protestant missions? Is His mighty voice stifled in the many
cultures where no mission penetrates? If the answer is an unequiv-
ocal no, then how has God been speaking in time and space ever
since creation?

God Speaks Universally through Creation

"The heavens declare the glory of God" (Psa. 19:1). The lavish sunset colors stroked by the Master Artist on the easel of the sky communicates God's majesty, intelligence and omnipotence. The rhythm of the seasons sings of His goodness and concern for men. The fertile valleys and snow mantled peaks echo their agreement. God is! "For the invisible things of Him from the creation of the world are clearly seen, being understood by the things that are made, even His eternal power and Godhead so that they are without excuse" (Rom. 1:20). Through nature God sings an anthem of Himself, and men universally hear. God's attributes are clearly seen. At all times God is being perceived. The message written in natural wonders strikes so forcefully that it leaves all men without excuse.

Think back to when God challenged Job to an intellectual battle (Job 38). He began, "Where were you when I laid the foundation of the earth?" and then multiplied that question with several dozen more. Those questions probed into stellar space and delved into the microscopic world of the snowflake. God could not quote Scripture because Job had no Bible. He could not remind Job of laws and covenants, but He could awaken Job's conscience with a whirlwind tour of many kinds of natural phenomena.

God still speaks to cultures without the Bible through the drama of wind, cloud, storm and thunder, through the panorama of galaxies and through the miracles of birth, blossom and fruit. Do primitive cultures jumble this message by insensitiveness to the light they do have, thereby inverting God's order? Do they become oppressively subdued under a harsh creation? They worship the creation rather than the Creator. Satan abuses creation and culture for his own ends, usurping man's vice regency under God (Kraft 1973:117).

God Speaks Universally through Conscience in Culture

Every culture recognizes some system of right and wrong. Paul speaks of "the work of the Law written in their hearts, their conscience bearing witness, and their thoughts alternately accusing or else defending themselves (Rom. 2:15). Conscience declares that the God of creation is holy and just. As C. S. Lewis has so poignantly expressed, " . . . when I open that particular man called myself, I find that I do not exist on my own, that I am under a law; that somebody or something wants me to behave in a certain way . . . we conclude that the Being behind the universe is intensely interested in right conduct - fair play, unselfishness, courage, good faith, honesty and truthfulness" (1959:32-36).

Since creation God planted a device in all men which sounds an alarm on sin. True, the device can be tampered with, as Cain did in attempting to escape responsibility for his brother. Human beings can rewire their consciences so that the alarm sounds only faintly or infrequently, as with the new moralists. Certain cultures pattern the conscience with blurry, inaccurate data concerning right and wrong. Still, because God conceived it, it works (Daane 1973:92). It demands response in obedience born out of faith in Him because of the kind of person He is (Uda 1974:90).

Let us not underestimate the power of God's voice in creation and in conscience. He speaks clearly and effectively through these media. He broadcasts the Gospel to the ends of the earth. Romans 10:18 says, "But I say, surely they have never heard, have they? Indeed they have: their voice has gone out into all the earth, and their words to the ends of the world". We find the evidence of the same universal message in Colossians 1:23, which directs our attention to " . . . the hope of the Gospel you have heard, which was proclaimed in all creation under heaven . . .".

But the Christian message had not yet permeated the globe, nor even the Roman Empire. What does Paul mean here? The Gospel written on the scroll of the heavens and in the hearts of men!

God Speaks Universally through the Church

Now, since the cross, for the first time in history, with successive expansions, Christianity has become universal (Winter 1975:4). In a sense, God has always been evangelizing the unbeliever next door and the unbeliever on the other side of the world. We never start from scratch with our witness (Freytag 1957:15). Our listener is never theologically blank or morally untutored. As colaborers with God we should reemphasize what God has already said, beginning where each person is (Kraft 1973:113).

When the Church encounters the lost, two things are known:

* They know God in some way.

* They do not honor Him as God intends, giving Him thanks (Rom. 1:21).

When we preach in the name of our Heavenly Father, we must require men to first, recognize and honor the Creator as the only, true and living God, in repentance born of the Spirit (Acts 11:18). Secondly, men must offer thanks to Him. This is the essence of repentance. Men must stop ignoring God and begin to worship Him. Men must turn from indifference and begin to praise their Maker in gratitude for life, food, family and goods, as God ordained since Adam. Martin Luther emphasized this same teaching in his ministry and writings (Forell 1954:67).

Often we try to explain the atonement, somehow expecting theological understanding to inspire repentance. Sometimes it does, especially in Christianized cultures. However, the man without the Bible (Schaeffer 1969:91-105) seldom understands and very seldom sees the need to repent. He sees no relation at all between the message he reads in his environment and the message he sees in the missionary's flannelgraph presentation. We fail to build on God's universal communication.

When the Apostles confronted their pagan audiences, they zeroed in on the great truths pregnant in creation and conscience (Glasser 1976:3). Paul and Barnabas asked, "Men, why are you doing these things? We are also men of the same nature as you, and preach the Gospel to you in order that you should turn from these vain things to a living God, who made the heaven and the earth and the sea, and all that is in them . . . He did not leave Himself without a witness, in that He did good and gave you rains from heaven and fruitful seasons, satisfying your hearts with food and gladness" (Acts 14:15,17 NAS). The pagan hearer is more likely to sense that he is in the presence of truth when he hears of the God who sends the rain and the crops and who made heaven and earth. He can understand the clear demand to "turn from these vain things to the living God" long before he can master the concepts of propitiation and justification (Rev. 14:6,7; Mark 13:10).

God's revelation in the outer universe and in the inner mind unite to call for repentance, worship and thanks. Paul makes this clear from Romans 2:14, "Or do you think lightly of the riches of His kindness, forbearance and patience, not knowing that the kindness of God leads you to repentance?" With a natural and moral revelation urging men to repent specifically of their ingratitude and indifference, should our Gospel fail to do likewise? If we are colaborers with God, then we should join His chorus. We preach the same message. Notice this in Paul's address to the Athenians, "What therefore you worship in ignorance, this I proclaim to you. The God who made the world and all things in it, since He is Lord of heaven and earth, does not dwell in temples made with hands . . . He gives to all life and breath . . . He made from one all nations of mankind to live on all the face of the earth . . . that they should seek God" (Acts 17:23-27 NAS). We too must challenge men to respond to God, the God of whom they instinctively, dimly already know. "God is now declaring to men that all, everywhere should repent" (Acts 17:30b) Repent, honor God as the only God. Give thanks for His goodness.

Consider Apollos, a man mighty in the Scriptures, a Spirit-directed preacher who knew "only the baptism of John". Was he saved? Certainly. Did he have an effective ministry? Yes. What did he preach? John's message: Repent! We do not prize theological ignorance, but we must insist that it does not prevent people from being saved. The minimum requirement for salvation is a heart-felt cry for the God who is there. Watchman Nee emphasizes, "For what is it to be reckoned righteous? It is to touch God" (1961:41). As men obey this summons, they call out and fulfill the divine promise, "Whosoever will call upon the name of the Lord shall be saved" (Joel 2:32).

Men Must Touch God in Repentance

When the publican cried, "God be merciful to me a sinner", his prayer reached the heart of God. The man was saved. We are not told how much theological knowledge he possessed. Certainly, it was less than that of the Pharisee. But we do know that he went down to his house justified (Luke 18:13,14).

The thief on the cross prayed, "Remember me". The Lord Jesus might have used this opportunity to explain the plan of salvation. He could have expounded on the significance of His death. He simply promised, "This day thou shalt be with me in Paradise" (Luke 23:42,43).

Are there heathen who are ready to touch God? Do some individuals and homogeneous social groups ripen under the influence of God's sermons in the cosmos? History answers in the affirmative. In the last century a young Japanese lad named Neesima renounced idolatry at an early age and began to search for God. Later, after reading Genesis 1:1, he prayed, "Oh, if You have eyes, look upon me; if You have ears, listen to me" (Glover 1953:165). Neesima became one of Japan's mightiest evangelists.

Nee records meeting a man who at the age of twelve, while worshipping an idol, began to think to himself, "You are too ugly and too dirty to be worshipped! What is the sense of worshipping you? The boy slipped away to touch the true and living God. Finding an open space, he poured out this prayer, "O God, whoever You are, I do not believe You can dwell in that shrine. You are too big, and it is too small and dirty for You. You surely must dwell right up there in the heavens. I do not know how to find You, but I put myself in Your hands; for sin is very strong and the world pulls. I commit myself to You wherever You may be (Nee 1961:43).

Entire peoples become receptive in a similar fashion. When an animistic Ayore tribe of Bolivia was reached by missionary, Bill Pencille, a large number trusted Christ. The Ayore chief told Pencille that missionary effort would have failed with an earlier generation. "They would have killed you." But the chief's prior observation of the marvellous majesty and rhythm of the seasons stirred him to cry out, "Oh God of creation, reveal Yourself to me". He dreamt that a white man would come with that very revelation. As his tribe searched and waited, his generation ripened to a new receptivity (Wagner 1967:234-50). Christ promised, "Ask, and it shall be given you; seek, and ye shall find; knock, and it shall be opened unto you. For every one that asks receives and he that seeks finds; and to him that knocks it shall be opened" (Luke 11:9,10).

The Decision Making Process

Individuals and groups of people as described above go through various steps in coming to Christ. It appears that the Great Commission can be broken down into four basic communication mandates: 1. Christian presence, 2. Proclamation, 3. Persuasion and 4. Discipleship. Part of the problem with the harvest comes from failing to discern where the audience is in this sequence.

Figure 24 below represents an attempt to place these four communication ministries in the perspective of a spiritual decision process, which brings people to Christ and maturity. This model

Figure 24

THE DECISION MAKING PROCESS

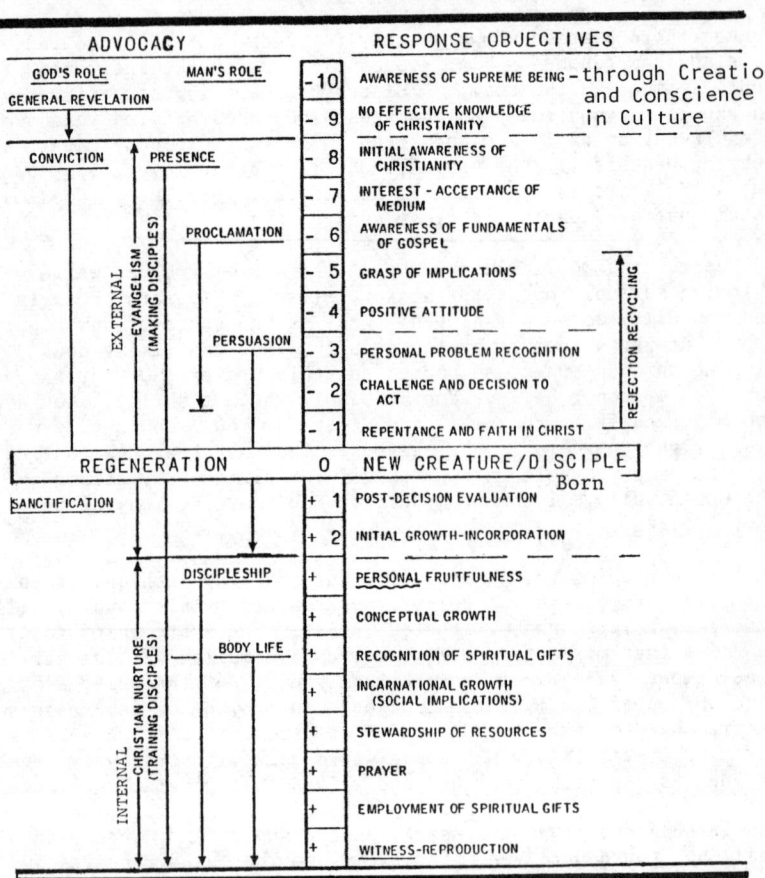

is similar to other decision models. James F. Engel of the Wheaton Graduate School, built this model as an adaptation to Viggo Sogaard's suggestion while he was a student (1973 *CGB* IX; 6:333 and Engel and Norton 1975:44-47). It represents a step beyond the mere secular models because it depicts the interaction of both God and His messenger with the receptor.

Every receptor appears somewhere along the sequence represented in Figure 24. All have some awareness of the Supreme Being through God's general revelation in creation and conscience. However, at this stage there is no effective awareness of the good news of the possibility of forgiveness of sins in Jesus Christ. Other receptors will have an awareness and grasp of the implications of the Gospel from exposure to Christian proclamation. Only when this awareness is accompanied by a strong felt need for change, designated as personal problem recognition, does the individual open his life to Christ. Prior to this moment of truth, there is neither sufficient understanding nor the felt need to allow a valid response. Once a person is persuaded to receive Christ, he enters a process of spiritual growth through obedience to the Word under the illumination of the Holy Spirit.

Figure 24 is later utilized in Chapters Six, Seven and Eight as a grid for defining where each receptive audience is found spiritually on the scale from -10 to +2.

The Pendulum of Responsibility for the Lost

To summarize this chapter, we may ask, "How swings the pendulum of responsibility for evangelizing the lost?". The same sustaining God of creation who causes the fields to ripen, wants to guide us to the repentant seekers, as He did Carey, poring over his crude maps and charts. When we arrive we must coordinate our mission to confirm and emphasize what God has been saying and doing. We must call out, "Turn to the true and living God", knowing well that the blood of Jesus Christ cleanses the sin of the ignorant as well as that of the theologian. Whoever truly cries out and touches God in repentance will be justified, even if he has never understood the doctrine of justification. Thus, every responsible witness must capture the universal message of the Innocent dying and rising again for the guilty. This is the supracultural significance of blood sacrifice (Gen. 3:21; Lev. 17:11).

This truth must be transmitted meaningfully in the culture to which God calls us, using redemptive analogies such as Don Richardson uses in *Peace Child* (1974:211). This is ethnotheologizing to contextualize the eternal Gospel (Kraft 1973:109-26). Further distinctive elements of the supracultural revelation in continuous mission will be discussed in the following chapters.

God shoulders the burden for world evangelization through us. Our responsibility is to obey the Lord of the harvest. He plants us where He wants us as we will lift up our eyes to go to His ripe fields. He does not depend on our frenzied saturation efforts. God works through obedient followers who conscientiously disciple into local congregations those God has ripened to repentance. We share with God in evangelizing the three billion. Responsible believers like Phillip, Peter, William Carey and Bill Pencille are led by the Holy Spirit in their daily "going, baptizing and teaching" of repentant Samaritans, Ethiopian eunuchs, Corneliuses, the heathens and the Ayores (Matt. 28:19,20; Acts 8 and 10; Morris 1960:78-80). The responsibility never was nor ever will be ours alone. Moreover, our failures and mistakes do not stymie God's program of redemption. We can either harmonize with Him in His harvest by discipling our neighbor whom He has ripened or strike our own discordant notes in a frenetic activity with the multitudes. Saturation may be a valid means of discovering the repentant for discipleship, but without meeting actual, felt needs, there can be no genuine discipleship (Smalley 1974:299). Superficial proclamation is not the accomplishment of the Great Commission. God calls us to disciple, not just to saturate (Stott 1975:55).

The International Congress on World Evangelization in Lausanne, July, 1974, focused on mission strategy and the dynamic process of reaping the harvests. No strategy is sufficient which does not begin with what God is saying and doing through cosmological media to reach each man where he is. World evangelization can be speeded; reaping can be accelerated when the Church understands God's prior ministry in every culture. Will the Lausanne Continuation Committees consider these issues? Will really serious thought dare to challenge some of the presuppositions of our twentieth century evangelical view of mission? Will we, like William Carey, learn to discern the discontinuous cultural assumptions from the continuous, biblical universals?

It is time for the Christian to recognize the biblical basis for his responsibility to the lost. We must not minimize or exaggerate our duties. We must not think of our guilt more solemnly than we ought to think. We have some theological repenting to do which will cause us to feel better, live healthier and work more fruitfully with God, as His colaborers. It is time to nudge the pendulum of Christian responsibility gently back into balance with what God has always been saying and doing. He is a jealous God. Until Christ's return, may we be found moving in rhythm with Him as we become more responsible in discipling the unreached 65% in Bolivia.

How can we more fully join in concert with the initiative and priorities of God in His continuous mission? The next chapter develops these biblical priorities around a dynamic, spiral model.

6

The Church in Continuous Mission: A Dynamic Model

Continuous mission originates with God. He creates man for Himself. Since the fall, He is recovering far more than what Adam lost in Eden by summing up all human history in Jesus Christ (Eph. 1:10; Heb. 13:8). Each man's conscience and culture tutor him to God if he will listen (Gal. 4:2-5). Now we are prepared to consider God's third step in His universal, cumulative self-revelation, not only through creation and conscience formed through culture, but also through the Church. The chasm between a holy Creator and His estranged creation was once, and yet again, will be filled by Israel as a "light to the nations" (Gen. 12:2,3; Isa. 42:4,6; 49:6; II Chron. 7:18 and Rom. 11:24-29). In the meantime, the Church must become better stewards of this grace temporarily entrusted to us to share with a hurting world. How can we resolve the tension between two segments of the Body of Christ engaged in fulfilling this Great Commission? How can we set proper, biblical priorities in God's continuous mission? Would a spiral model help to prioritize the sequence of mission?

Creative Tension between Church and Mission

For the first time in human history the sun never sets on the Christian movement. Christianity is now universal (Winter 1975:4). With such phenomenal growth to the ends of the earth in this generation, we need as never before to more clearly define our terms. We need to sharpen our focus on the unreached three billion (Winter 1975a:228). Only then can we more effectively synchronize our strategy for evangelism world wide, hastening the return of the Lord of the harvest (II Pet. 3:9-15a). Remember why He is waiting. He is giving us time to get His message of salvation out to others. It is crucial to recognize the distinct functions of the apostolic band ministry in harmony with those of the local church (Cook 1975:233-240; Murphy 1975:207-221; Stott 1975:11-20).

There is a battle of confusion in Christian missions because of our fuzzy impreciseness in defining our tasks (Cook 1975:234; Peters 1970:43). Secondly, we are still guilty of forcing Scripture into our own inflexible mold (Gothard 1971:7; Murphy 1975: 51). Would it be too much of a dream to work towards some kind of universally accepted frame of reference upon which we can hang our church - mission concepts, still allowing for the balanced flexibility of the Spirit (John 3:8)?

Tension stems from man as the variable in human history. Unfortunately, this tension carries over into the Christian movement with its extensive, untapped resources, both spiritual and material. These resources could be more effectively channeled if we better understood and appreciated one another's roles in the Body of Christ. Then we would be free to be accountable to each other and to move on (Gee 1963:1-12). Otherwise, the clashing accumulation of the gifted in one place overseas often produces the frustrated cry, "Missionary, go home!" or "Submerge yourself in our national church". With just cause they shout, because the missionary becomes so enmeshed that he pushes the nationals to one side (Wagner 1974:103; 1973:1-13). Must the confusion and conflict continue? Or is it possible to develop some kind of a flexible grid to guide us? Certainly God is too big to systemitize; however, He helps us maintain biblical tensions in the church - mission controversy creatively for greater accountability (Fuller 1971:33).

Sharpening our Focus

Green Lake 1971 sparked a lot of new thinking after the shock of being confronted with the topic of Third World Missions, not included on the agenda (Wagner 1974:105). That experience spurred me to prepare a paper for our Bolivian Field Conference in August, 1972, attempting to wrestle with this problem by suggesting a gradual work load transfer of mission functions to the national Church (Smith 1972:20). The following table summarizes my thinking.

Table VIII

WORK LOAD TRANSFER FROM MISSION TO CHURCH

Work Load Subject to Review and Change	Characteristics
1. 3/4 mission; 1/4 church:	Mission paternalism of the 50s followed by the conflict of adolescence and separation of 60s

2. 1/2 mission; 1/2 Church: Adult partnership projected for the 70s. Mission should begin a new cycle to the unreached.

3. 1/6 mission; 5/6 Church: Redeployment of mission scaffolding to areas less than 20% reached during the 70s.

4. "0" foreign mission; All Church, spawns own mission: National Church spawns own mission, sending own missionaries, leaving "no room" for outsiders, as in Romans 15:22 and I Thess. 1:5-10; projected for the 80s.

Earlier, at the Park Street Congregational Church Missionary Conference in April, 1972, Peter Wagner dissuaded me from including the last stage of "0" mission, since the concept of mission continues until Christ comes. Later, he developed his Full-Circle 360° concept (Wagner 1974:103-4). Could this be a possible grid to serve as a handle for focusing and synchronizing so many of the nebulous concepts relating church to mission? As a modality and as a sodality, we must learn to harmoniously integrate our efforts and resources for the completion of the Great Commission in this generation (Mott 1900:196; Winter 1973:121-39).

The remainder of this chapter attempts to order the contributions of various authors on the Full-Circle Evangelism model previously developed by the author in Figure 25 (Smith 1975:21-32). This is the type of theological model suggested by Hodge and Montgomery for objectifying supracultural, biblical truth. It may be subsequently applied cross-culturally (Hodge 1965:I 3; Montgomery 1966:67-98; Barbour 1974:45-48). In addition, Dr. Glasser, in perusing this model, suggests that it might even be extended from the Gospels and the Acts of the Apostles to the present as an accordion-type fold-out. This would illustrate a continuous spiral relationship of the Church and its mission until the coming of Christ. In fact, by building on my previously derived spiral of the Continuous Supra-Cultural Biblical Principles vs the Discontinuous Covenantal Cultural Forms Old Testament Model (Smith 1969: 118; 1976:24), this "centrifugal" spiral may be traced from Adam to Christ as in Figure 26 (Blauw 1962:10; 1974:41; Stott 1975:21, 22; Kraft 1973:113). The combined result would be a three dimensional model from Adam to the present, demonstrating God's redemptive mission through His people in each successive generation. A New Testament application of this model is made, beginning with the Apostles, after discussing three primary commitments in church and mission.

Figure 25

FULL-CIRCLE EVANGELISM PROCESS

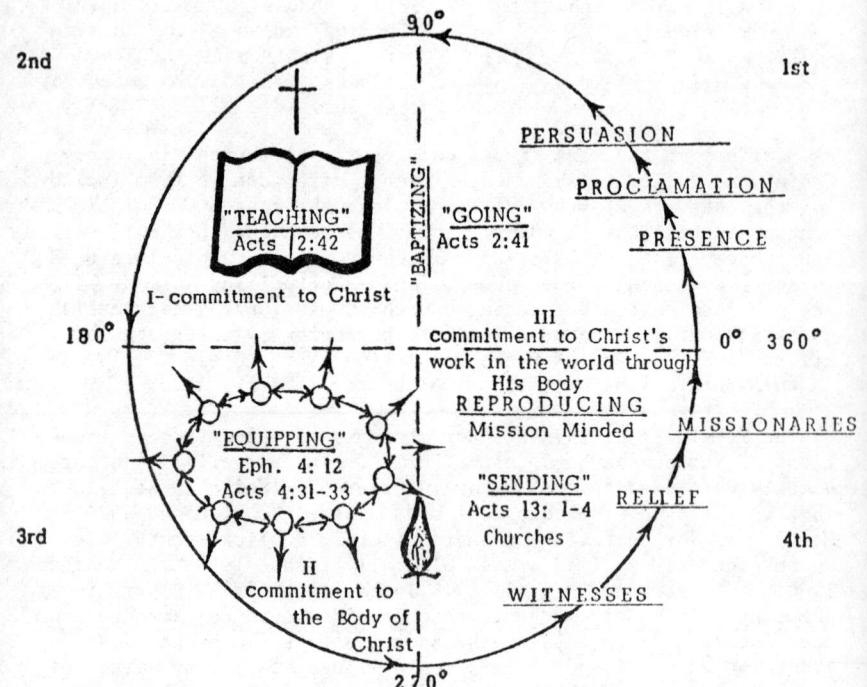

Figure 26

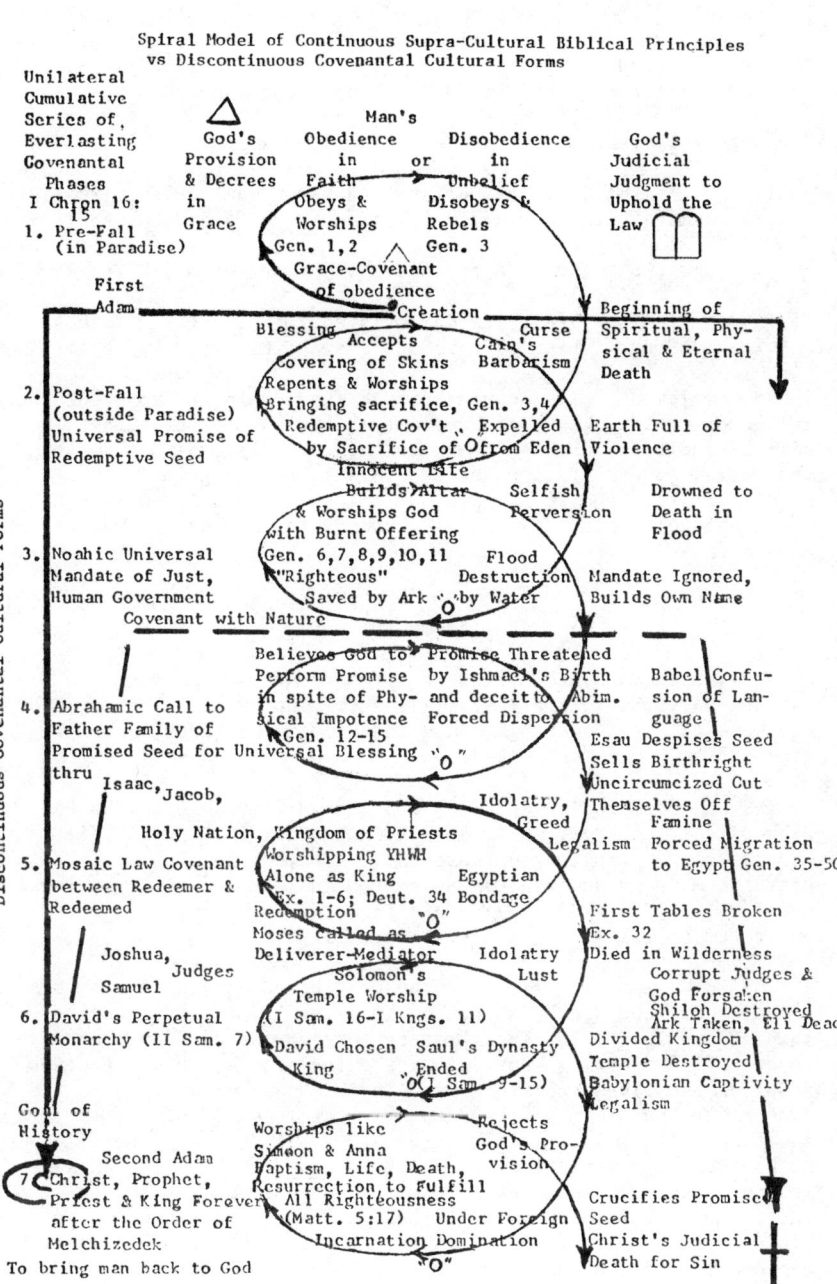

(Smith 1969:118)

The Three Commitments in Church and Mission

Pastor Raymond Ortlund cried out to God to deliver him and his Lake Avenue Congregational Church from mediocrity (1974:1-151). God gave him three commitments which are superimposed on Figure 25 to show a possible application of the spiral model process. The three commitments are:

I. Commitment One: to Christ. Wherever you are spiritually, commit your heart again to God. From 90° to 180°.

II. Commitment Two: to the Body of Christ. From 180° to 270°.

III. Commitment Three: to Christ's work in the world through His Body. From 270° to 360°, starting a new cycle to 90°.

These commitments will be used as the three main headings for the remainder of the chapter. The contributions of other authors will be indicated as they speak to the topic discussed throughout the spiral process from 0 to 360° through the Gospels and the Epistles. This should sharpen our focus on the relationship between apostolic bands and local churches for harmonious world mission.

COMMITMENT I - TO CHRIST (90° - 180°) Reached by the Apostolic Band in Mission (0 - 90°)

The first quadrant in Figure 25 represents the *going* of Matthew 28:19,20 (Oliver 1973:17). Zero represents the origin of the New Testament Apostolate and the "apostolic bands" who make disciples.

The unique Apostle sent from God was our Lord, according to Hebrews 3:1 (DeRidder 1971:148-180; Rengstorf 1964:424,28,43). He was fully entrusted to represent His Father in this world. In His circumcision and baptism He shared in Israel's election for service (DeRidder 1971:162). His judicial authority will be demonstrated to all (Titus 2:12-15; Rev. 11:15).

The word "apostle" is not to be considered equivalent to "missionary" or "one sent", although the Greek literally suggests this (Blauw 1962:77). The first century Jewish missionaries were never called apostles, but rather the *shaliach*. Thus, the Greek supplies the linguistic form used in the New Testament while the content of that form is determined by the function of the *shaliach* of late Judaism (Rengstorf 1964:421). They were fully authorized representatives of the Lord God Jehovah. In the same way the disciples were sent out with the power and authority of the Lord Jesus in Matthew 28:19,20. With this background, the missionary concept of apostle burst into its full meaning after Pentecost with the power of the Holy Spirit working through the

The Church in Continuous Mission

first century Church to the very ends of the earth in fulfillment of Acts 1:8 (Hahn 1967:9-39).

Ed Murphy recently highlighted the continuing apostolic function by tracing the roles of three types of apostles (1976:107-110). However, his second and third types may be combined to emphasize that the basic difference exists between the original twelve apostles and those who have followed.

1. The initial group, known commonly as the twelve apostles, was authorized by Jesus as He had previously been authorized by His Father. They were to uniquely share in His mission to Israel, witnessing both His earthly life and His glorious resurrection (John 20:21). The word "apostle" occurs twenty times in the Gospels and twice in the Acts. With Judas eliminating himself, the group's first joint act was to become the twelve again (Acts 1: 15-26). The number twelve for the Jew symbolizes the indwelling of God in the human family (Coleman 1969:25). The importance of this number is seen by its reoccuring use for the twelve patriarchs, tribes and in the foundations of the twelve gates for the heavenly Jerusalem.

Thus, twelve is very much a Jewish number, historically and eschatologically representing the true spiritual Israel (Ladd 1974:109). The apostles will judge the twelve tribes of Israel from twelve thrones (Matt. 19:28; Luke 22:30). As long as the missionary outreach was limited to the Jews, only these twelve were necessary. Their apostleship ended with death and does not reappear until Revelation 21, where they judge Israel in the coming kingdom. No doubt the Apostle Paul primarily had in mind these first century apostles in Ephesians 2:20 when he spoke of the Church being founded upon Jesus Christ and His apostles and prophets. That foundation continues through their inspired writings to provide a unique skeletal form until the coming of Christ. Succeeding groups of apostles take and build on this singular foundation (Stedman 1972:70,71). Biblically, the word "apostle" was used to include more than just the original twelve. However, although the original apostolic role to Israel disappeared with the death of the twelve, the apostolic function continues to the "nations" (McGavran 1955:13).

2. The continuing group of apostles outshown the outreach of the original twelve, even in the first century. Spontaneous expansion of the Christian movement through local synagogue-type congregations and individual Christians gave way to a new pattern, beginning in Acts 13 (Cook 1975:236). The seal of the continuing apostleship is this special call, spiritual authority and leadership from the Holy Spirit, to cross new frontiers. This is recognized by God's people until we all become like Christ at His coming (Eph. 4:12; Rom. 8:29). Stedman affirms, "It is a part of the apostolic gift to start new churches. We call those who

do this 'pioneer missionaries' today. In the course of Church history, there have been many such secondary apostles as Adoniram Judson in Burma, William Carey in India, Hudson Taylor in China, etc. These were men who had the apostolic gift and were made responsible for imparting the whole faith to new churches (1972:72).

The Holy Spirit called Barnabas and Saul from among the gifted men ministering to the Antioch Church. By Acts 14:4,14, they were declared apostles even though they did not form part of the closed college of the twelve (I Cor. 15:5). They became the first of the cross-cultural bands of apostles to the Gentiles. Paul never counted himself as being among the twelve nor as taking Judas' place. He simply called himself an apostle to the Gentiles (Rom. 11:13; Gal. 2:8). The other messengers, *apostoloi*, of the churches (II Cor. 8:23), Epaphroditus (Phil. 2:25), Silvanus and Timothy (I Thess. 1:1; 2:6), may also be considered as part of this secondary apostolic group.

Bocking affirms that an apostle is sent through barriers in the name and with the authority of Christ to win new territory to Him (1961:12). This cross-cultural church planting function is what Wagner calls the missionary gift today (1974:34,35). Why not view the continuing apostlate as fulfilling this role instead of drawing a new term into an already crowded theological vocabulary? We should not confuse the apostle with the evangelist like Philip (Acts 21:8; II Tim. 4:4; Eph. 4:11) who worked along with a church planting apostolic band.

This missionary structure or sodality (Winter 1973:121) soon smothered the church structure or modality, in fulfilling the Great Commission. There are eleven easily-identifiable apostolic bands in Acts listed chronologically:

1. Barnabas-Saul-Mark (13:4-13).
2. Paul-Barnabas and their "companions" (13:13; 13:13-15:12).
3. Paul-Barnabas-Judas-Silas (15:22-34).
4. Paul-Silas (15:40f).
5. Barnabas-Mark (15:37-39).
6. Paul-Silas-Timothy (16:1-9).
7. Paul-Silas-Timothy-Luke (16:10).
8. Paul-Silas-Timothy-Luke-Aquilla-Priscilla (18:2-23).
9. Paul-Silas-Timothy-Luke-Aquilla-Priscilla-Apollos (18:24-29).
10. Paul-Silas-Timothy-Luke-Erastus-Gaius-Aristarchus (19).
11. Paul-Silas-Timothy-Luke-Sopater-Aristarchus-Secundus-Gaius-Tychicus-Trophimus (20:4; Murphy 1976:113).

Continuous mission starts with making disciples, as shown in Figure 27. It goes on from the first century through Church history until today. It acts as a continuous spiral. This process is essentially unchanged (Stedman 1975:158-184; Murphy 1976:114-117). The cultural applications vary widely. Each apostolic band

Figure 27

CONTINUOUS MISSION PROCESS: MAKING DISCIPLES

1. MAKING DISCIPLES (Mt. 28:19, 20)

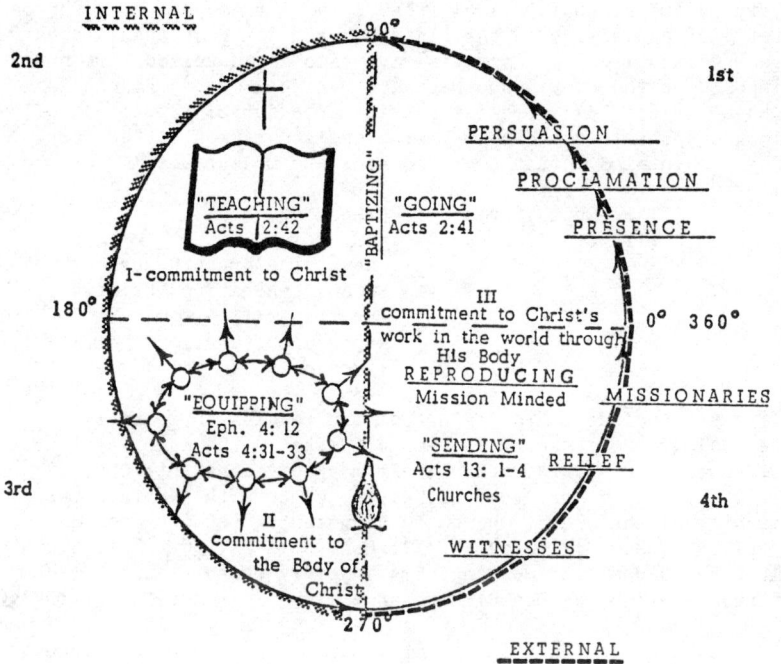

learns to serve its own generation according to the will of God
(Acts 13:36), assuming its God-given function in the Body of
Christ. The apostles were not only pioneer church planters to the
four corners of the globe (Stedman 1974:30,31), they were present
to proclaim and to persuade men to repentance and incorporation
into a local expression of the Body of Christ, passing through
baptism (Acts 2:1-11, 41; 11:18, 20,21; Wagner 1971:124-138; 1972:
14; 1974:103-4; Stott 1975:23, 37-56; Green 1970:40,49,58; Martin
1964:98-109; Moule 1961:47-66). Dr. Tippett, following Van Gennep's
"Rites of Passage" (1961), emphasizes the importance of the turning from idols to the living God (I Thess. 1:9). He developed a
very useful ethnohistorical research tool from analyzing the patterns of conversion in the Fijian Church for more than a hundred
years (1963:1-28). Tippett's five time-depth periods are superimposed on the Continuous Decision Making Process, Figure 28
(Engel 1975:45-47). This emphasizes the spiral repetition of various responses to the Gospel from one generation to the next.
Engel maintains that these responses are measurable.

> Time-Depth Period 1: Precontact
> (Tippett 1963:5) 2: Awareness
> 3. Conversion breakthrough
> 4. Second generation Christianity
> (next spiral)
> 5. Rapid acculturation
> (successive spirals)

Tippett concludes, "The nature of man remains the same, while
technology progresses. The Gospel works in the same way; patterns
of acceptance and rejection are remarkably constant (1963:28)."
It is important for every witness to capture the supracultural
meaning of the cross, where the "Innocent" died once for the
"guilty" (Gen. 3:21; Lev. 17:11; Heb. 9:11-15,26). This truth
must be transmitted meaningfully in every culture, using redemptive analogies, as Don Richardson employs in *Peace Child* (1974:21).

The apostolic band in *teaching*, from $90°$ to $180°$, is demonstrated by the second quadrant in Figure 27. These church planters
cooperate with God in His process of progressively bringing the
new believer closer to His ideal of Ephesians 4:13 (I Thess. 4:3;
Col. 1:28). The newly baptized are folded into a local body of
the Saints, preferably into a new neighborhood congregation where
their needs will be met (Silvoso 1974:399-407). The church planting band as a team is responsible for consolidation in quality
growth. The apostolic teams are God-given resources for both *internal* and *external* growth (Tippett 1967:111; Wagner 1976:139-40).
Evangelism always requires effective follow up. Conversion growth
demands quality growth. McGavran calls this couplet "discipling"
($90°$ - $180°$) and "perfecting" ($180°$ - $270°$) (1955:13-15). The
former involves the rejection of idols while the latter represents
the maturing process by progressively enthroning Christ as Lord.

Figure 28

CONTINUOUS DECISION MAKING PROCESS

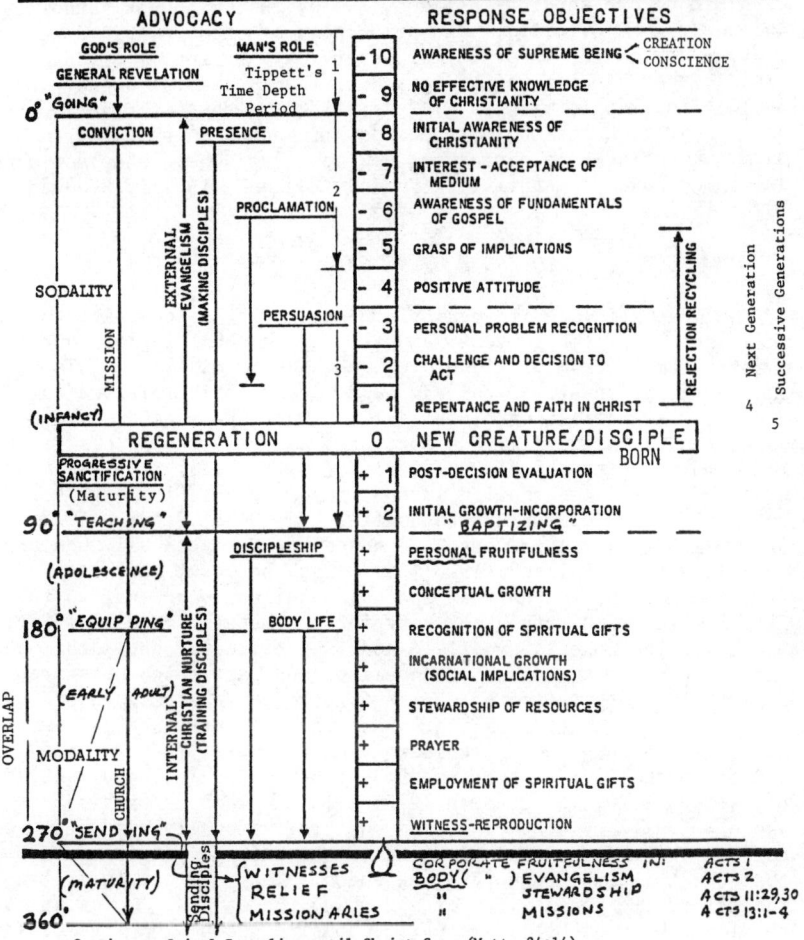

Continuous Spiral Recycling until Christ Comes (Matt. 24:14).

This kind of discipleship is one of the most neglected aspects of the Christian mission today (Kuhne 1976:13ff; Ortiz 1975:4-9). Evangelists by and large cannot seem to afford the time nor do they seem able to mobilize the necessary team to work with them through the second and third quadrants to produce an indigenous church. This process demands time and makes us vulnerable as we share our lives in a close group relationship (Lk. 1:15-17). Jesus called out the twelve from the multitudes around him to be with Him before sending them out, two by two, with His authority and power (Mk. 3:14,15). The principles of obedience in discipleship are caught in practical, every day sharing of living examples; they are not taught in school (Hanks 1973:3; Wagner 1971b: 5-8). The example of Acts 2:42-47; 11:20-24 shows the seriousness of the early Church and of the apostolic bands in providing a warm, accepting home church for new believers where they could be discipled towards maturity in Christ (Magbanua 1971:2; Stedman 1972:115).

COMMITMENT II - TO THE BODY OF CHRIST ($180°$ - $270°$)

The apostolic band in *equipping* and exiting is demonstrated in quadrant three of Figure 29, emphasizing the building of continuous commitment from mission to church back to mission. This sequence is the result of the *equipping*, previously referred to by McGavran as "perfecting" (Eph. 4:12). Once the repentant becomes committed to Christ (I), the next most natural step is his growing commitment to the Body of Christ (II). This is the way that the Lord Jesus' incarnation is continued today. His Body is a mutually caring community (Bonhoeffer 1949:24-6; Stedman 1972:37-39; 1974:32-33). This Body Life concept was practically unheard of before 1945 (Kilinski 1973:138). Each believer has received from the Lord of the harvest special enabling, *charisma*, to fulfill his function within the Body for the benefit of all (I Cor. 12:4,7). The Ephesians 4:11-16 model emphatically shows that the gifted apostles, prophets, evangelists and pastor-teachers are like trainers given to the Church for the express purpose of *equipping* the gathered Saints. Then these Saints take the initiative to continue the Church's work in the world ($270°$ - $360°$) and the mutual edifying of the Body ($180°$ - $270°$) (Judge 1960:40-61; Peters 1970:175; Stedman 1972:80-114). This is precisely where we fail, by depending upon our professionally paid staff to perform these functions belonging to the Saints. It is no wonder that the trainers become over extended. They are not fulfilling their first responsibility of *equipping* the Saints. McGavran sees the local body of believers as a composite group with five classes of leaders, simultaneously fulfilling all of these biblical roles harmoniously (1974:89-96 and Feucht 1974:34-149). They involve:

1. Volunteer maintenance of existing church programs: Sunday School teachers, ushers, choir members, elders, expositors, etc.

2. Volunteer outreach to neighboring community of the unconverted.
3. New home church leadership.
4. Professional staff: pastor-teachers, secretaries, youth and social workers, etc.
5. Denominational executives, missionaries.

Only by maintaining a balanced representation in each of the above five categories can a church maintain its spiritual health and truly discover its "Six-Self Identity" (Speer 1902:49; Martin 1964:55-65; Tippett 1973:154-8). Then it is ready for reproducing itself externally, as described by the fourth quadrant.

Figure 29

CONTINUOUS MISSION PROCESS: BUILDING COMMITMENT

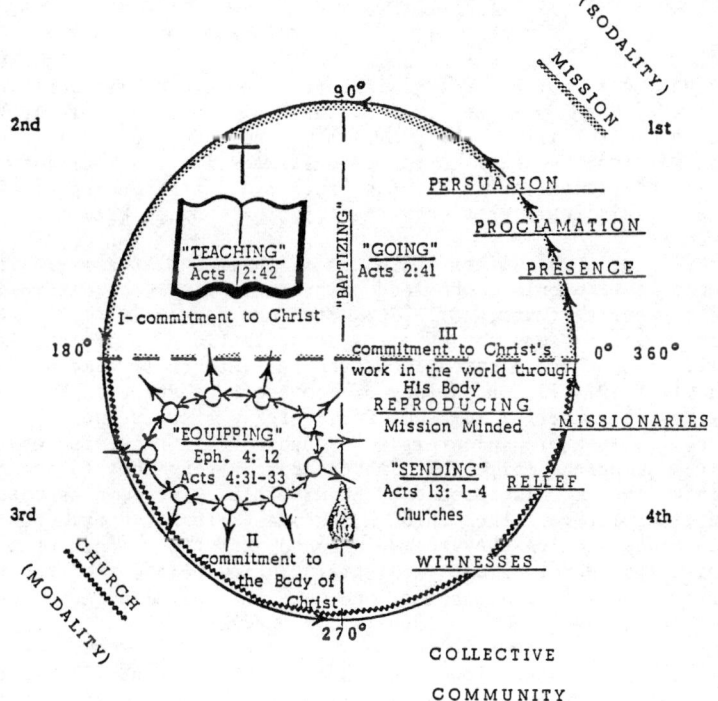

The maturing process takes time. It needs periodic, apostolic attention, but always without smothering. As soon as possible before reaching the 270° *equipping* of the Saints, the apostles left the new congregations on their own for awhile to allow the spiritual gifts among them to emerge and blossom. Upon returning (Acts 14:21-23), they not only confirmed and exhorted the believers but also recognized the elders raised up by God in every church. Then they returned to Antioch, their original launching base, to report (Acts 14:27).

The apostles began a new missionary cycle at zero to the unreached areas beyond. They visited the fledgling congregations on the way, expanding their missionary vision by enlisting some promising helpers from among the emerging churches to participate in some of the eleven teams previously described. This strategy was so effective that after approximately twelve years and three missionary journeys throughout the eastern Mediterranean, Paul claimed that there was no more room for him (Rom. 15:23,24). As he was to pass through Rome, no doubt he was seeking their sponsorship for his new cycle of missionary enterprise to the western Mediterranean, to the very ends of the earth in his day (Glasser 1976:100).

COMMITMENT III - TO CHRIST'S WORK IN THE WORLD THROUGH HIS BODY (270° - 360°, Recycling to 90°)

The local church *sending* witnesses, relief and missionaries from 270° to 360° is depicted in the fourth quadrant of Figure 30, a composite of all of the previously mentioned processes in continuous mission. A local church demonstrates its level of maturity by its participation in witness, relief and the sending of missionaries. This represents only the first half of Commitment III.

Every believer witnesses to his faith in Christ as he daily touches the repentant whom God brings into his life, discipling the responsive (Matt. 28:19,20; Acts 1:8; Wagner 1974:37). But every believer does not have the evangelistic gift of Ephesians 4:11. When the committed 120 moved out into their community (Schuller 1974:15) on the Day of Pentecost to share in body evangelism the wonderful works of God, Peter was surrounded by a host of available church planters. No doubt the 120 distributed themselves among the first three thousand to average out to about twenty-five new disciples to each discipler. As soon as possible, the discipler took them through the same internal continuous mission process which they themselves had just experienced with Christ from 90° to 270°, in Figure 30. New neighborhood churches sprang up all over Jerusalem, and thus the spiral process continues (II Tim. 2:2; Howard 1969:175; Murphy 1975:312; Kennedy 1970).

Relief is another important aspect of Commitment III (Stott 1975:25). Barnabas and Saul carried relief to Jerusalem from

The Church in Continuous Mission

Antioch (Acts 11:29,30). Paul took the eastern Mediterranean's love gift to Jerusalem (Rom. 15:25-27).

Missionaries being released for foreign service from the local church is found as a principle in Acts 13:1-4. The Holy Spirit spoke to the sensitive Antioch church about its responsibility for freeing the apostles, Barnabas and Saul, from local responsibility in order to begin a new Spiral Evangelism Process at zero (Cook 1975:236). Thus, Commitment III involves external services and reproduction, both in our home community (270° - 360°) and abroad (0 - 90°) among the unreached.

Figure 30

COMPOSITE OF THE CONTINUOUS MISSION PROCESS

1. MAKING DISCIPLES (Mt. 28:19, 20)

2. BUILDING CONTINUOUS COMMITMENT FROM THE:

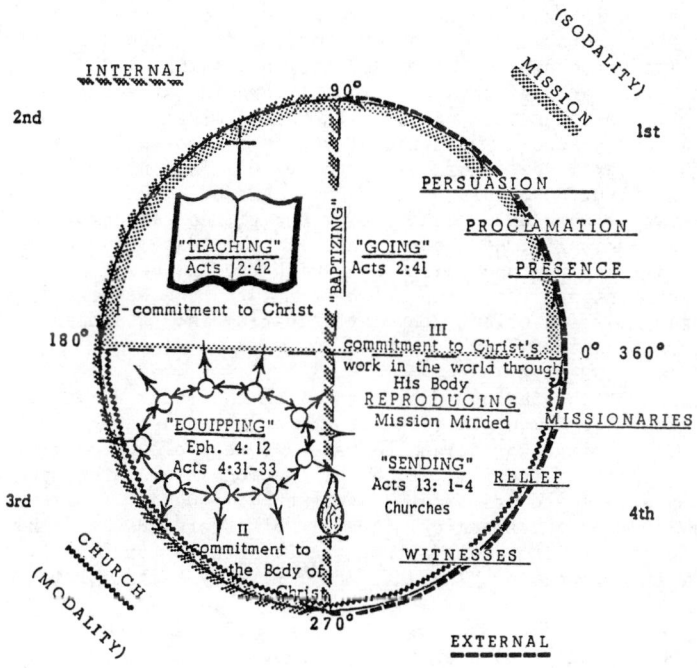

COLLECTIVE COMMUNITY

The continual spawning of new apostolic bands in new cycles is demonstrated by coming full circle to the first quadrant in Figure 30. In this way the spiral model emphasizes the continual *going* of Matthew 28:19,20 until Christ comes. There are two structures which God has continually used throughout history for completing His redemptive mission in anticipation of the coming King (Winter 1973:124).

The first structure may be defined by the term *modality*, which indicates a public mode or arrangement of people. Applied to the Church, a *modality* represents an inclusive Christian community of all ages, including both sexes, as a biologically perpetuating organism. Historically, Paul went to the synagogues across the Roman Empire, convincing the gathered Jews and Gentiles alike that their Messiah had arrived in Jesus Christ, the One prophesied by Moses. Out of the Messianic converts from these synagogues he forged new synagogues that were not only Christian but also Greek, each one reflecting the local culture.

The second structure may be defined by the term *sodality*, which describes a private, exclusive, voluntary fellowship, restricted by age and sex and requiring a commitment to a common purpose, like the Scouts, the YMCA or the Rotary. Although Dr. Winter, in "The Two Structures of God's Redemptive Mission" (1973:124), says that later forms of this widely-proliferating structure undoubtedly had no connection at all with Paul's missionary bands, Paul set a good precedent with the eleven or so apostolic teams within which he participated or helped to spawn. Paul never stayed around to suffocate his newly formed churches. Once they were on their way toward being equipped by the gifted teachers, he moved on. Periodically, he checked on their progress between 270° to 360°, forming new apostolic bands with those showing promise in church planting. In this way he stimulated the new churches into becoming mission oriented by participating in his apostolic bands (Wagner 1971b:5-8).

From that beginning, Christians from the later Roman period drew from the Roman military structure in emphasizing discipline, allowing nominal Christians to make a more profound commitment. And in spite of the limitations of the monastic system, because of its skills and its ordered, settled life which it preserved from Egypt to the Benedictines, to the Cistercians and finally to the Germans, Luther could study the Scriptures for himself to discover the principle, "The Just Shall Live by Faith" (Latourette 1938:379-80).

Symbiotically, both structures are essential to each other. This is because of the relative weakness and nominality of the diocesan, denominational and local church modal structure. Fortunately, the church does supply volunteers for the sodality (monastic order, mission agency or task force), which in turn spawns committed leadership for the modality itself as well as volunteers for the formation of new modalities and missionaries for cross-cultural planting of new modalities and sodalities until Christ comes. Figure 31 describes the measurable progress made by these two redemptive structures in the spiral continuous mission process. Work is continually transferred from the older to the younger structure. As each becomes mature, each reproduces the other (Wagner 1971:176; Winter 1977:18).

Figure 31

CONTINUOUS WORK LOAD TRANSFER

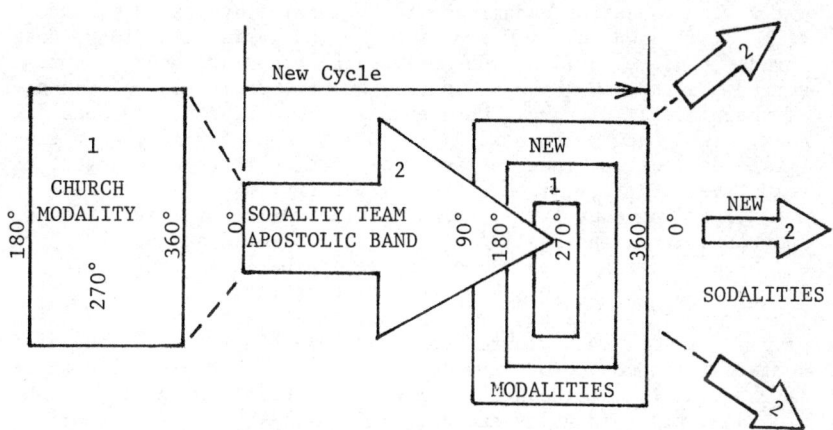

Where Are You in Continuous Mission?

Why not attempt to pinpoint where you are presently located around the circumference of the continuous mission sequence in Figure 30. Once finding your position, immediately you may discern what should be your next priorities. Your long range goals are outlined in the successive quadrants lying just ahead of where you are now. McGavran describes the process of turning over the work to the national church. He recommends our going on just a few miles beyond their outreach. Then we should plant another church all over again (1977:1-5). These concepts all taken together and applied locally will effectively help to double performance over the next five years.

This chapter concludes Part Two. We have prioritized biblical goals to stimulate improved participation in God's continuous mission. Clarity of priorities is crucial to successive doubling. Now we are prepared to actually apply the trends of Part One with the priorities of Part Two in rural and urban mission developed in Part Three.

SUMMARY AND APPLICATION

Part Two demonstrates the second missiological moment of prioritizing biblical goals for continuous mission around the four quadrants of a dynamic spiral. God cumulatively reveals Himself through creation, conscience, culture and the Church. We never begin from zero in our witness. God is always ahead in ripening the harvest. We work together. He is summing up all human history in our unchangeable Lord and Savior, Jesus Christ (Eph. 1:10; Heb. 13:8). In the interim He is giving us time to get His message of forgiveness, acceptance and liberation out to others in contextualized mission (II Pet. 3:9-15a).

Man has always been the variable in history. The failure of our first progenitor, Adam, led to successive cycles of a reductive spiral down to a few choice men. God worked with Seth, Noah, Abraham, Moses, David, Zerubbabel, Ezra, Nehemiah, etc. He preserved the race in these few until the Man, Christ Jesus, appeared as the hinge of history. He stands at the center as the Second Adam, like a new mustard seed, restoring to us far more than the first Adam lost. Since the incarnation of Christ, He changed the reductive, centripital mechanism of history. Now, a continuous, ever-expanding centrifugal spiral of redemptive history has been successfully unwinding like a drama on the world stage. In spite of the oppression of the Roman Empire, Barbarians, Vikings, Mongols or whatever plagues have hurled themselves against the Christian movement, it has now emerged universal. Such is the dynamic process of love that flourishes under hardship while wilting with comfort. The conquerors are conquered by the superior life style of the vanquished, the weak whom God has chosen to overpower the wise and strong in every culture (I Cor. 1:27,28). The majority of the unreached three billion are among the poor (Snyder 1975: 37-53; McGavran 1970:198; Whittaker 1977:17-21).

God is moving His continuous mission into a new phase with the rise of third world missions. How are we responding? As we focus on the prophetic handwriting over our times (Dan. 5:22-28), many see the demise of the West (Winter 1970a:31-42; 1970b:11-53; Broek 1968; Cole 1973; Ehrlich 1970; Meadows 1972; Mesarovic and Pestel 1974). The incoming cast of rising third world nations are overshadowing the declining West. God is directing these third world mission protagonists in playing out the final lines as they reach to the very ends of the earth (McGavran 1955:64). Since ours is the first generation to see all the biblical prophecies regarding Israel as the fig tree of Matthew 24:33 being fulfilled simultaneously, I believe the Lord is speaking strongly to us in the West. We must humble ourselves to voluntarily sacrifice in giving our rising third world Christian brethren the help they need to generate as many New Testament apostolic bands as possible. Paul did this at his own expense. We also should move ahead strongly before impending crisis surprises us. If we do not harmonize in moving out voluntarily with God toward a simpler life style, we may well lose out even as participants in a supporting role (Wilkerson 1974:13,17,119-21).

The Church, both as modality and sodality, must learn to further synchronically strategize its efforts for completing its responsibility to God in the Great Commission during this generation. As each of us is caught up in the continuous mission process, we will become more keenly aware of our interdependent roles and functions. We can move with greater accountability to one another, especially to our brethren in third world emerging missions. We can look forward to hastening the return of the Lord of the harvest (II Pet. 3:12-15).

Part Three now develops two examples of the third missiological moment of strategizing for doubling both rural and urban mission.

Part Three: Strategizing

Ethnic Participation in
Continuous Mission

7

Rural Mission to the Aymara-Quechuas

Part One emphasized the importance of seeing the trends among the Bolivian people from the perspective of the national Church and the associated missions. This is ethnohistory. Part Two demonstrated the necessity of theologizing from the people's point of view, answering their felt needs. This is ethnotheology. Now, Part Three proposes the wedding of the trends of Part One with the biblical priorities developed in Part Two under the rubric of God's continuous mission. How do these two concepts come together to form a meaningful doubling strategy for both a rural and urban context? Bolivia is divided between the two. This chapter will show how to apply newly developed church growth methodology to the rural 100,000 Aymaras. As these people move up the social acceptability scale, they are being absorbed by the Quechuas to the east as described by Hamilton's maps in Figures 1 and 2 of Chapter One. Joint strategizing by nationals and foreigners in mission is not optional if we take Jesus and His Lordship over us seriously (I Cor. 4:1,2; Matt. 25:14-30 and Wagner 1974:76). This is ethnostrategy. It speaks to the needs of each definable homogeneous unit in the language and culture of that group. It expects a response appropriate for that group.

According to Dayton and Engstrom (1976:14), strategy simply stated is:

1. Deciding what God wants you to do and be. SET GOALS.
2. Discovering the more important goals. ESTABLISH PRIORITIES.
3. Analyzing the best way to reach your goals. PLAN.
4. Working toward your goals according to plans. START LIVING.
5. Using what you have learned to set new goals. KEEP ON LIVING.

Aymara-Quechuas, Buffer or Bridge for Church Growth?

The homogeneous unit of 100,000 Aymara-Quechuas in Bolivia has been selected for this area study to serve as a reproducible model for examining other homogeneous unit churches throughout the Andean zone. The advancing Kingdom of God among the Andean highlanders will thereby hopefully be speeded forward. Ten million largely Christo-pagan Quechua speakers still await the Good News, while one and a half million animistic Aymaras have been responding at 17% per annum over the last fifty years.

The Quechuas who had once subdued the Aymaras, were subjugated by the Incas in the 14th century. Both were brought under a centralized government system that controlled their lives. The 16th century Spanish imposed even greater hardships. The conquerors gave the fertile valleys to the Spanish overlords while forcing the natives up into the barren, chilly mountains. Later, the feudal hacienda system of farming reduced them to a cheap labor force with minimal legal rights.

The relationships among the Aymara, the Quechua and the Spanish-speaking *mestizo* are complex. In addition to linguistic differences between the first two groups, there are also socio-economic and cultural differences between the *mestizo*, on the one hand, and the Aymara-Quechua on the other. The Aymaras and the Quechuas are economically, politically and culturally subordinate to the *mestizos*. The disadvantaged position of the Aymaras and the Quechuas compared to the more permeable *mestizo* class creates a strong, continued movement from the former to the latter. Such "passing" is a long-term process. Thus, people are found at various stages of acculturation, preventing the defining of sharp demarcation lines between these groups. See Figures 1 and 2 in Chapter One to appreciate this process. Since the Aymara has accepted the Gospel more readily than the Quechua, the Evangel is more closely associated with the Aymara in the Quechua mind. This has impeded Quechua acceptance. Moreover, the Roman Catholic Church has traditionally concentrated more on the Quechua population, providing more religious material in Quechua than in Aymara. Notice the high incidence of syncretism registered among the Quechuas in Figure 21 of Chapter Four. Primov sees the conversion of the Aymaras to the Protestant movement as the response of a marginalized group to a more promising and functional moral order (1974:58).

Spanish Catholicism superimposed itself upon native animism. Syncretism resulted. Today, this is demonstrated in a variety of feasts to ancient community gods, venerated as guardian saints. For years the Church and State used this means to control the helpless and despised Indians. However, the Church suffered setbacks under the liberators, Sucre and Bolivar. Bolivia gained its independence in 1825 while the northern republics followed

Figure 33

BOLIVIAN POPULATION DENSITY

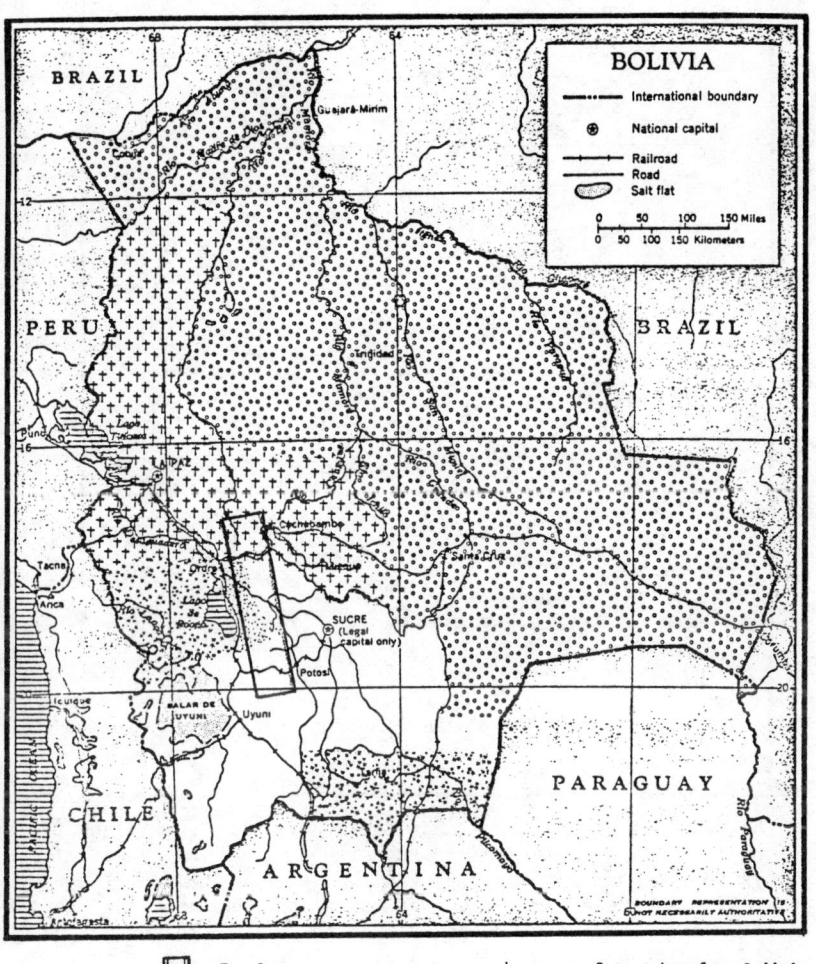

	7 - 9	persons per sq. km.
	4.5-5.5	" " " "
	3 - 4	" " " "
	less than 1	person " " "

Data taken from Bolivian National Census, 1950

Figure 34

BOLIVIAN COMPOSITE

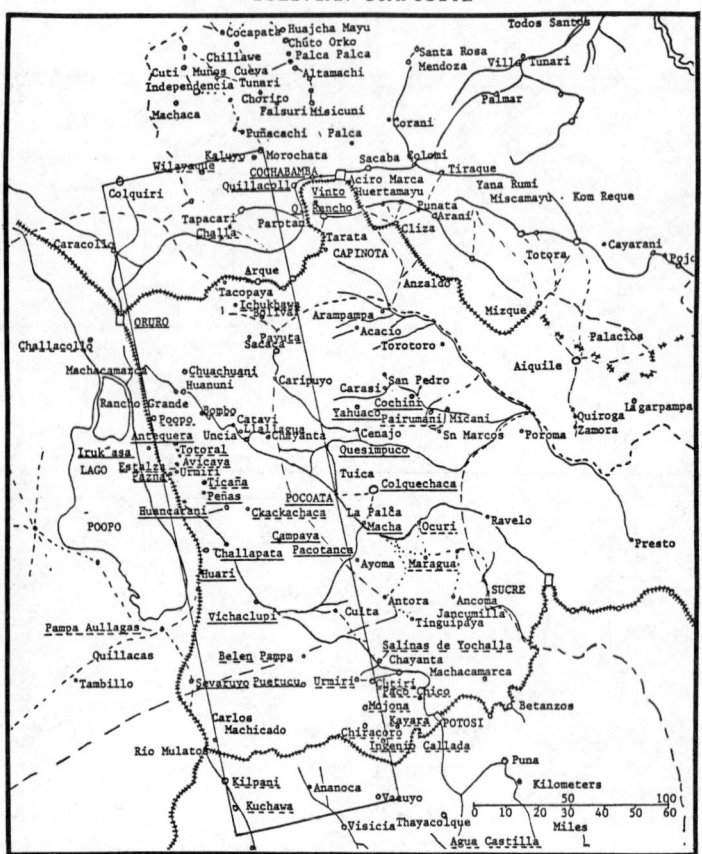

The people feel that they must constantly make sacrifices to the place spirits living under the earth's crust. They must always be vigilant for anything that would make their gods unhappy. Otherwise, sickness, crop failures, or animal and household thefts would be signs of their protector's displeasure. These gods also uphold moral good and are displeased with laziness, carelessness, greed and marital infidelity. They are constantly on the look-out that no wrongdoing escapes their attention (Tschopik 1951:192-3).

The Aymara-Quechuas worship through an individual supplication of their localized place deities. Beyond this, the concept of the gods becomes more distant and impersonal while the Christian God, whom they have learned of through Catholicism, is the most remote.

there is no apparent heirarchy of deities; rather, immediate needs press the people into selecting the appropriate deity to act on their behalf. Despite the influence of Catholicism and of the Incas, the ancient Aymara gods and spirits still are the most revered (Nordyke 1972:21). Land, illness and fear of thievery are their primary concerns (Nordyke 1972:119).

7. Spiritually describe the target as summarized in Figure 35. It is a profile of 100,000 Aymara-Quechuas in Bolivia during 1976, showing their spiritual distribution along the Continuous Decision-Making Process Scale from -10 to +2 (Engel and Norton 1975:45). This process has been explained on pages 72 and 73 of Chapter Five. Figure 35 graphically shows the ripe 30% Aymara-Quechua animists like fruit ready to be picked, spreading from -7 to -4. Above them are the remaining 55% green, resistant syncretists and pagans hanging tenaciously at -8 and -9. Below, are the 15% God-fearers who range between -3 and +2. One percent of these, or 1,000 believers, are members of the newly-formed ECU churches previously listed, while the remaining 1% belong to other groups.

Overcoming Nominalism with New National Missions

A desired goal of this chapter is to see at least twenty of these most vital new congregations going on to maturity by immediately reaching out in continuous $360°$ mission. This is emphasized at the bottom of Figure 35 between $270°$ to $360°$ by the diagonal line drawn between these boundaries. Otherwise, they may tend to grow fat with an increasing number of spiritual infants accumulating at +1 and +2 on the scale. They tend to lose their way when their spiritual parents fail to help them on down through the remaining phases towards maturity at $360°$ mission. The old distinction between home missions and foreign missions is becoming obsolete. Replacing it is the more precise designation of E_0, E_1, E_2 and E_3 evangelism. E_0 designates the evangelization of nominal church members. E_1 means winning unbelievers among those of one's own culture, or the 20% nominal and 10% practicing Roman Catholics. E_2 crosses a cultural barrier and plants new churches in a different culture, as among the 45% syncretists. E_3 signifies that the second culture is much more different from the original culture than was E_2 (Costas 1976:1,6; Wagner 1976:3). Therefore, E_3 evangelism is needed among the 20% animists appearing in Figure 21 on page 55, summarizing the above breakdown. Notice that both E_2 and E_3 are cross-cultural despite Stott's continued confusion of these terms at Urbana'76 (Howard 1977:57).

Focusing these terms and goals is crucial in order to avoid the gradual demise of new spiritual children from spiritual malnutrition. Once-thriving congregations in Tacopaya, Arque, San Pedro and other places where the AEM began its Bolivian ministry, are now dead because of parental neglect and failure to generate new national missions. God wants us to be responsible, cross-cultural

E_3 missionary parents, procreating as many E_1 maximum power communicators in their own culture. These national teams will help to improve the present waning 10.6% per annum growth among this target people.

Producing a successful Aymara-Quechua model in continuous mission could help speed the harvest across the entire Bolivian and Peruvian population mosaic, where the AEM is presently working. The same supracultural, biblical principles are applicable to other similarly responsive homogeneous units (Winter 1975:219).

Figure 35

PROFILE OF 100,000 AYMARA - QUECHUAS IN BOLIVIA, 1976

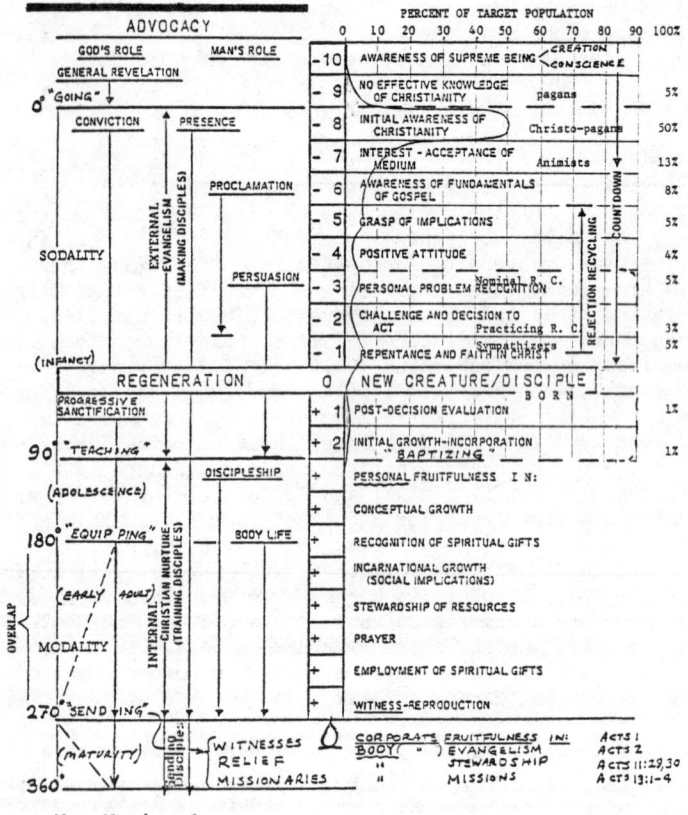

New National
Mission Born

ETHNOSTRATEGY

Foreigners and Nationals in Continuous Mission

The AEM is a fellowship of spiritually and cross-culturally gifted church planters, teachers and support personnel from six western homelands. We have been called by God to help the Body of Christ in the nations of Bolivia and Peru make disciples. Practical experience shows that we tend to meet our expectations. This section proposes specific ways for reaching the goal of doubling the growth of those churches desiring to participate in continuous mission over the next five years. This process is summarized in the full-circle spiral of Figure 36. Notice the increasing difficulty in crossing successive barriers to witnessing as we move around the circle from E_0 witnesses to E_2 and E_3 cross-cultural communicators.

Figure 36

CONTINUOUS MISSION COMPOSITE WITH MISSION-CHURCH OVERLAP

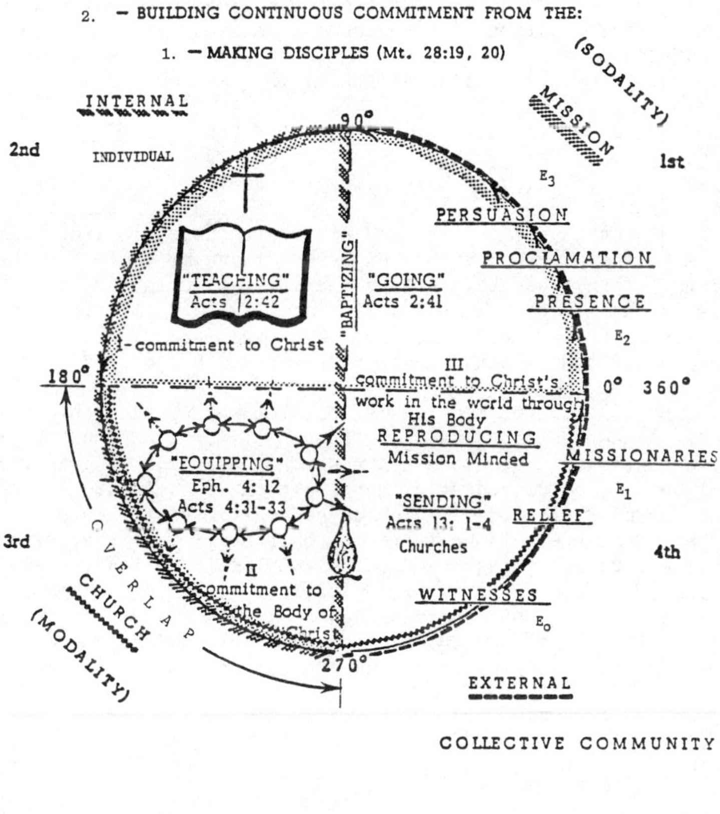

2. — BUILDING CONTINUOUS COMMITMENT FROM THE:

1. — MAKING DISCIPLES (Mt. 28:19, 20)

(SODALITY)
MISSION
1st

INTERNAL
2nd   INDIVIDUAL
90°
E_3

PERSUASION
PROCLAMATION

"TEACHING"   "GOING"   PRESENCE
Acts 2:42   Acts 2:41
"BAPTIZING" E_2

I—commitment to Christ

180°   III   0° 360°
commitment to Christ's
work in the world through
His Body
REPRODUCING
Mission Minded   MISSIONARIES

"EQUIPPING"
Eph. 4:12
Acts 4:31-33   "SENDING" E_1
Acts 13: 1-4   RELIEF
Churches

3rd   II   4th
OVERLAP   commitment to
CHURCH   the Body of
(MODALITY)   Christ   WITNESSES
E_0
270°
EXTERNAL

COLLECTIVE COMMUNITY

Reviewing and Applying Continuous Mission

1. *Going* is represented from $0°$ to $90°$ in Figure 36. God calls and sends apostles to those He is bringing to repentance (John 16: 7-15; Acts 11:18). These apostles must be directed, not by personal whim, but by the Lord to His heavy harvest fields (John 4:34,35) This involves constant availability for ethnotheologically meeting the felt needs of the people as the Lord Jesus Christ did with His compassionate:

    a. Presence - to help each person, beginning where he is.
    b. Proclamation - of liberation from all that separates man from God (Isa. 61:1,2a). God forgives man on the basis of the substitution of the Innocent for the guilty.
    c. Persuasion - of the repentant to commitment to Christ, then to His Body, and finally to His work in the world as responsible, reproducing members of a caring fellowship of believers caught up in mission.

2. *Teaching*, or discipling, is represented from $90°$ to $180°$ in Figure 36. The repentant must be instructed by our life and teaching to obey all received from the Lord Jesus in a profound commitment to Him, starting with incorporation into a local congregation by baptism. Here, needs are met and internal growth toward spiritual maturity is experienced (Eph. 4:13).

3. *Equipping*, or perfecting, is represented from $180°$ to $270°$ in Figure 36. The gathered Saints in each church, according to Ephesians 4:11-16, must be *equipped* to do the *external* work of the ministry and the *internal* edifying of the Body. The gifted apostles, prophets, evangelists and pastor-teachers are like trainers given to the Church for this express purpose of *equipping* the Saints. Then these Saints take the initiative to continue Christ's work of the ministry in the world, as witnesses, agents of relief and missionaries themselves, from $270°$ to $360°$! They simultaneousl edify one another in the local Body, from $180°$ to $270°$.

4. *Exiting* of the missionary apostles should occur by at least $270°$. A new cycle begins among the 65% from $0°$, beyond the reach of the national Church and its newly begun teams. The Apostle Paul set a good precedent with the eleven or so apostolic bands in which he participated or which he helped to start. He never stayed around to smother his newly formed churches. Once they were on their way toward being *equipped* by the locally gifted, emerging teachers, Paul moved on. Periodically he checked on their progress between $270°$ and $360°$, forming new apostolic teams from among those showing promise in church planting. In this way he stimulated the new churches into generating other missions from the outset.

By this process a national, indigenous Church is created which itself then becomes a 270° to 360° mission-generating Church, represented by quadrant 4 in Figure 36. New apostolic bands are born for continuing the full circle evangelism spiral process throughout the Bolivian and Peruvian population spectrum, in cooperation with other like-minded groups of believers (Acts 13:1-4). This will hasten the return of our Lord as He completes His glorious Body, the Church, through us as colaborers with Him in His waiting harvest (Smith 1976:4-16; Tippett 1973:155-8).

The following account by John Lloyd, a key Quechua worker with the AEM, illustrates how he is carrying out this 360° mission process with his national teams among the target people.

1. *Going*, 0 to 90° - We landed in a potato patch and discovered that the adjoining town was called Payuta, with one believer. He was lonely and without fellowship. We gathered the leaders of the village who told us that they were interested in hearing the Gospel. However, they did not feel they had time to clear a landing strip for our departure, so Benedicto and I had to walk out. When we flew in the second time we offered the village men fifteen pesos each to clear a piece of runway. We also gave them the option of accepting a Quechua New Testament instead of the money. Of the twenty-one workers, eighteen chose New Testaments.

After many months of visiting Payuta and patient teaching of the Gospel, we felt that they were ready to make a decision. We were expecting a great response, so we told them that they had to make a decision either for or against the Lord Jesus. They said they would decide together and let us know in the morning. You can imagine our disappointment when only one man said he wanted to accept Christ. In fear of reprisals from the place spirits, they had called the witch doctor in during the night. He told the group that if they accepted Christ, they would get a fever and many would die. We were dumbstruck and could do nothing more than to leave sadly, praying for a breakthrough.

During our absence from Payuta the Holy Spirit continued to work in their hearts. After much prayer, we decided just what we should do. Benedicto taught on the necessity of obeying God rather than man and of the importance of eternity compared to the present. Then we took a bold step in the power of the Holy Spirit, declaring categorically that the witch doctor had been lying. No fever would come nor would anyone die for accepting Christ. With that, twenty-five adults professed faith in Christ!

2. *Teaching*, or discipling, 90° to 180° - Immediately we organized a church with a three-day celebration. Five more adults received Christ during this festival, meaning that about half the adults in the village were now Christians. Four families brought their idols and destroyed them in a public power encounter - with

no ill effects. This action by inside advocates is very important
to sealing a public decision among animistic peoples (Nordyke
1972:169). Baptisms were performed by the nationals.

3. *Equipping*, or perfecting, 180° to 270° - Following the New
Testament pattern, we acted as outside advocates and named the
new elders according to the following process. As a team we
prayed together to reach perfect agreement regarding the choice
of three men who had emerged as leaders. We called them aside,
asking them if they felt that God had called them to this ministry
and if they felt they met the biblical requirements for elders in
I Timothy 3. Having answered affirmatively, we left them alone
while we met with the other believers. They agreed that these
three met the biblical standards, giving them unanimous approval.
Even some of the unbelieving spectators added their approval.

4. *Exiting* and surveillance, 270° to 360° - The believers continued to grow rapidly qualitatively and quantitatively in Christ
under their own leaders in their own way (I John 2:27). Upon our
return, we were surprised to find that the new believers had
called a day of prayer and had then gone as E_1 evangelists to a
neighboring village to share their new faith. We continue periodic
visits to further encourage them in the Scriptures, which gradually
allays their anxieties centering around their land, illness and
fear of thievery (Nordyke 1972:119-27; Lloyd 1976:5,6).

Just as the Apostle Paul periodically checked on the progress
of the new churches between 270° and 360°, we too as cross-cultural
E_2 and E_3 missionaries are responsible for a similar, periodic
ministry among our fledgling churches. They must be stimulated
to give birth to as many E_1 maximum-power communicators as possible
Otherwise, new believers tend to become ingrown and fat from introspection. The Lord Jesus commissioned His disciples to reach out
in 360° mission (Matt. 28:19,20). Bruno Frigoli, an *altiplano*
missionary to the Aymaras, does this well, as proved by the phenomenal sustained 17% AAGR among his mushrooming congregations.
His slogan is, "Each church a new church each year" (1975:6,7).
Such responsible parenthood requires purposeful planning and work
to succeed.

To summarize this part, some possible strategy goals which
could result from regional workshops are to:

1. Harmonize with God to increase the 10.6% to 14.8% AAGR among
the target churches, mostly through E_1 evangelism and church planting. As E_2 and E_3 evangelists and church planters, we can best
join with our successful national brethren in accelerating the
growth of new congregations with 360° mission vision.

2. Bring each of the five cooperating subdirectorates and their
new congregations through a regional 360° workshop to spur on sustained growth.

3. Determine how well their spiritual needs are being met to better meet these needs during the coming year through theological education by extension at their level.

4. Set a faith projection for at least doubling the present performance of each church over the next five years, based upon:

   a. Annual number of converts won.
   b. Resistance of various sectors of the surrounding population.
   c. Amount and quality of church growth compared to others.
   d. Total financial and human resources available for pursuing church growth in this area.

5. Select twenty new, promising churches from among the five cooperating subdirectorates showing the highest potential for growth. Trimestral monitoring and special theological education by extension (TEE) will be given during the coming year to enable each one of these twenty pilot churches to reach its $360°$ mission goal after having become equipped itself from $180°$ to $270°$. Each pilot church will be responsible to reproduce itself annually.

6. Publish and circulate the results of God's blessings on this continuous mission process in the Christian newspaper, *El Faro* and on the Christian radio station, *Cruz del Sur*. This will stimulate others to want to grow also.

7. Evaluate progress annually to encourage the sustained reproduction of new churches and to motivate other interested churches to also participate in this continuous mission process across the entire Bolivian and Peruvian population mosaic.

COMMITMENT OF HUMAN AND FINANCIAL RESOURCES

Motivated personnel will be enlisted at the regional workshops, based upon their voluntary desire to participate in continuous mission in their own locality. The following people, money and organizations are needed to carry out this plan:

1. The approval of AEM General Director, Ron Wiebe, has been requested for conducting church growth workshops. Proposals were submitted 19 December 1975, 22 April 1976 and 3 June 1976.

2. The approval of the AEM Field Council was requested 3 June 1976. A response is expected by September, 1977.

3. The approval of the Aymara-Quechua Team Director, John Lloyd, was requested by September, 1977.

4. The approval of the ECU President, Tito Montero, and of the ECU Executive Board, confirming their invitation of 27 April 1976, for sixteen regional workshops, was requested.

5. The approval of the leadership of the five following subdirectorates chosen to initiate the workshop series will be requested upon return to Bolivia:

a.	Cochabamba	October, 1978
b.	Oruro	November, 1978
c.	Challapata	December, 1978
d.	Pocoata	January, 1979
e.	Potosi	February, 1979

6. The approval of our homeland supporting churches will be sought during deputation this summer.

7. All other national and missionary colleagues involved in this continuous mission project continue to receive their present support from their own sources.

8. The actual expense of conducting the workshops is budgeted at $5,000.00, in addition to an equal amount to be raised locally.

9. Other organizations like the Bolivian Evangelical Social Action Commission (COMBASE), Latin American Literacy and Literature Movement (ALFALIT), Andean Communications Center, Every Home Literature Crusade and Christian Nationals' Evangelism Commission can promote participation as they become interested in the new church growth proposed by this plan.

EVALUATION

The progress of this continuous mission evangelism strategy for the 100,000 Aymara-Quechuas may be measured annually against the projections shown in Figure 37. This semi-logarithmic graph compares a possible projected, five-year 50% AAGR ECU Aymara-Quechua growth with:

1. The 16.6% AAGR of the nearby Baptist Aymaras in Carangas among 100,000 people during the last fifteen years.

2. The 54% AAGR of the mushrooming evangelical Quechuas of Ecuador among 200,000 people during the last ten years.

Field reports should be submitted to the ECU central office by 1 July of each year so that the November National Assembly may be advised of progress. Necessary readjustments may be made to improve reaping.

Table IX gives the actual annual steps projected to approximate a 50% AAGR upper limit from 1975 to 1985. It also gives the lower limit of 14.87% AAGR for doubling growth every five years. This reflects the same order of magnitude as the Baptist 16.6% AAGR to the west. Notice the number of people per thousand in the

Figure 37

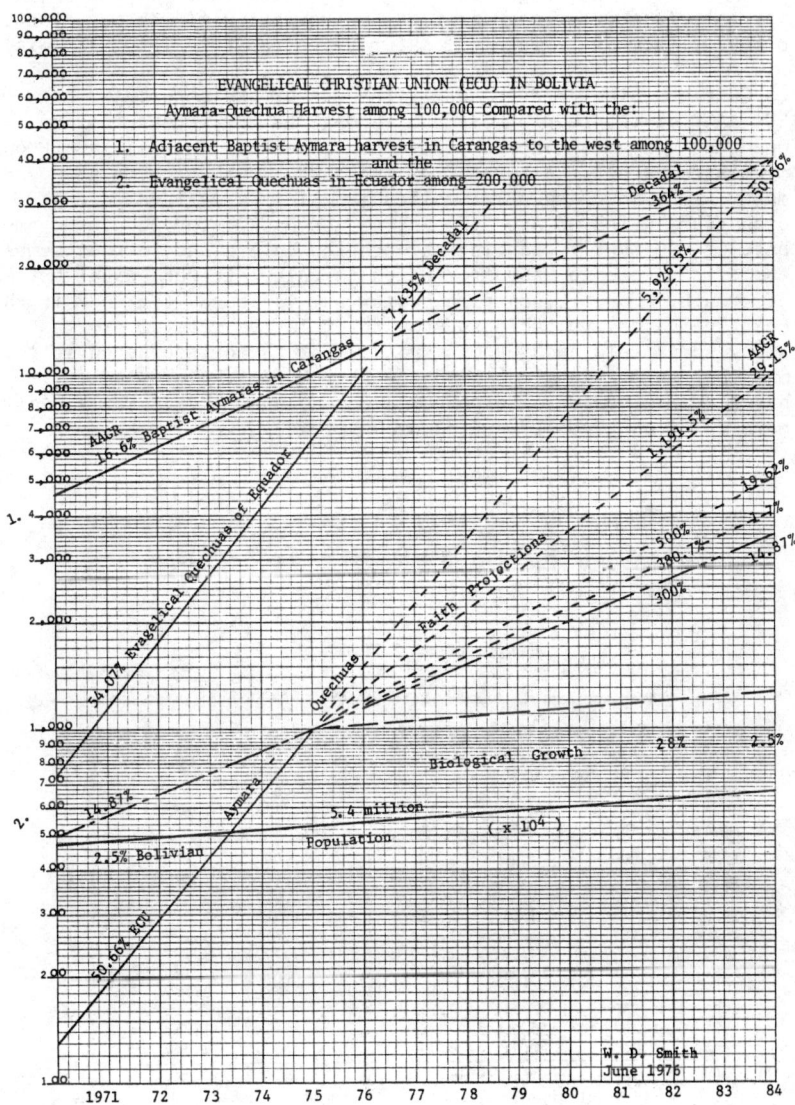

last column who must be added annually just to keep up with the population growth alone. Somewhere between the upper and lower limits lies the faith projection which will come out of the proposed five initial regional workshops. Goal ownership is crucial for the effective evangelization and equipping of the repentant, bringing them on to integral maturity in the Lord (Eph. 4:11-16).

Caution is advised regarding the use of the abnormally high 50% AAGR of the people movements among the 200,000 Ecuadorian Quechuas and among the 100,000 Aymara-Quechuas in Bolivia. People movements do not exactly follow the same growth pattern as does money. The money base multiplies itself by a certain percent each year, which we are defining as the AAGR. The people movement base is constantly changing through the influx and loss of members. There is no stable base from which to calculate the annual percent of growth. However, until a better way is found, the AAGR is the best indicator available to show the relative rate of growth among comparable homogeneous units. For those interested in the mathematical rationale behind the church growth formula, it is based upon a series of exponential equations already explained more fully on pages 17 and 18 of Chapter Two.

Table IX

POSSIBLE FAITH PROJECTIONS: 1975 to 1985

between 50.66% and 2.5% AAGR

Year	Average Annual Growth Rate (AAGR)				Doubling Every 5 Years	Bolivian Biological Growth	
	50.66%	29.2%	19.62%	17%	14.87%	2.5%*	
1970	130	278	408	456	500	884	
1971	190	359	488	534	574	906	
1972	292	464	584	624	660	929	
1973	441	599	699	731	758	952	
1974	664	774	836	855	871	976	
1975	1,000	1,000	1,000	1,000	1,000	1,000	25
1976	1,507	1,292	1,196	1,170	1,149	1,025	26
1977	2,270	1,668	1,431	1,369	1,319	1,051	26
1978	3,420	2,154	1,712	1,602	1,516	1,077	27
1979	5,153	2,782	2,048	1,874	1,741	1,104	27
1980	7,763	3,594	2,449	2,192	2,000	1,131	
1981	11,696	4,641	2,930	2,565	2,297	1,160	29
1982	17,622	5,995	3,505	3,001	2,639	1,189	29
1983	26,550	7,742	4,193	3,511	3,031	1,218	29
1984	40,000	10,000	5,016	4,108	3,482	1,249	31
1985	60,265	12,915	6,000	4,807	4,000	1,280	31
	5,926.5%	1,191.5%	500%	380.7%	300%	28%* Decadal growth	

People per 1,000 required to keep up with the population growth annually.

* 1975 World Population Data Sheet of the Population Reference Bureau, Inc.

Rural Mission

Only because of the loving sacrifice and vision of those pioneering the way before us, since the time of George and Mary Allan, can we make these suggestions and dream of doubling church growth every five years. May the Lord of the harvest spur us all on to greater accountability and faithfulness. His return is near.

In the meantime, as we harmonize with Him until His return, may we foreigners be increasingly used of God to encourage the national Church in generating its own missions. May many new E_1 maximum communicators form apostolic bands, accelerating God's continuous mission across the entire Bolivian and Peruvian mosaic. This will hasten the return of our Lord Jesus Christ as He completes His glorious Body, the Church, through us as we work with Him.

Remember why He is waiting. He is giving us time to saturate the hurting world with His healing message of forgiveness of sin. We accept the replacement of our guilty lives by His innocent life given on the cross. Are we equally ready to accept His universal mandate? We cannot betray the 65% unreached. This will require a growing synchronization of our efforts.

In conclusion, the possible doubling strategy proposed in this chapter must be evaluated in field workshops to secure the goal ownership of those desiring to grow. The ultimate Aymara-Quechua ethnostrategy will be derived by the workshop participants themselves. All we can do is suggest a range of possibilities. They must:

1. Decide what God wants them to be and to do.
2. Discover the more important goals.
3. Analyze the best way to reach their goals.
4. Work toward their goals as planned.
5. Measure progress and set new goals based upon experience.

Seven steps were followed to locate the target area inhabited by the 100,000 Aymara-Quechuas. Now we hope for greater coordination of the reaping by the five ECU area subdirectorates involved. These same steps will be adapted in the next chapter to urban mission.

8

Urban Mission to the Mestizos

This chapter concludes Part Three on strategizing. It is designed to enable the reader to develop his own church growth ethnostrategy. The Bolivian *mestizos* provide the background for this study. Any one of the nine capital cities or mining towns may equally be chosen. Each will eventually be involved in regional church growth workshops. At that time, the five-step process for locating urban target areas will be field tested and further honed. Most of the AEM personnel are working among this group of people.

Luis Palau United Campaign, 1974: Just the Beginning

Nine thousand city *mestizos* responded to Luis Palau's tri-city campaign during November, 1974. Those cities were Oruro, Cochabamba and Santa Cruz (Smith 1974b:5). The campaign in Cochabamba saw 2,501 decisions. One month later, only 25% of those making a profession of faith in the crusade were attending local churches. In comparison with previous campaigns, this was hailed as a success. However, in comparison with the 63% follow-up experienced by the recent Rosario Plan, '76 (Silvoso 1977:1), we need to anticipate the 1978 harvest with Palau, who says, "Up to now, we've talked about follow-up as something that takes place after the evangelistic campaign is over" (Gerber 1976:516). The difference between follow-up and harvest is far more than quibbling over words. It's the basic difference between *gathering grain into barns or leaving it in the fields*.

On the basis of past involvement with Luis Palau, he has asked me to coordinate the preparation of home churches to serve as these barns for the La Paz harvest. Modeled after Rosario, the La Paz experiment will be aimed at a crop of more than 900,000 people concentrated in Bolivia's functional capital. See Figure 1 in Appendix A to appreciate the 3.6% AAGR of this city since the turn of the century, making it one of Bolivia's top priorities for harvest. Two examples of the spiritual openness in this city over the last two years are:

1. John and Orlene Maze's pioneering Christian television programming receiving free time and national viewing.

2. Jonathan and Thelma Forsythe's home Bible studies growing to ten a week.

These examples merge with many others world-wide, demonstrating that the changing cities are ready for the Good News (Greenway 1976:21-76). But even though cities are ready, each ethnic group within the city must be considered unique. Urban church strategy requires a distinct approach for each homogeneous unit.

What is Urban?

Roger Greenway in his hailed *Urban Strategy for Latin America* (1973:27) arbitrarily cites 20,000 or more inhabitants as his index for determining whether or not a concentration of people is urbanized. However, urban anthropologist, John Gulick, disagrees (1973:983-4). He shows why as he traces the historical development of this type of reasoning, beginning with Robert Redfield's 1941 Folk Urban Bi-Polar Moralistic Model (Gulick 1973:981-7).

Cities are man-made environments with constant human interaction. The natural environment surrounding a village tends to counter balance the human element more than it does in cities. The larger the city, the more intense the life style.

Intuitively, people feel that a relatively large population is an important factor for classifying a settlement as being urban. Since population size can be measured rather accurately, should it not be an objective index or urbanization? However, no one can agree on what the minimum size should be. The U.S. Bureau of Census says 2,500; the U.N. cites 20,000, along with Greenway; the renowned demographer, Kingsley Davis, says 100,000 (Breese 1969:5ff). Such lack of objective criteria has not stopped the invention of an accumulation of qualitative, urban life characteristics.

Many have contributed to Redfield's moralistic Bi-Polar Model, which follows in Table X (Gulick 1973:984). These arbitrary, ideal polar concepts are merely hypotheses to be tested. They are not yet set in concrete (Fox 1977:11).

Table X

MORALISTIC BIPOLAR RURAL-URBAN MODEL

	Rural		Urban		Rural		Urban
0r	Country (village)	0u	Town (city)	11r	Particularistic	11u	Universalistic
1r	Community (Gemeinschaft)	1u	Noncommunity (Gesellschaft)	12r	Homogeneous	12u	Heterogeneous
2r	Folk	2u	Urban	12rx	Few alternative modes of behavior	12ux	Many alternative modes of behavior
3r	Primitive	3u	Civilized				
4r	Natural ("true")	4u	Spurious, superficial, artificial	13r	Personal	13u	Impersonal (anonymous)
5r	Simple	5u	Sophisticated	13rx	Constrained	13ux	Free
6r	Provincial	6u	Cosmopolitan	14r	Integrated	14u	Disintegrated (anomic)
7r	Tribal society	7u	Mass society				
8r	Moral	8u	Corrupt	14rx	Conformist	14ux	Nonconformist
9r	Inherently stable	9u	Inherently changing	15r	Sacred	15u	Secular
10r	Human in scale	10u	Dehumanized	15rx	Superstitious (myth-oriented)	15ux	Rational

Basically, this model is anti-urban. Here are some examples.

1. Urban life lacking constraining personal relationships, category 13, is one of the many easily refutable implications of this model.

2. Not one critic has yet worked out an adequate substitute with equal appeal. The Bipolar Model stereotypes camouflage reality by oversimplification.

3. The assumption that urban and rural represent a single, uniform type of settlement is a major flaw.

4. Glaring internal inconsistencies are seen among the urban traits. If cultural heterogeneity is one of the few traits that all can agree upon, then anonymity and anomie cannot characterize all city dwellers (Lewis 1965:496).

5. Hauser (1965) shows that moralistic bipolar traits taken at face value and applied cross-culturally do not fit well.

Since "essential urban" characteristics elude us when considering complex, larger cities, why not consider some smaller, simpler samples called "city" or "urban" by the inhabitants themselves and by observers? Gulick does this by abstracting the seven following essential urban characteristics from the work of seven other anthropologists (1973:993-4).

1. Local residents and institutions serve as *brokers* between the larger society upon which the settlement depends and the surrounding region that the settlement dominates. The brokerage or middleman functions are primarily those of government administration, transportation, industry, communication and commerce. These middlemen act as conduits of information, power, money and prestige (Fox 1977:159).

2. In carrying out these functions between an ethnic settlement and a larger city, strangers and *outsiders* frequently visit the settlement.

3. Social *classes* arise among the inhabitants, whereby they relate to each other according to stereotypes (Mitchell, 1969:10).

4. Personal *connections* in other larger cities lend prestige and power to the uppermost class. They may behave with a sophisticated, cosmopolitan, cultivated, universalistic and urbane air. However, the fact that the lower class city dwellers do not display such traits does not exclude them from being urban (Richardson and Bode 1969:2).

5. Urbanites in categories 1,2 and 3 of Table X are often characterized as being impersonal, rationalistic, *goal-oriented* and single stranded in their interpersonal relationships. However, they are also intensely personal, multiplex or with many-stranded relationships.

6. The life style in a settlement is subject to *change* because of dependence upon the larger society over which they have no control.

7. Cultural *heterogeneity* in various forms is present in all of the above characteristics. (See Bruner 1973:374).

Some exceptions do exist. None of the above traits is wholly rural or urban. The idea of "pure" types and polar opposites is rejected. All traits may be equally found in both villages and in cities. The important differences among them are in style and degree (Gulick 1973:997). The primary motivation for migrations to the cities is to share in the new and exciting way of life, not primarily for obtaining a job (Gulick 1973:998). This statement spurs the missionary on to find out how he can better identify and meet the growth needs specified by Maslow (Goble 1970:52). This is best accomplished through kinship lines (Gulick 1973:1006). Therefore, it is essential to localize the groups having self-awareness. Then it will be possible to meet the crisis of hurt and pain that is overwhelming and frustrating this group. The "melting pot" myth about the absorption of homogeneous groups has been shattered. See Chapter Three, pages 34-36 for the "stew pot" alternative model put forward by Wagner. Seaton shows how to creatively meet health needs (1976:19ff), especially in third world mission.

Hopefully, this analysis helps to clear the fog on the meaning of urban being that of attitude. In conclusion to this section, urbanism may be defined as a predisposition to share in the work and the life of an interdependent community built around mutually committed, largely non-related families. Empirically, this level of community life requires a concerted effort of over 2,000 people to produce the necessary urban services. This is in keeping with the U.S. Bureau of Census minimum urban size of 2,500, provided the seven essential urban characteristics enumerated above are included in this definition. The missionary must capitalize on the attitude of interdependence and commitment to relate a meaningful Gospel in the urban context.

What is *Mestizo*?

Since the turn of the century Indians constitute a slowly increasing majority of the Bolivian population. See Figure 11 of Chapter Three to appreciate the trend from 60% in 1910 to 64% by 1980. The majority are Aymaras and Quechuas who live in the highland plateau and intermountain valleys. The balance are whites of Spanish descent, 10%, and *mestizos*, 25%. The latter are a mixed people of Spanish and Indian descent. As a result, the people are divided today ethnically, linguistically, geographically and religiously. Since the 1952 Revolution, successive governments have attempted to improve the Indian status and political consciousness for more effective integration into the national life.

As the *mestizo* population grew since the Spanish arrival in the second quarter of the 16th century, they developed an increasingly strong sense of social identity. By the middle of the 17th century, they composed a third recognizable ethnic grouping.

Gradually, the concept of race has come to have more of a social and cultural meaning rather than biological. Thus, whites are often racially mixed, and a *mestizo* can be racially Indian and culturally Spanish. The term *indio* technically means Indian. But unfortunately, it describes social characteristics of a person living in an indigenous community, speaking an indigenous language, going barefoot, wearing homespun clothes and bearing an Indian surname. Historically, it has been an epithet implying racial inferiority.

The 1952 Revolution officially substituted the word *campesino*, or peasant, for the title *indio*. This heralded the government's attempt to raise the Indian status from a powerless tenant farmer to a landholding participant of the national society. The effects of the reform are most obvious in the highlands. Especially the Aymaras are working through their local peasant syndicates to effect changes in education and public welfare. Their increased dynamism and the fluidity of the social structure have worsened interethnic relations, ranging from mild paternalism to bitterness and animosity (Weil 1974:78).

Geographically, the *mestizos* are the most pervasive of all the ethnic groups. Economically and socially their position is equivocal in Bolivian society. The ambiguity surrounding their status also surrounds their rubric. *Mestizo* and *cholo* are applied indiscriminately, often interchangeably. A wealthy, upper class *mestizo* may be regarded as white whereas a poorer *mestizo* trucker might be called *cholo*. An urbanized Indian might be called *campesino* in one village and *cholo* in another. There is little apparent physical difference among the three classes. The terms chosen refer to social status rather than to biological race.

Regardless of differences in status between *mestizo* and *cholo*, both are defined by the cultural criteria of language, urban orientation, occupation, manners and dress. The most outstanding characteristic of this complex group is its ability to speak Spanish along with one or more Indian languages. A close corollary to speaking Spanish is the ability to read it. As they move up the social acceptability scale, they are turning to Christ at 10% per annum, demonstrated in summary Table V on page 46 of Chapter Three. Most *mestizos* are marginally literate. There is a great disparity between the *cholos* who have had two years of primary education and the fully literate. Education, like speaking Spanish, is crucial to upward mobility and is widely encouraged. Furthermore, *mestizos* and *cholos* are basically urban-oriented. They are generally not *campesinos*. Though they are highly adaptable to western ways and dress, they rarely abandon their folk religion, magic and curing techniques. However, while carryovers are merely traditions for the *cholo*, they are community rituals for the Indian. Thus, this accounts for the high degree of syncretism shown in Figure 21 of Chapter Four on page 57. How is it possible to get beyond the *mestizo*, *cholo* and *campesino* biases to produce effective urban church growth?

Beyond *Mestizo* Bias to Becoming Christians

Folk religion, magic and native curing techniques must be confronted in a public power encounter by an accepted, inside advocate of the living Gospel. Can we dare to organize such an encounter and more effective follow-up in anticipation of a miracle like that of 1973, which touched twice as many people as did Palau in 1974? God unexpectedly shook Bolivia with the preaching and healing ministry of newly converted nineteen-year-old Roman Catholic, Julio Cesar Ruibal. Without promotion or much organization, from December, 1972 to February, 1973 during three-day campaigns in La Paz, Santa Cruz and Cochabamba, God touched over 200,000 people through this young man. This represents about 5% of the population at that time. Allowing for nearly 10% professing Christ, as commonly occurs at mass campaigns in Bolivia (Smith 1974b:5), the Church was faced with the need to incorporate 20,000 new believers. Why can only the Assemblies of God today report 2,000 discipled in their congregations compared to an insignificant number of Ruibal converts spread throughout the remaining Bolivian denominations (Wagner 1974b:12)? When the harvest came in, only the Assemblies of God were ready for church growth through previous training of the laity (Frigoli 1975:1-4). Since 1970, the reality of each church planting one new church each year has become increasingly a way of life for the Assemblies of God among the Bolivian Aymaras. Bruno Frigoli makes a threefold promise to the emerging churches:

1. One-half of the galvanized steel roof (the most expensive part of the building) once they have organized the new group of believers and put up an adobe church.

2. A supply of Bibles and hymn books in their own language.

3. Where needed, a mule or bicycle for their pastor to facilitate planting another church within five miles.

However, no degree of preparatory organization or incentives can ensure success. The dynamic power of the Holy Spirit so evident in world-wide awakenings (Orr 1973:vii-28), produces the actual miracle of gaining the attention and convicting so many Bolivian people of their need of Christ. They turn to God from their past enslavement when we speak relevantly to their *mestizo* bias. Western Christian missions and churches can no longer be blind to the world view of the *mestizo* emerging from the 65% unreached pagan pool.

Western Christians have been heavily secularized and saturated with scientific thinking over the last one hundred years. We are taught to think that disease is not caused by God's will but by germs. Disease is cured by drugs, colds by Dristan and malaria by quinine. Western missionary physicians have moved out across the globe effectively praying for and healing many in the name of the Lord Jesus Christ, using drugs and modern technology. Rationalists say that there is no God. The physical, chemical and psychological causes measured and manipulated by man are the *only* reality. They work equally as well for atheists and theists.

Thus, faith healing to a twentieth century thinker is a delusion. The healer is either self-deluded or a clever manipulator. People claiming to be cured were not really sick, or they had temporary feelings of well being. Perhaps some were even planted among the group to build the reputation of the healer. Westerners and other modern secularists are skeptical about any power available to men outside the human realm.

McGavran says that most people in Asia, Africa and Latin America believe that disease is inflicted by spirits and gods. It is cured by superhuman power. Witches "eat up the life force" of other men. An angry neighbor casts an evil eye on a woman. She grows weaker every day until she dies. A wandering evil spirit devours a baby. The baby dies. A demon causes an illness which no medicine can cure. Western medicine may help some people, but

all of these countries are full of mysterious powers about which
the white man knows little. Only those who do know the secret of
black power can heal African afflictions. Evil powers must be
overcome by superior powers. In Latin America, the healer has
great power. His incantations, potions, sacrifices and medicines
amazingly heal the sick (1977b:2).

McGavran continues to affirm that perhaps 98% of these people
believe that a superior power drives out an inferior power. In
Europe and Asia, the impersonal, mechanistic system of scientism
fails to satisfy millions. They too eagerly believe in occult
extra-human powers. Satan worship flourishes. The mysterious
influence of magic words, rites, robes, stars, yogis and gurus
fascinate many (1977b:3).

Western Christians have a special problem with faith healing.
It definitely occurred in Bible times, but it conflicts with their
science today. The emerging Church ministry was characterized by
continual faith healing, according to Acts 5:12-16. Missions must
re-think their position on healing in order to be relevant among
people with this world view.

Here are five attitudes some Christians take towards faith healing, according to McGavran (1977b:4):

1. Although God ordinarily operates through His observable laws,
   He is not bound by them. When He pleases, He intervenes to
   meet each person within his cultural view.

2. Healings are a mixture of God's acts and man's acts. Incomplete healings and failures are from a lack of faith or sincerity. Genuine deliverance does occur.

3. An overwhelming number of valid cures is convincing some of
   the skeptical that healing campaigns can be valid.

4. Some abuses and demonic cures are causing other skeptics to
   brush healing campaigns aside as being totally invalid.

5. God has called some to actively engage in healing and exorcising, resulting in the multiplication of sound churches
   with responsible, reproducing Christians.

Since healing campaigns are a part of today's context, missionaries must ask what should be our biblical response. What do we
do with those who decide to become Christian, as occurred during
the Ruibal campaigns? Even though Ruibal touched twice as many
people as did Palau a year later, the permanent results were the
same because the Church had not decided what to do with the converts. The Church cannot afford the luxury of further indecision.
Perhaps the following seven steps suggested by McGavran would help

to overcome evangelical indecision. These seven steps answer the *mestizo* needs as they become Christian out of a pagan society (1977b:8,9):

1. Converts or inquirers, speaking for as many as possible of their village, invite leaders of a nearby church to hold a mission.

2. At the height of the series of meetings, the accepted inside advocate encourages the villagers to burn both individual and community fetishes at a public ceremony.

3. The converts representing most of the village, if possible, build a church at once within their means.

4. The congregation chooses a responsible local man to lead them while studying through extension. He is supported by local church offerings.

5. Christians recently converted buy Bibles, worship during the week and on Sunday, learning at every service.

6. New converts are baptized as soon as they complete the baptismal course and possess an intelligent faith in Christ.

7. The new congregation of baptized believers selects deacons and elders based upon their emerging gifts and spiritual maturity. A guiding committee is formed and delegates are sent to the annual meeting of the Church.

These seven steps may not exactly apply in all situations since conditions differ among villages and denominations. It is of primary importance that leaders of existing churches and missions do not spend their time debating what to do or discussing whether God indeed heals today. We must not betray the 65% unreached while discussing whether or not the *mestizo*, emerging from the pagan pool, is genuinely converted.

Adapting Seven Urban Characteristics for Church Growth

Having clarified how to meet *mestizo* bias biblically and relevantly, we are now ready to adapt Gulick's seven essential urban characteristics for church growth.

1. The middlemen *brokers* are key people to win for Christ at the outset. Once they become inside advocates, the whole region can eventually be claimed through their witness. Paul seems to have used this strategy in his missionary journeys as narrated in the Acts of the Apostles.

2. The *outsiders* like Ruibal who visit an ethnic settlement may gain the confidence of the group by meeting their felt needs. Their *mestizo* bias can be overcome as these needs are satisfied. Inside advocates for Christ will emerge. They should be encouraged to follow their connections along kinship lines with the Gospel.

3. The social *classes* of each community must be respected by inaugurating homogeneous unit churches.

4. Personal *connections* should be followed along kinship lines for spontaneous church growth.

5. The *goal orientation* of urbanites lends itself well to faith projecting. The intensely personal, multi-stranded web of interrelationships serves church growth well.

6. The rapid *changes* in life style through migration requires a dynamic decision-making process. The urban evangelical church must re-think and re-design to improve its participation in this same process. We must be relevant.

7. Cultural *heterogeneity*, present in all of the above characteristics, may be helpful to church growth after each homogeneous church has matured enough to begin reaching out to those who are different from them.

With a better understanding of what is urban, *mestizo*, and how to overcome *mestizo* bias, we are now prepared to begin ethnostrategizing through the five-step process of locating ripe urban targets.

Five Steps in Locating Urban Target Areas

The methodology used here is essentially similar to that of the previous chapter. Both follow the Missions Advanced Research and Communication Center (MARC) Workbook entitled *Planning Strategies for Evangelism* (Dayton 1977). This Second Revision expands on the "Engle Scale Process" of ethnic decision making. Also, it introduces a quantified receptivity-resistance axis similar to what I have already demonstrated in Table V on page 46 of Chapter Three.

The MARC Workbook is an excellent tool for facilitating analysis. It focuses on a specific group in an attempt to understand the perceived needs of each people. Step by step, the ethnic planner is led to consider the most appropriate people, methods and strategies for more effective communication of the Gospel. He is continually reminded that he is actually part of the process, not just an outside observer. As you use your copy of the Workbook, you will find the following five steps helpful in locating your urban target areas.

1. *Ethnolinguistically*, locate the suspected responsive *mestizo* group that interests your mission in Figure 38, the Bolivian Ethnolinguistic-Religious Population Distribution, with the crusades of Ruibal in 1973 and of Palau in 1974. Palau conducted an E_1 evangelism type crusade while Ruibal entered the E_2 category among the *mestizo* syncretists. Of the nine thousand registering decisions for Christ with Palau in 1974, notice in Figure 38 how most remained suspended among the 20% nominal Roman Catholic population. Palau did not touch the Roman Catholic syncretists who comprise 45% of the population. Approaching 1980, the general characteristics of the responsive *mestizos* moving up socially toward the white class which Palau represents, are (reading a vertical swath from top to bottom in Figure 38): 15% syncretists, out of ordinary evangelistic range; 55% nominal Roman Catholics; 26.6% practicing Roman Catholics and 3.4% committed Protestants for a total swath of 100%. A separate ethnostrategy must be worked out on the field in the upcoming workshops to effectively reach each of these homogeneous units.

2. *Geographically*, subdivide a city-wide map like that of Cochabamba, shown in Figure 39, for distribution of responsibility among participating churches, as tabulated in Table XI. In order to participate in the 1978 effort with Palau, each church should be required to commit itself to a 1977 church growth workshop. This will validate its growth history over the last five years and enable the believers to project a faith commitment for the next five years, including the beginning of new home churches in their new neighborhoods. These new home churches will serve as granaries for receiving the expected '78 harvest, as was so effectively done during the Rosario Plan (Gerber 1976:566).

3. *Demographically*, define the 1978 population of the target city of Cochabamba from Figure 2 of Appendix A. This will be in the vicinity of 210,000 at a 3.395% AAGR. These people must be broken down into their respective ethnic subunits. Each should be accounted for by one of the committed participants in the first regional church growth workshop.

4. *Socio-economically*, Cochabamba has been the most progressive of Bolivia's rural areas. Language, dress, occupational activity, wealth and productivity determine the social stratification of the *cholos* and *campesinos* in the Cochabamba valley. Urban *mestizos* are closely related to this dominant class. They have nearly identical life styles. They exalt hard work, placing no value on leisure, which is in direct contrast to the prevalent, Hispanic tradition among the whites (Weil 1974:114-119). Being poor is equated with being lazy. The Church could well capitalize on the cooperative spirit that characterizes the dominant *cholos*.

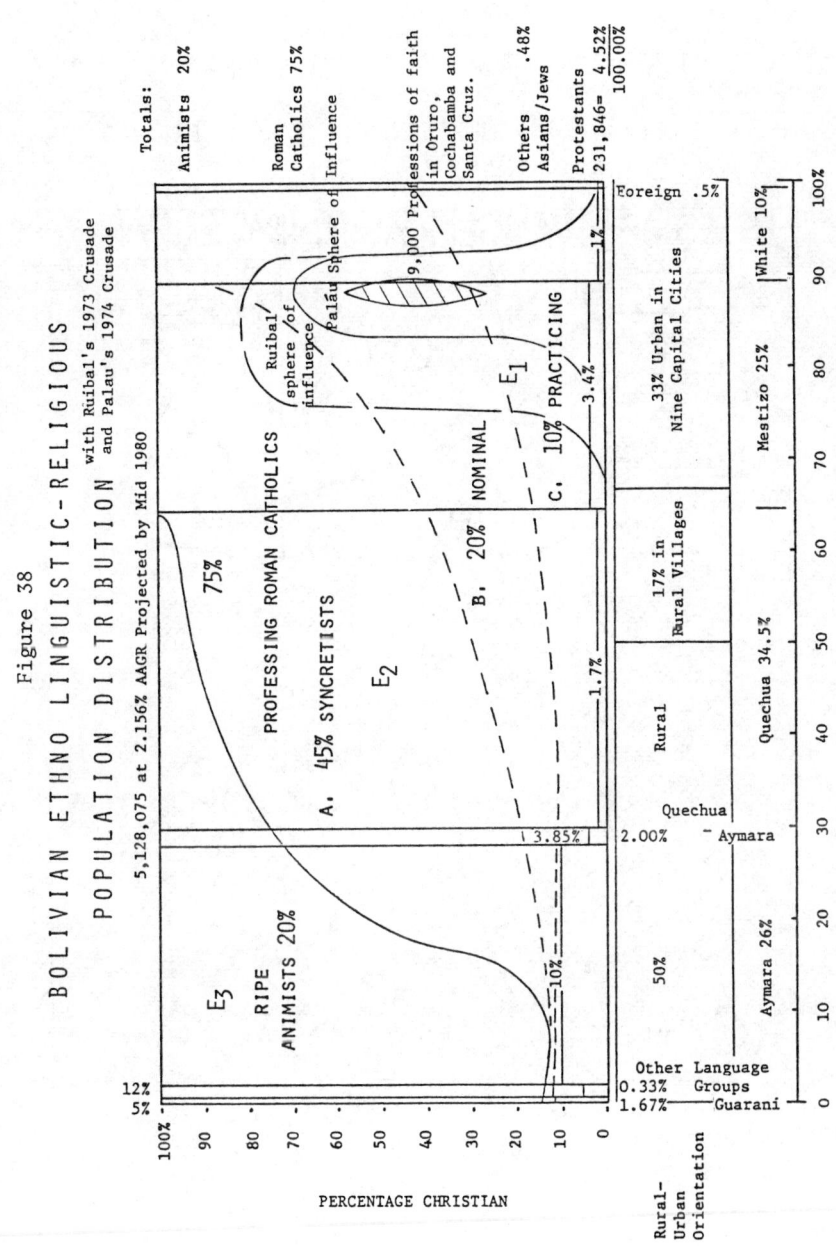

Figure 38

Figure 39

EIGHTEEN RESPONSIBILITY AREAS FOR
COCHABAMBA CHURCHES

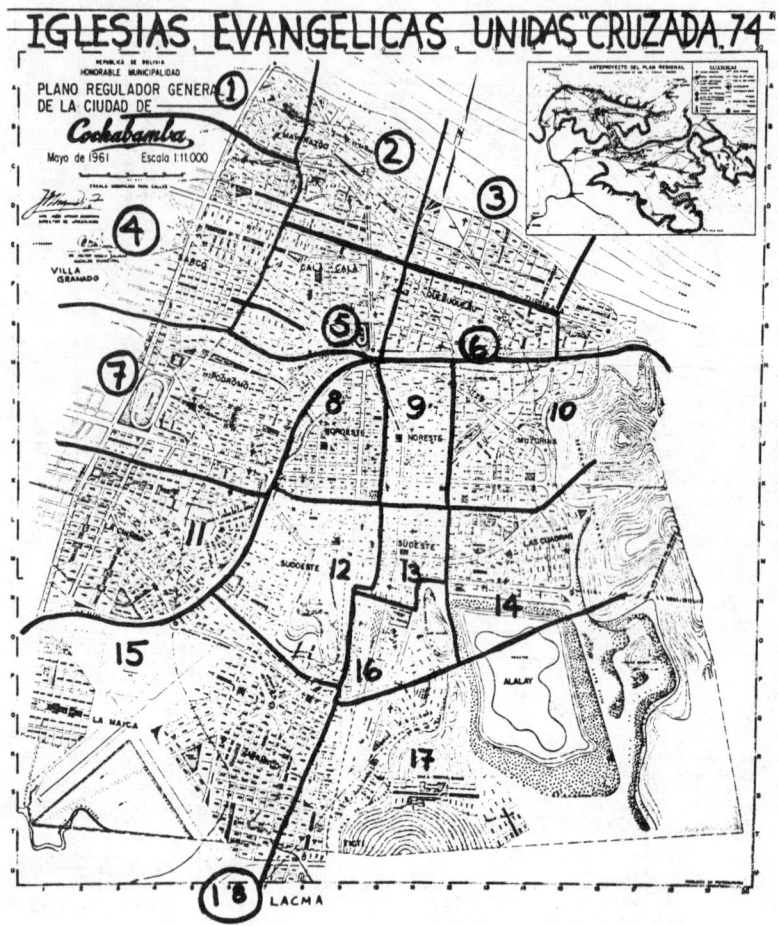

Table XI

Forty-Two Participating Cochabamba Churches in Palau 1974 Crusade

1 ZONA MAYORAZGO
IGLESIA EVANGELICA "MAYORAZGO"
Cuadro #391 - Tel. 7563

2 ZONA CALA CALA (NORTE)
IGLESIA BAUTISTA (TEMPORAL)
Avenida Siles s/n y Avda Circunvalación

IGLESIA de DIOS SANTIDAD
Enrique Arze 210

3 ZONA QUERU QUERU (NORTE)
IGLESIA EVANGELICA "EMMANUEL"
Instituto Americano Tel. 8330

4 ZONA SARCO - VILLA GRANADO
IGLESIA EVANGELICA METODISTA
"Cristo Rey"
Villa Granado Tel. 7773

5 ZONA CALA CALA (SUD)
IGLESIA EL LIBERTADOR
Avenida Libertador Bolívar frente el Estadio

6 ZONA TUPURAYA
IGLESIA EVANGELICA "ARANJUEZ"
Callejón 5 (Barrio Basilio)
Tel. 8233
Esq. Melchor Urquidi y Av. Portales

IGLESIA EVANGELICA "EL NAZARENO"
Esq. Florian Zambrana y
Venancio Jimenez

7 ZONA VILLA GALINDO
(Hipodromo)
IGLESIA EVANGELICA PENTECOSTAL
Esq. Nueva Castilla y Lorenzo
Anexo Villa Berdecio

IGLESIA EVANGELICA BAUTISTA
Virreynato de Lima y San Alberto s/n

IGLESIA PUERTA ABIERTA
Avda Blanco Galindo Tel. 7231

IGLESIA BAUTISTA INDEPENDIENTE
Plaza Virrey Tolado - Tel. 1005

EJERCITO de SALVACION "ANEXO"
Esq. Oswaldo Canedo y Nueva Castilla

8 ZONA NOROESTE
IGLESIA ASAMBLEAS de DIOS
14 de Enero 4571 - Tel. 2353

IGLESIA EVANGELICA METODISTA
Mayor Rocha y Baptista
Tel. 1541

9 ZONA NORESTE
IGLESIA CRISTIANA EVANGELICA
Bolívar 3640 - Tel. 3439

10 ZONA MUYURINA
IGLESIA BAUTISTA "MUYURINA"
Perú 2081
Tel. 3807 (San Pedro)

IGLESIA BAUTISTA INDEPENDIENTE
Calle Pol Tel. 1005

11 ZONA LA CHIMBA
IGLESIA EVANGELICA PENTECOSTAL
Anexos: Calle Victor Ustares s/n
Calle Alinata s/n
desde 1 (de Enero '75, Cornelio Saavedra

12 ZONA SUDOESTE
PRIMERA IGLESIA BAUTISTA
Calama 3935 Tel. 5539

IGLESIA EVANGELICA PENTECOSTAL
Uruguay 3792 Tel. 1358

CONGREGACION BAUTISTA "EL MESIAS"
Mama Ocllo y Tiahuanaco s/n

Iglesia

IGLESIA BAUTISTA INDEPENDIENTE
Plaza Osorio final Calama
Tel. 1005

13 ZONA SUDESTE
EJERCITO de SALVACIÓN
Lanza 6543 Tel. 7123

IGLESIA EVANGELICA
"Cristo es la Respuesta"
16 de Julio y Uruguay

14 ZONA LAS CUADRAS
IGLESIA del NAZARENO
Gustavo Otero 347
Tel. 5381

IGLESIA CRISTIANA EVANGELICA
"Getsemani"
Avenida 9 de Abril 3058

IGLESIA ASAMBLEAS de DIOS BOLIVIANA
Avda. 9 de Abril y Nicaragua

15 ZONA JAIHUAYCO
IGLESIA EVANGELICA PENTECOSTAL
Playa de ganado
(Parque Canata)

IGLESIA CRISTIANA EVANGELICA
Av. Cabildo y Plaza Libertad

16 ZONA ESTEBAN ARZE (SUD)
Y SAN MIGUEL
Congregación Bautista San Miguel
Moxos y Cerro San Miguel

Iglesia de DIOS SANTIDAD (Norte)
Avenida República 679

Iglesia CRISTIANA EVANGELICA
Esteban Arce 1367 (Sud)

17 ZONA CERRO VERDE
IGLESIA EVANGELICA PENTECOSTAL
Canini entre Moxos y Avda Rep.
Tel 5644

IGLESIA EVANGELICA METODISTA
"Bethel"
Avenida República
(Villa Santa Cruz)

IGLESIA CRISTIANA EVANGELICA
Villa Huayra Khasa

18 ZONA LACMA
CONGREGACION BAUTISTA "NAZARETH"

IGLESIA CRISTIANA EVANGELICA

IGLESIA DE DIOS SANTIDAD

IGLESIA CRISTIANA INDEPENDIENTE

Generally, the wealthier, more urban and westernized the individual, the greater his tendency to perceive himself as *mestizo*, comply with Spanish norms and follow the upper class. However, the closer he imitates, the greater is his frustration at not being assimilated. Bitter relationships result between the upwardly mobile middle class members and the elite who consider them to be ostentatious social climbers.

Of all the peoples in Bolivia, the *cholos* come the closest to being a synthesis of the Indian and the Spanish. They value education and material comforts, and yet, unlike the upper and urban middle classes, they do not resent working for these goals. In fact, they can often be heard criticizing the upper classes for laziness.

There seems to be a dichotomy between the sexes concerning their roles. The *cholo* men are much more dissatisfied with their position than are the women. The men are more oriented toward the Spanish values, wearing European styles and attempting to adopt

Spanish norms regarding sexual adventure and the love of leisure. These desires are sharply curtailed by economic reality. The *chola* women often control the family purse strings by their hard work in earning the major portion of the income. In contrast to their husbands, *cholas* have adopted a self-identity far removed from the Spanish norm. They constitute a unique and unified enclave within the Bolivian middle class. They are aggressive and self-assured business women possessing formidable business acumen. In the Bolivian society, where few people realistically assess their status, the *cholas* are an exception to the rule. They are not deluded regarding their relationship to the upper classes. They tend to ridicule those among them who would put on airs or western clothes in hopes of changing their status. They are fiercely energetic in pursuing education for their children, encouraging them to use Spanish and become literate (Weil 1974:116). All these factors help to mold the ethnostrategy that must be designed to meet the need of each ethnic subunit.

If desired, both the denominational and integrational maps outlined in steps five and six of Chapter Seven may be developed here. After doing so, we are prepared to go on to the last step, which now follows.

5. *Spiritually*, define the target *mestizo* group along the Continuous Mission Decision-Making Process Scale in Figure 40. The figures used are based upon the breakdown under step one above. Immediately the ethnostrategist has a profile of the target people. He can then plan together with his local church or voluntary, second commitment maximum E_1 Gospel communicators the steps to follow to gradually bring these people on down the scale to new birth and incorporation into a new neighborhood church.

Ethnostrategy

The ethno (cross-cultural) strategist must work together with his team members through this continuous mission process in order to achieve goal ownership. Otherwise, all is in vain. The continuous mission, four-quadrant ministry of going, teaching, equipping and exiting with surveillance, has already been developed on pages 80-91 of Chapter Six and 108-110 of Chapter Seven. Here is a summary of our experience in starting a home church in the new neighborhood of Aranjuez, appearing as section six in Figure 39.

1. Began with a new neighborhood Bible study in 1970.
2. Attempted to meet the needs of the community as determined by house to house visitation.
3. Focused ministry on adults and parents as heads of families.
4. Discovered, developed and discerned the spiritual gifts of the laymen.
5. Reached out in social and missionary witness (Greenway 1976: 74-6).

Figure 40

CONTINUOUS MISSION DECISION MAKING PROCESS SCALE
For Urban *Mestizos*

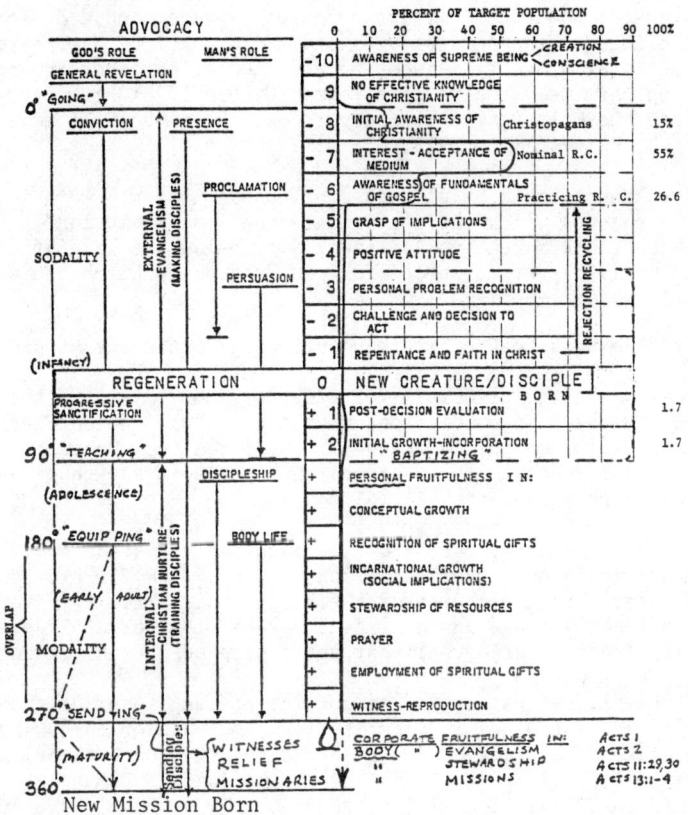

Now it is your turn to apply the same process to your ethnic group, working through the implications with your colaborers, both missionary and national. Then you can summarize your goals and secure both financial and human commitment.

Evaluation

Continual measuring and monitoring of progress is essential for good stewardship (Matt. 25:19-21). We check our bank balance and interest payments monthly. Why should we not be even more concerned about checking the progress of the harvest? The possible/probable upper and lower limits of growth have already been worked out for the Evangelical Christian Union nationally in Table IV of Chapter Three on page 41. This, along with the ECU Aymara/Quechua graphs in Figure 37 of Chapter Seven, may serve as models for you to follow.

Changes do not occur without purposeful prayer and a desire to obey the Lord of the harvest with a will to work. Piaget notes that the total process of adopting new thought patterns and action takes approximately two to five years (Gruber 1973:78). Ever since Pentecost the Holy Spirit is ready to use those who will move with Him to the harvest (Orr 1973:vii-xviii).

What changes could help speed continuous mission? A review of possible changes which could stimulate continuous mission in Bolivia for the ECU/AEM team now follows. Try using the same grid for writing a similar prescription for your national Church and mission to consider for adoption.

Suggested Changes to Facilitate Doubling in Continuous Mission

To carry out the principles of effective $360°$ mission, the ECU and the AEM governing bodies and missionaries will need to eventually implement some policy changes. These can best be realized through involvement in the regional church growth workshops and the growing process that will follow.

1. Recognize that the E_0 and E_1 evangelistic passion and skill of the new indigenous churches, launching out from $270°$ to $360°$, is one of the clearest measures of their spiritual vitality, growing at or above an average annual growth rate of 10% (or 200% decadal growth). Indigenization will not get a stopped church growing.

2. Acknowledge that it is not sufficient just to print theologically sound statements in constitutions, manuals or in news release Nothing takes the place of day by day discipling of both neighbors in E_1 evangelism ($270°$ to $360°$) and the nations in E_2 and E_3 evangelism (0 to $270°$). God will judge us by how we have spent our time and budget. He will also judge us as to how our partnership in the witness of the Gospel of Jesus Christ to men whom He has ripened, produced results that remain. The responsive people whom God has prepared have priority.

3. Recognize that $360°$ mission is a function of the whole Church. Even more fundamentally, it is the function of the missionary and his mission society. Training younger churches in $360°$ mission can never be done by a society whose missionaries themselves do little evangelism, from $0°$ to $270°$, especially in the neglected follow-up process from $90°$ to $180°$. Motivated and equipped laymen are the key to a people movement. Every $360°$ mission has a chief function of proclaiming Christ so that men are persuaded to become responsibl

reproducing disciples, who themselves continue this 360° discipling process until Christ comes.

4. Refuse to substitute the indirect and often unintentional "witness" of medicine, education, agriculture and relief for purposeful persuasion as a normal part of the life of every missionary, pastor and Christian in his field of responsibility, from 0° to at least 270° before beginning a new cycle.

5. Recognize that some populations are so resistant, that in them missions must satisfy themselves with preparatory work. Eventually, some may accept Christ. In highly resistant populations, as among university students, there is a legitimate place for seed-sowing and "gradualistic activities" (0° to 180°).

6. Recognize that such "gradualism" is often carried on long after it has ceased to be necessary. Thus, consider all gradualistic enterprises as schools, hospitals, clinics, print shops, radio, etc. as temporary expedients to be involved in until qualified national leaders come forward to take over. Younger churches and all missionaries constantly work for Christian commitment now, to 90°, resulting in new churches now, to 180°, where new believers are equipped to 270° and go on to reproduce to 360°.

7. Be serious about church growth as good stewards. The numbers of the redeemed are important now as they were in New Testament times (II Cor. 4:15). The ECU and AEM will attempt to account for not only the conversions but also the reversions; the transfers, both in and out; and finally, for biological additions and losses of believers.

8. Keep careful records of each homogeneous unit church membership. Each church and its assisting missionary should have uniform rules and forms for securing a continuingly meaningful record of membership increase and decrease. These statistics should be included in the minutes of each Church's and subdirectorate's annual meeting. This data is also brought to the November assembly for the department of historical data to record and later correlate nationally.

9. Make continued assistance dependent upon the younger church providing the national board with an accurate profile of membership and progress towards continuous mission.

10. Use the AAGR as a chief factor in determining the amount of assistance which will be given to younger churches.

11. Utilize the AAGR also as a chief factor in choosing what missionary work, institutions, and efforts will be maintained, reduced, or reinforced. Evangelistic potency will be a primary consideration

of the ECU and the AEM administrations in establishing priorities.

12. Begin working towards the realization of an annual church growth workshop with each subdirectorate among the homogeneous unit churches. The related missionaries should also be involved in these workshops, helping to determine the evangelistic potency, with an eye to discovering the inception of vigorous new people movements. The following should be determined:

   a. The annual number of converts won and lost besides the number of new churches established and lost, according to the following pattern:
      1.) conversions and reversions.
      2.) transfers in and out.
      3.) biological additions of believers' children and deaths.
   b. Resistance of various sections of the population.
   c. The amount and quality of church growth compared with others in the same area, evaluated against the faith projection.
   d. The total financial and human resources available from both the national churches and the mission for pursuing church growth in this area.
   e. Suggestions for improved church growth.

A copy of these findings will be sent to the central administrative office of the ECU, with a copy to the AEM.

13. Agree that the ECU and AEM have a continuing responsibility, shared in varying degrees with the younger churches, according to their maturity and resources, to train laymen, pastors, missionaries and churches in both internal E_0 and external E_1, E_2 and E_3 effective evangelism. This includes the preparation of abundant, indigenous evangelistic materials. The teaching and equipping of the Saints occurs between $90°$ and $270°$ in Figure 34. An overlap between the mission and the church occurs between $180°$ and $270°$ at the local level. This may become a source of tension if the missionary stays around too long smothering national initiative and expression of gifts.

With rising literacy, a sizeable proportion of mission resources should go into the preparation of effective tracts, books, posters and theological education materials, which proclaim Christ as the only Savior and Lord. The repentant must be persuaded to become responsible, caring disciples of Jesus Christ in a dynamically reproductive community of the Saints.

14. Cooperate in evangelistic enterprises conducted jointly with other evangelical denominations whenever possible. The Gospel preached by several churches simultaneously has considerable impact.

Urban Mission 135

Others often plant while we reap, or we plant while they reap. Rejoice in the growth of any segment of the Church of Jesus Christ. Share in joint efforts provided the committed are folded into local congregations as an integral part of the $0°$ to $180°$ thrust of the campaign. Do not stop short of baptizing at $90°$, which so often occurs in Latin America. A fresh start in a new community is preferable, where it is possible to emphasize the baptism of entire families together and their formation into homogeneous unit home churches.

15. Do not delay evangelistic effort unduly, pending a possible cooperative effort. While we pray for united cooperative efforts, in most situations the initiative is clearly ours. This is especially so when no other evangelical church is present in remote areas. And even where other churches may be present, often they cannot be enlisted for a cooperative $360°$ mission. Waiting for a united effort must never be used as an excuse for not evangelizing.

16. Under ordinary circumstances our churches and mission should utilize at least fifty percent of their budgets for direct evangelism. In view of the large field receipts obtained for educational and medical work, the total percentage of the field budget marked for evangelism is generally less than fifty percent. It is the intention of the ECU and AEM that the churches aided and the missionaries sent out will everywhere expedite the completion of the Great Commission and avoid short-range "rice Christians" and "gimmickitis" (Winter 1966:126-8).

17. Evangelism and cooperative efforts with other organizations like Christian Nationals' Evangelism Commission (CNEC), Bolivian Evangelical Social Action Commission (COMBASE), Latin American Literacy and Literature Movement (ALFALIT), Andean Communications Center, Every Home Literature Crusade, etc. must be constantly measured against achieved church growth. An evangelism which does not produce steady growth should be scrapped. In its place a more effective evangelism should be inaugurated to multiply churches in their own context.

18. Stewardship at home and abroad is crucial. The faith-promise plan, effective in so many churches, "will work anywhere", affirms Dr. Paul Smith of Peoples Church, Toronto, Canada (Palmer 1976:110). I have seen it work in Bolivia on a small scale in our newly started church at Aranjuez also. Here is what is involved. Try it!

   a. The biblical basis of missions and associated needs are made known during a week of special annual meetings.
   b. Faith promise cards are distributed. Each is encouraged to contribute monthly during the coming year as God provides the gift of love to pass on.
   c. Primary children are taught the joy of giving.
   d. Faith in God and in His work through missions grows over the years as records are kept and consulted.

SUMMARY

Part Three develops a strategy for both rural and urban ethnic participation in continuous mission. The goal is to double the present church growth within five years among those with growth potential and the desire to expand. A seven-fold process has been developed by defining each component of the harvest ethnolinguistically, geographically, demographically, socio-economically, denominationally, integrationally and spiritually. Finally, some suggestions were made to facilitate doubling in continuous mission.

The following steps have been taken to facilitate the movement of the Andes Evangelical Mission and the Evangelical Christian Union towards continuous mission:

1. The AEM General Director, Ron Wiebe, was given a proposal for sixteen regional church growth workshops with the ECU, in December, 1975. He was also given a copy of the $360°$ mission document found in Chapter Six for his evaluation on 22 April, 1976. The field response as of this date has been for us to go ahead in La Paz with our first church growth workshop, November, 1977. This would be in conjunction with the coming of Luis Palau in 1978. My responsibility would be to coordinate the preparation of home churches as granaries in La Paz as did Ed Silvoso in Rosario, Argentina from 1974 to 1976.

2. The AEM Aymara-Quechua Department Director, John Lloyd, in charge of three apostolic teams, working among the receptive target people described in Chapter Seven, was consulted 13 May regarding his participation and approval of this project. His permission was given 30 May, 1976 to cite his materials. This team continues to move ahead on its own, using church growth principles among the 100,000 target group.

3. A copy of Chapter Seven in draft form, upgrading the ECU historical data, was sent to ECU President, Tito Montero and to John Lloyd for continued feedback and updating. This document was considered 26-29 October, 1976 by the Aymara-Quechua Workers Conference, and Ron Wiebe reported their five-point reaction in December, 1976.

4. Based upon field evaluation and feedback of various drafts mentioned above, the first draft of this study was completed in April, 1977.

5. The ECU President, Tito Montero, indicated on 27 April, 1976 the interest of the national Church in my eventually conducting sixteen regional church growth workshops upon return to the field after September, 1977. One idea of this study is to select responsive target areas as described in Chapters Seven and Eight to produce working models.

6. Approximately twenty pilot churches, showing the most promise for growth in selected target areas, will be selected from those attending the initial workshops. This will be done on the basis of their willingness to reproduce another daughter church within one year after becoming equipped themselves.

7. Other helping agencies as the Christian Nationals' Evangelism Commission (CNEC), the Bolivian Evangelical Social Action Commission (COMBASE), the Bolivian Literacy Association (ALFALIT), Every Home Literature Crusade and the Andean Communications Center will be invited to participate in these church growth workshops to interest them in cooperating with their services in balanced, continuous mission.

8. Continuous mission progress will be monitored annually at the national assembly. As a result, it is expected that others will be stimulated to participate in the same growth process.

Conclusion

This three-part study is both a pilgrimmage and an appeal for more responsible participation in God's continuing mission. It comes at the end of one pilgrimmage of searching out the facts. It comes at the beginning of another pilgrimmage of sharing a vision that God has given. He says, "Clearly write the vision" so that those who hear may also run with you as messengers (Hab. 2:2,3; Heb. 10:37,38).

I appeal to my colleagues:

First, with the Andes Evangelical Mission, for improved recruiting and deployment of human and financial resources. We need closer matching of the reapers with the harvest. This is in accord with the three basic objectives of the mission.

Second, with the Evangelical Christian Union National Church for improved accountability from each of the homogeneous unit churches within the denomination. Now that the upper and the lower growth parameters are established, we know more clearly what God expects of us now and in the future. We should forge ahead together in obedience to the Lord of the harvest to develop church growth eyes within each of the five principal ethnic groups. This will involve:

1. Faith goals to double present performance over the next five years.

2. Growing evaluation and accountability for each phase of the harvest at the annual national assembly.

3. Baptism of the remaining one-half of the uncommitted believers attending regularly. Our goal should be approximately 25,000 baptized believers by 1980. This goal can only be realized as it is mutually owned by the participants in the regional church growth workshops.

4. Discovery, development and discernment of the use of each member's spiritual gifts for edifying the Body of Christ and for approaching each one's potential. Only then can we effectively reach out in Body evangelism and in church planting, especially to the 65%. Each church should attempt to plant a new church each year. Voluntary, second-commitment special evangelism task forces should be spawned with maximum power E_1 Gospel communicators to work among each cultural and subcultural group, especially focusing on the unreached.

Third, with the other forty missions in Bolivia to define a similar accountability showing where each mission and national church is participating in the evangelical commitment to Bolivia's continually expanding five million.

Could we possibly inaugurate a Bolivian Cross-Cultural Research and Training Center for measuring church growth progress and for providing in-service training of local personnel interested in reaching the 65% who are largely animists and syncretists? This center would show where the priority needs are and generate many more cross-cultural reapers.

Fourth, with those involved in world mission to reach some kind of agreement that would give us increased uniformity in reporting:

1. Where each one is in his particular harvest, ethnolinguistically, geographically, demographically, socio-economically, denominationally and spiritually. Each should show the percent yet unreached.

2. How much longer it will take to reach that crucial 20% discipled into responsible, reproducing indigenous churches capable of reaching the remaining population.

Fifth, with our supporting churches for continued upgrading in missions stewardship.

1. We missionaries need to be held more accountable for better matching of our workers with the harvest (John 4:34,35). Please ask us how much remains to be done and how long it will take.

2. Local churches need to be more accountable in communicating with their missionaries and the missionaries with the churches.

As all of us focus on reaching the 65%, the Lord of the harvest will show each one what He wants us to do. All of us will eventually stand before Christ's tribunal and account for what we have done. We know some of the questions that He may very well ask. For example, "How many times during your life did you double the investment of My gifts and talents in you (II Cor. 5:9-11)?"

Appendix

A.

Statistical Data

TABLE I

A. Nine Bolivian Departments and Capitals - 1950 Hinge Year

Department	Population 1950 Census	Area in sq. mi.	Pop. per sq. mi. in 1950	Capital City	Population 1950 Census
La Paz	948,446	51,732	18.3	La Paz	321,073
Cochabamba	490,475	21,479	22.8	Cochabamba	80,795
Potosí	534,399	45,644	11.7	Potosí	45,758
Santa Cruz	286,145	143,097	2.0	Santa Cruz	42,746
Chuquisaca	282,980	19,893	14.2	Sucre	40,128
Tarija	126,752	14,526	8.7	Tarija	16,869
Oruro	210,260	20,690	10.2	Oruro	62,975
Beni	119,770	82,457	1.5	Trinidad	10,759
Pando	19,804	24,644	0.8	Cobija	1,726
	3,019,031	424,162			622,829

B. Nine Bolivian Departments and Capitals - 1900 Boundary Year

Department	Population	Area in sq. mi.		Capital City	Population
La Paz	445,616	53,777		La Paz	54,713
Cochabamba	328,163	23,328		Cochabamba	21,886
Potosí	325,615	48,801		Potosí	20,910
Santa Cruz	209,392	141,368		Santa Cruz	15,874
Chuquisaca	204,434	26,418		Sucre	20,967
Tarija	102,887	33,036		Tarija	6,980
Oruro	86,081	19,127		Oruro	13,575
Beni	32,180	102,111		Trinidad	2,556
Pando (Nat. Territory)	9,000 (31,883	23,861 192,260)			
	1,766,451	640,226			157,461

C. Nine Bolivian Departments and Capitals - 1970 Boundary Year
(Projected from Official Estimates)

Department	Population			Capital City	Population
La Paz	1,364,125			La Paz	652,081
Cochabamba	632,460			Cochabamba	157,553
Potosí	698,194			Potosí	69,000
Santa Cruz	357,147			Santa Cruz	116,200
Chuquisaca	363,685			Sucre	50,700
Tarija	158,288			Tarija	23,500
Oruro	315,103			Oruro	98,800
Beni	217,262			Trinidad	17,500
Pando	28,718			Cobija	2,400
	4,134,982				1,187,734

Source: Encyclopedia Britannica (1959 III:818-19; 1910 IV:171)

Table II

GROWTH OF NINE BOLIVIAN DEPARTMENTS - 1900 TO 1980

Source: Corrected 1900, 1950 Census and 1969, 1970 Official Estimates

		1900	1910	1950	50 Yr. AAGR	1970	1980	30 Yr. AAGR	Receptivity Rating
	HIGHLANDS 86%					→	85%		
1.	LA PAZ	445,616	507,004	849,588	1.299%	1,364,125	1,728,565	2.396%	4
2.	COCHABAMBA	328,163	347,872	439,336	.585%	632,460	758,882	1.839%	6
3.	ORURO	86,081	100,671	188,337	1.578%	315,103	407,548	2.606%	2
4.	POTOSI	320,500	347,291	478,680	.806%	698,194	843,202	1.905%	5
5.	CHUQUISACA	187,800	199,417	253,475	.609%	363,685	435,655	1.822%	7
6.	TARIJA	83,400	88,708	113,536	.619%	158,288	186,910	1.676%	8
	Sub Total	1,451,560	1,590,963	2,322,922	.945%	3,531,855	4,360,761	2.122%	
	LOWLANDS 14%					→	15%		
7.	BENI	32,180	40,941	107,282	2.437%	217,262	309,174	3.591%	1
8.	PANDO	9,000	10,308	17,739	1.366%	28,718	36,539	2.438%	3
9.	SANTA CRUZ	202,700	212,432	256,310	.470%	357,147	421,601	1.673%	9
	Sub Total	243,880	263,681	381,331	.898%	603,127	767,314	2.358%	
	CORRECT TOTAL POPULATION:	1,695,440	1,854,644	2,704,253	.938%	4,134,982	5,128,075	2.156%	

Table III

GROWTH OF NINE CAPITAL CITIES

Source: Corrected 1900, 1950 Census and 1969, 1970 Official Estimates

		1900	1910	1950	50 Yr. AAGR	1970	1980	30 Yr. AAGR	Receptivity Rating
	91% of urbanites in highlands					→ (85%)			
1.	LA PAZ	54,713	77,950	321,073	3.603%	652,081	929,289	3.606%	2
2.	COCHABAMBA	21,886	28,420	80,795	2.647%	157,553	220,000	3.395%	3
3.	ORURO	13,575	18,452	62,975	3.117%	98,800	123,748	2.277%	5
4.	POTOSI	20,910	24,457	45,758	1.579%	69,000	84,731	2.075%	6
5.	SUCRE	20,967	23,874	40,128	1.307%	50,700	56,988	1.176%	9
6.	TARIJA	6,980	8,328	16,869	1.781%	23,500	27,736	1.671%	7
	Sub Total	139,031	181,481	567,598	2.853%	1,051,634	1,442,492	3.158%	
	8.2% of total population found in highland capitals 28.2%									
	9% of urbanites in lowlands					→ (15%)			
7.	TRINIDAD	2,556	3,407	10,759	2.916%	17,500	23,319	2.462%	4
8.	COBIJA	767	902	1,726	1.634%	2,400	2,830	1.662%	8
9.	SANTA CRUZ	15,874	19,352	42,746	2.001%	116,200	232,400		1
				(20 yr. AAGR	5.127%)	(7.177%	10 yr. AAGR)		
	Sub Total	19,197	23,661	55,234	2.136%	136,100	258,549	5.28%	
	1.1% of total population found in lowland capitals 5%									
	TOTAL URBAN	158,228	205,142	622,832	2.778%	1,187,734	1,701,041	3.406%	
	POPULATION	1,695,440	1,854,644	2,704,253		4,134,982	5,128,075		
	PER CENT URBANIZED IN 9 CAPITALS:	9.33%	11%	23%		28.72%	33.2%		
	RURAL VILLAGES:	6.17%	9%	14%		16.28%	17.0%		
		15.5%	20%	37%		45 %	50.2%		

Figure 1

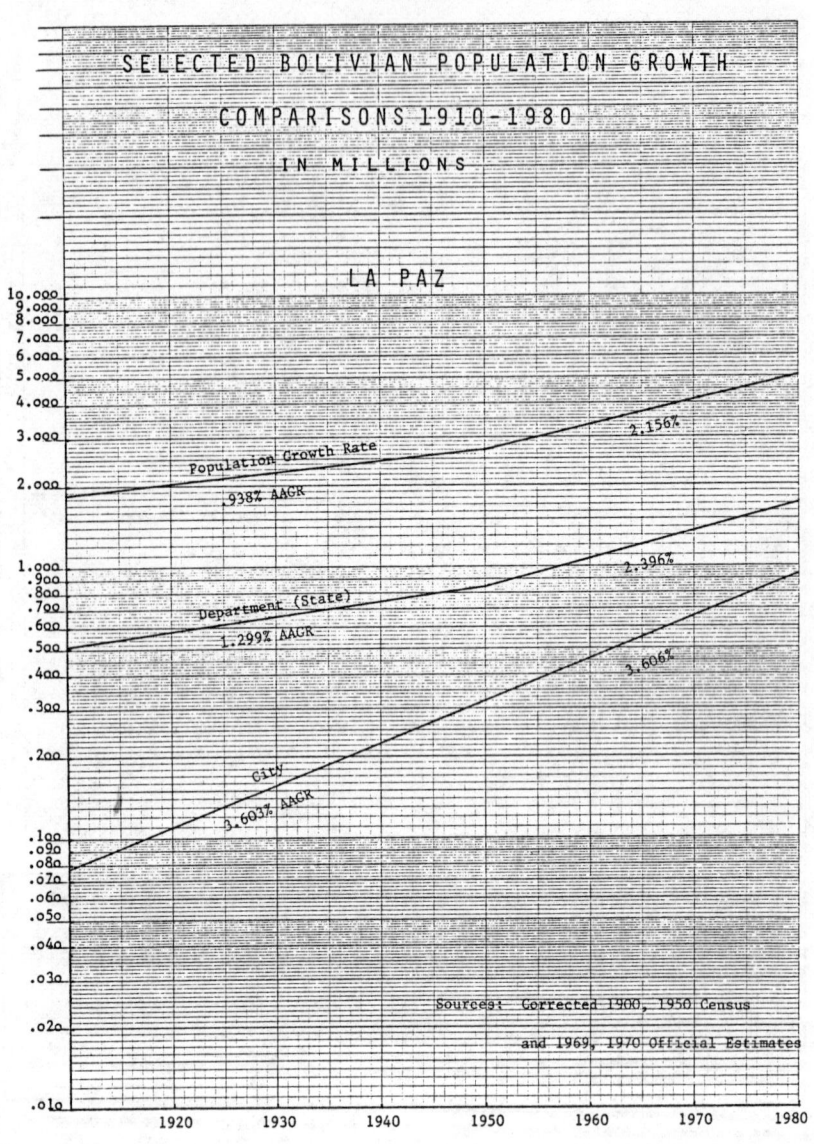

Figure 2

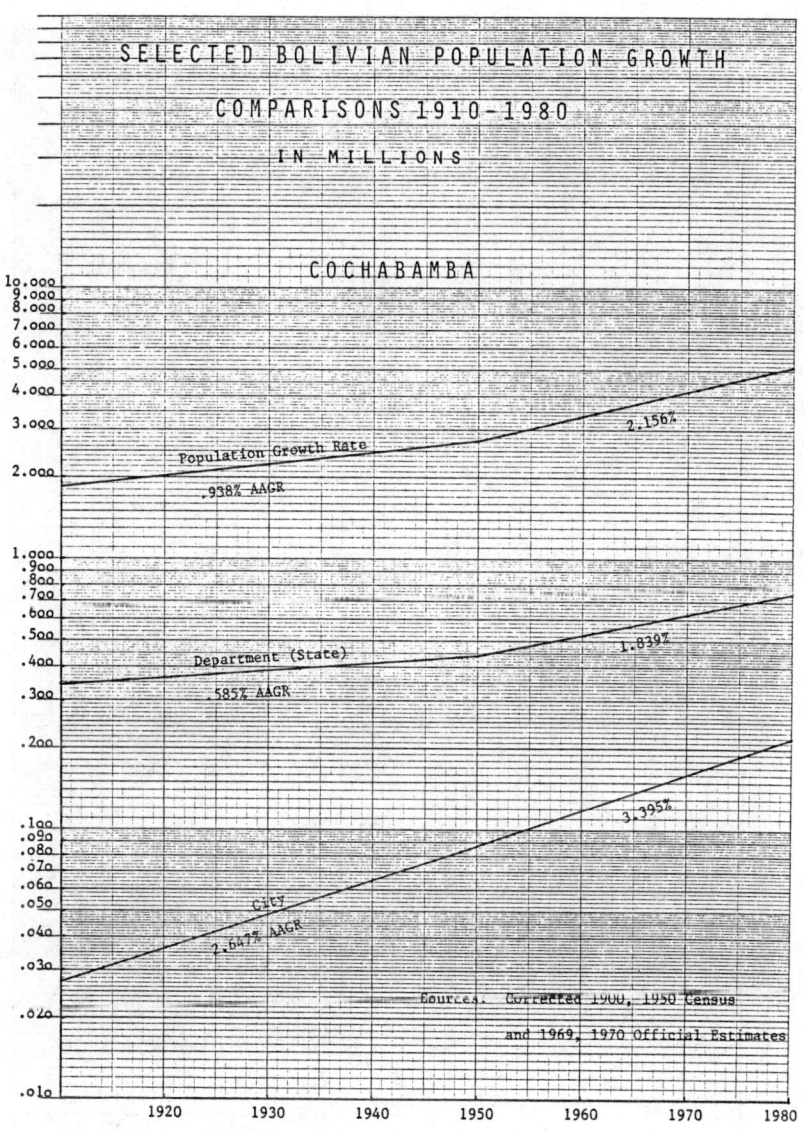

Figure 3

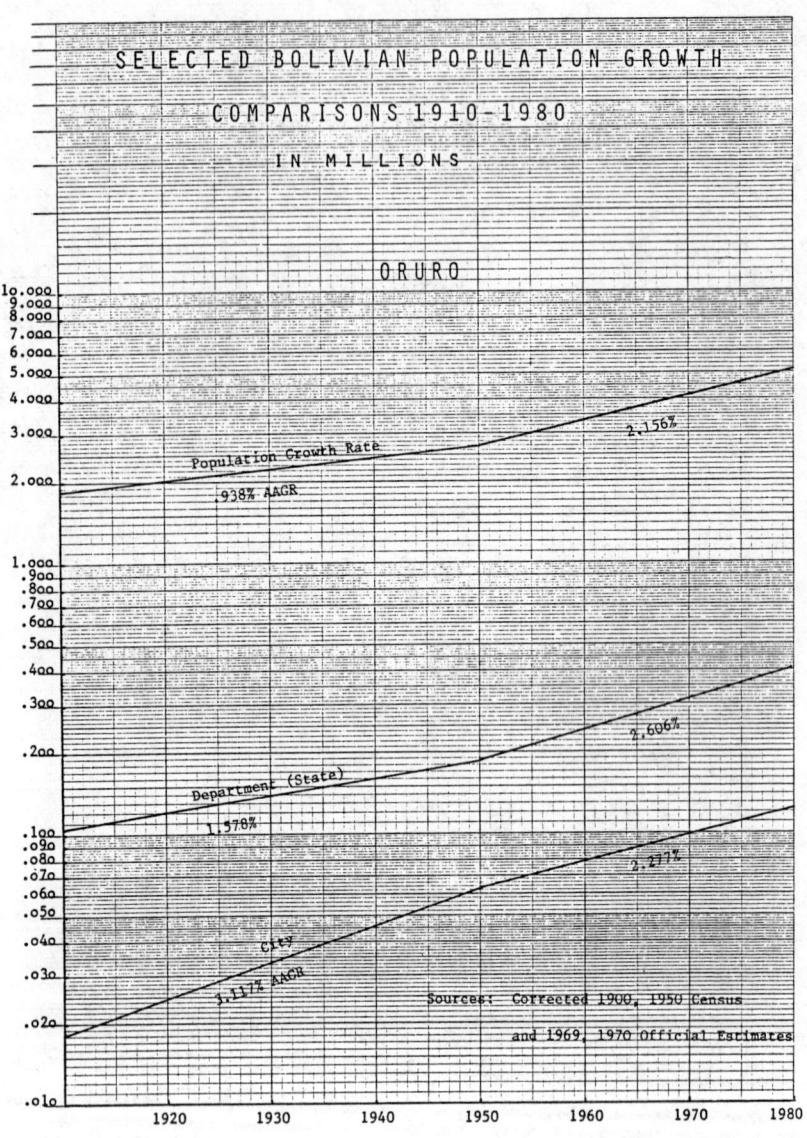

Figure 4

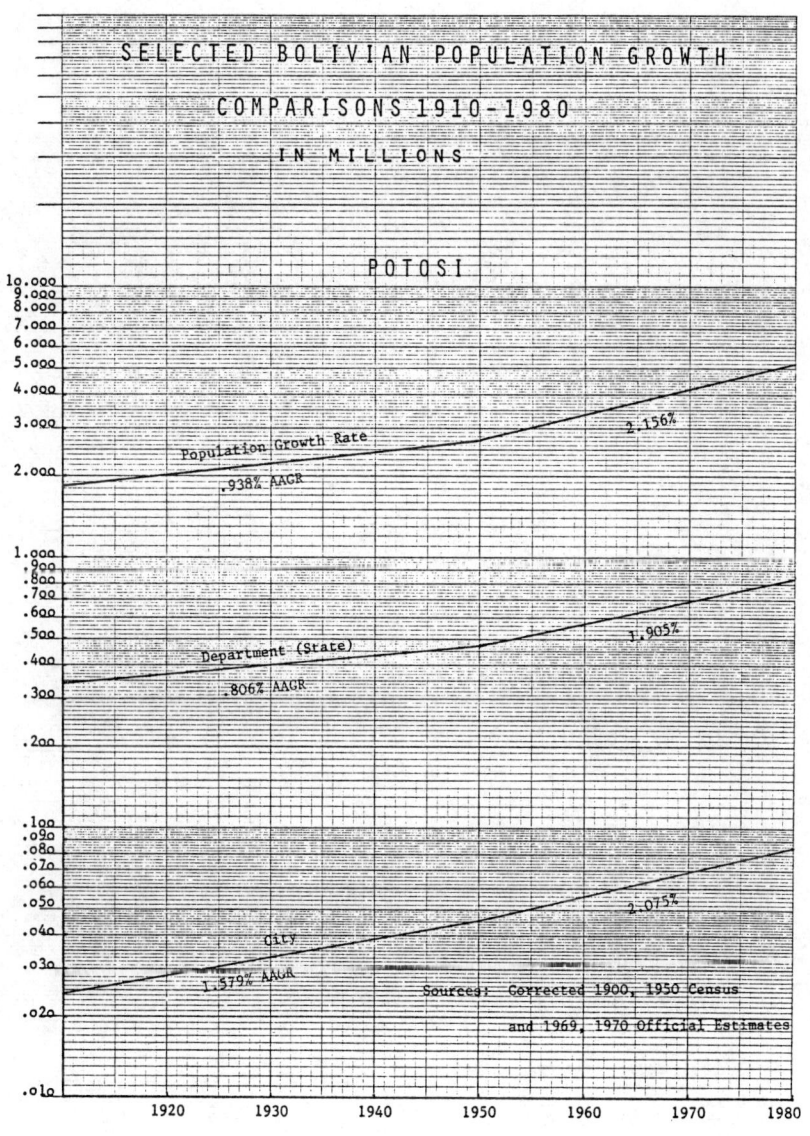

Figure 5

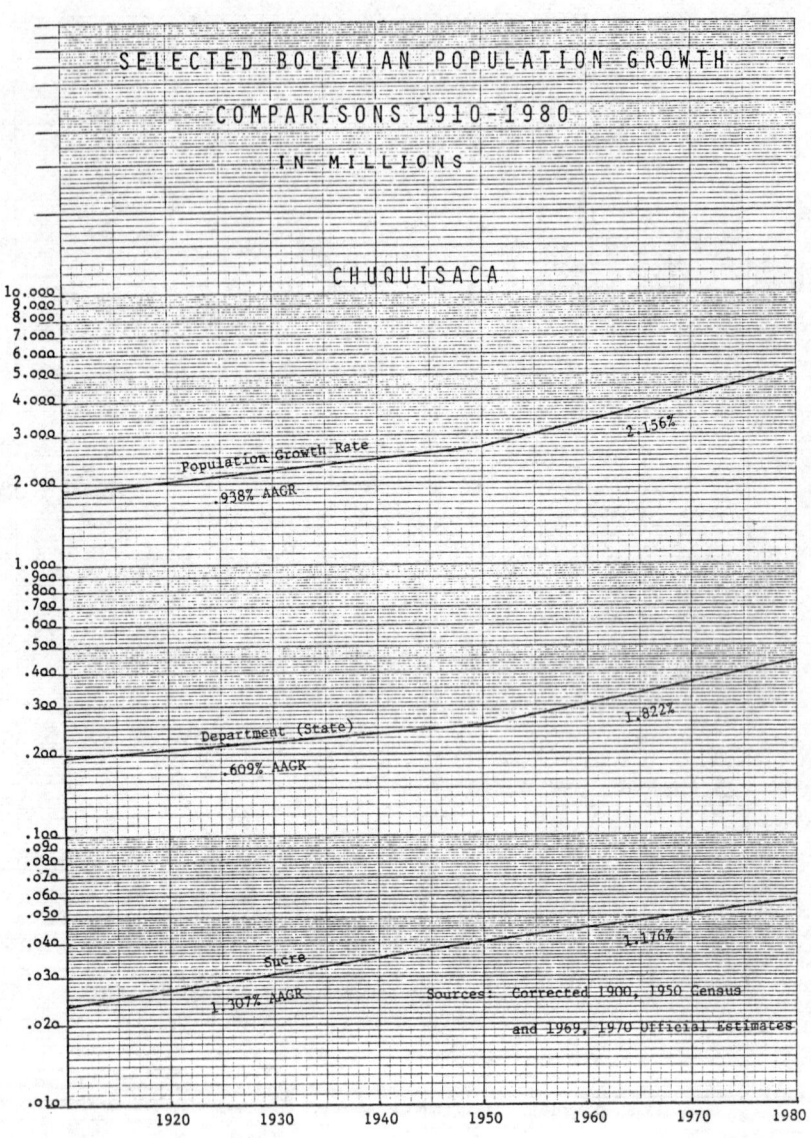

Figure 6

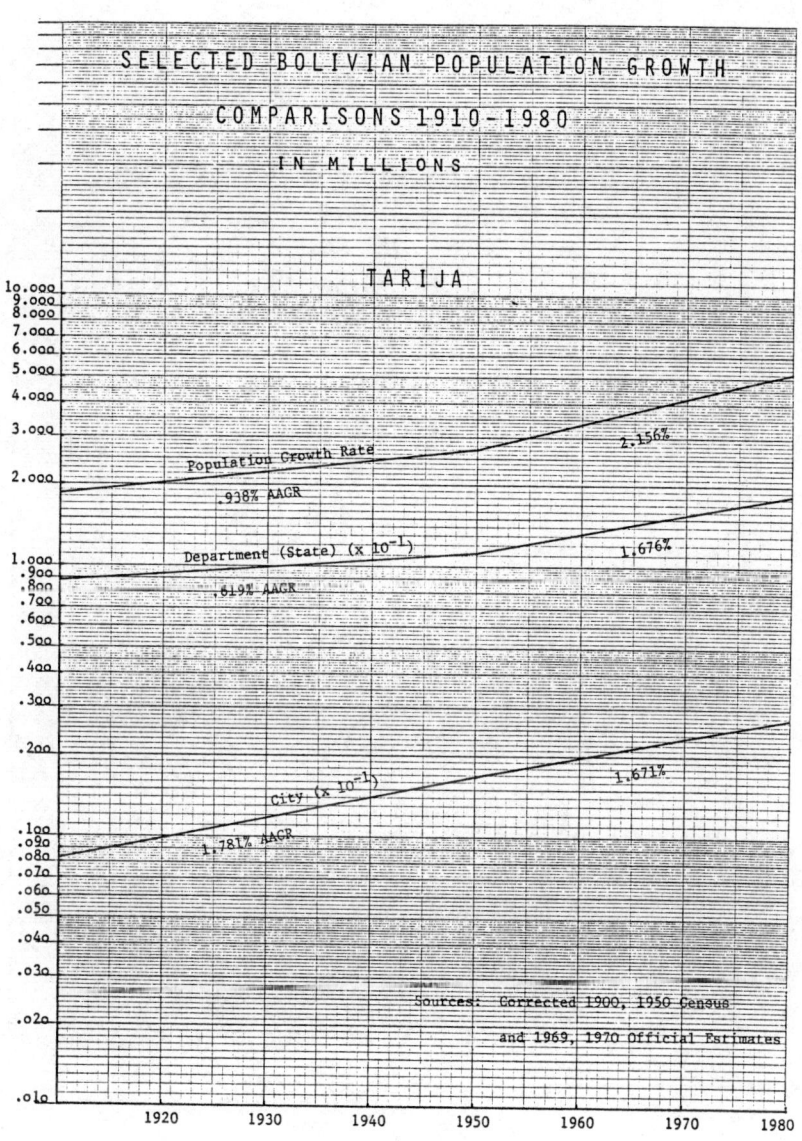

Figure 7

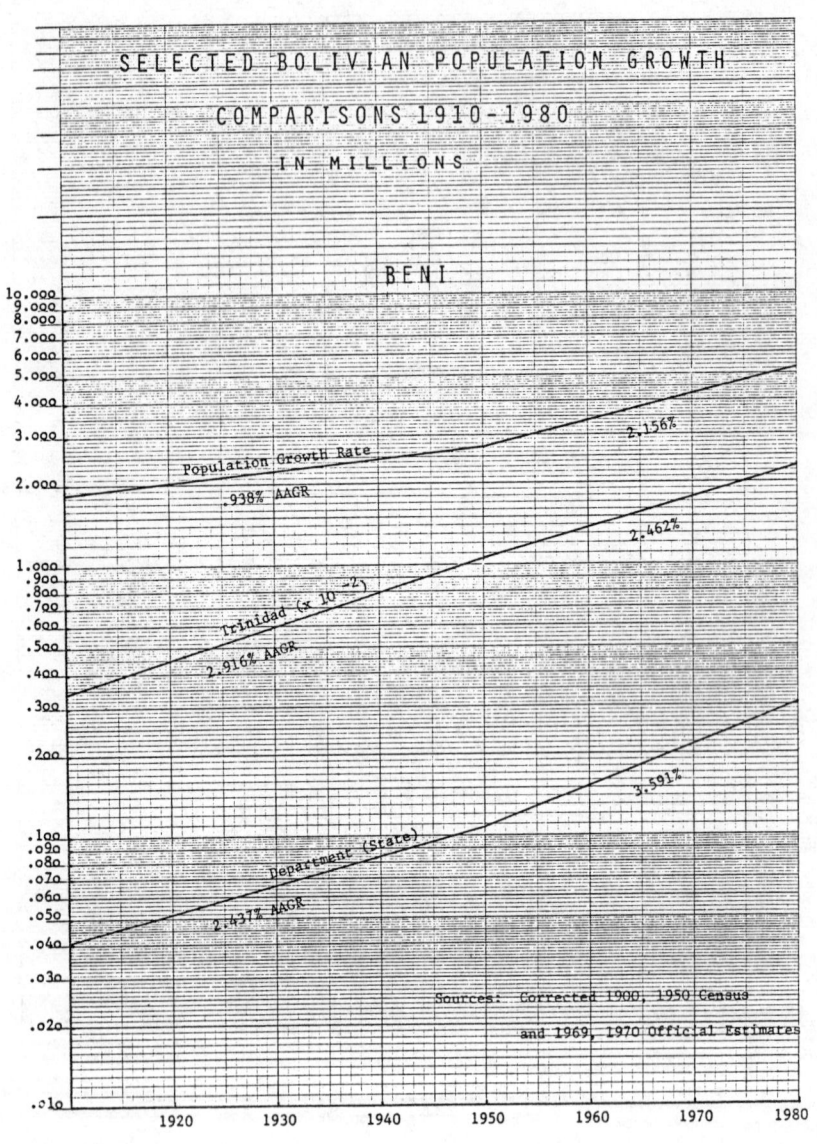

Figure 8

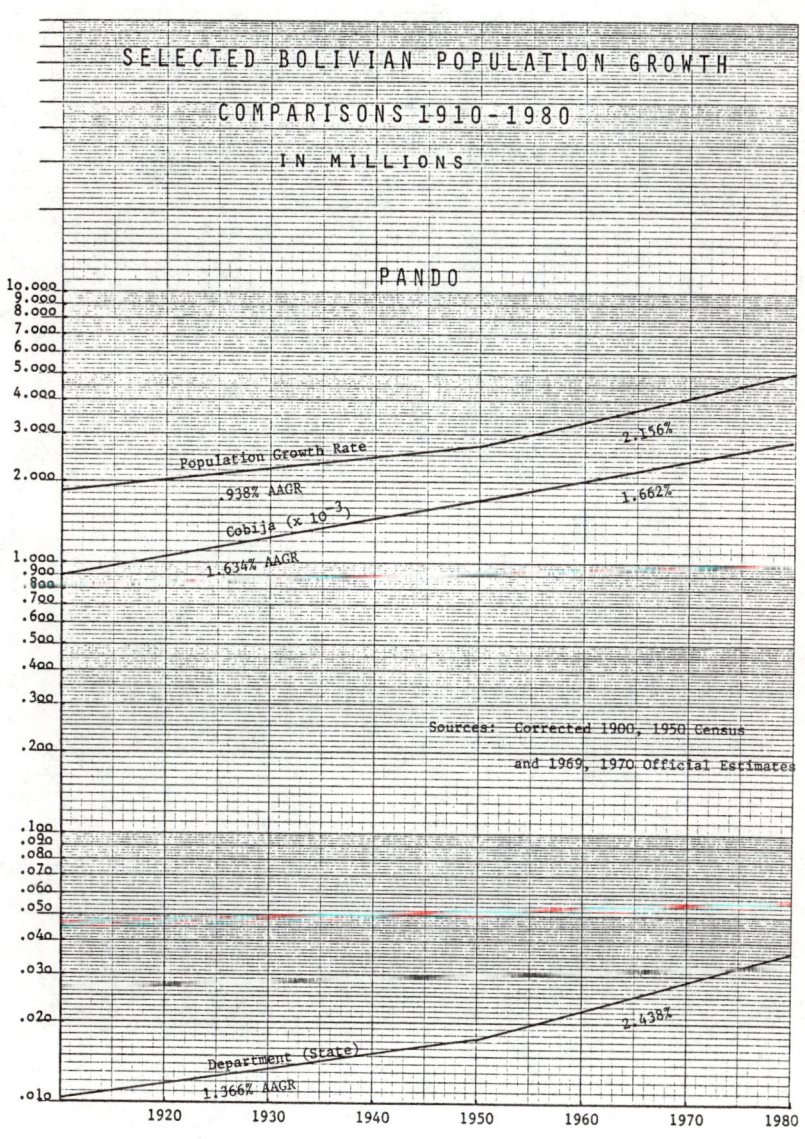

Figure 9

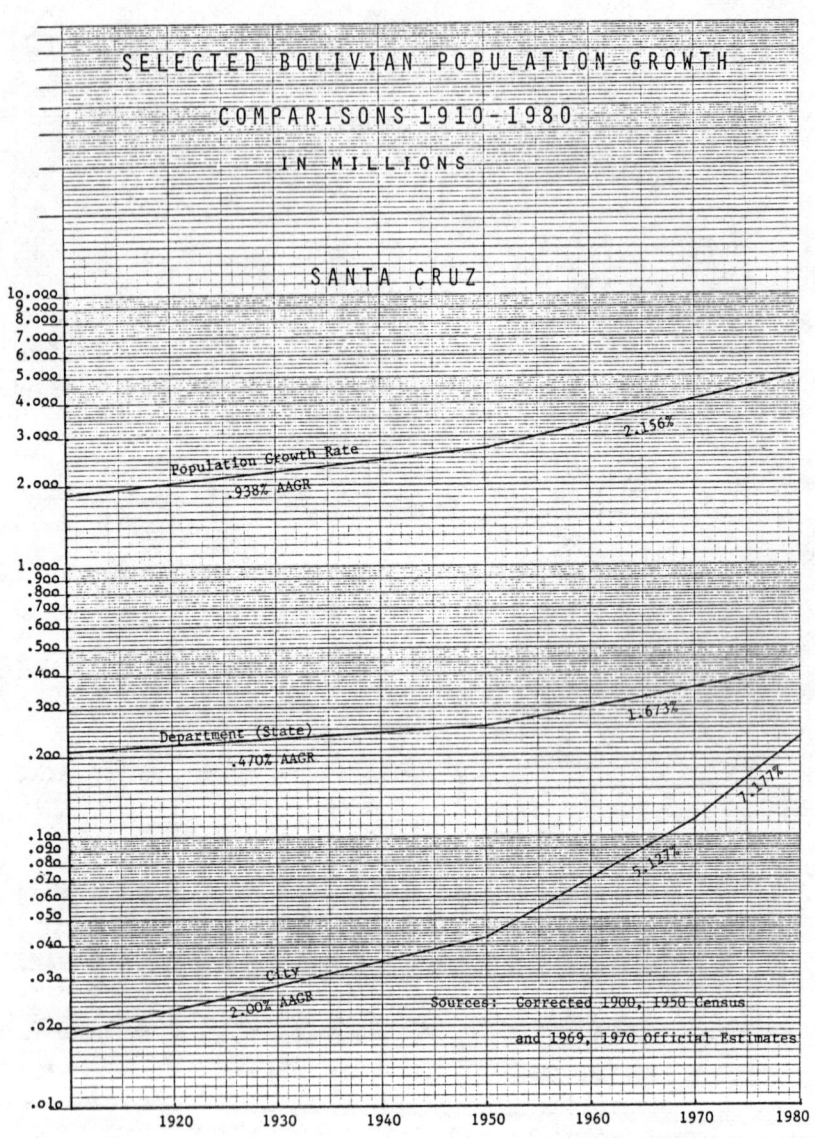

Table IV

BOLIVIAN ETHNIC GROUP TRENDS

	A % of 1910 Population 1,854,644	B 1910 Absolute Number	C 40 Yr. AAGR 1910 to 1950	A % of 1950 Population 2,704,253	B 1950 Absolute Number	A % of 1980 Population (projected)	B 1980 Absolute Number	C 30 Yr. AAGR 1950 to 1980	Receptivity Rating
GUARANI	.43%	8,000	.559%	.37%	10,000	.33%	17,000	1.784%	7
OTHER LANGUAGE GROUPS	4.57%	84,732	-.167%	2.93%	79,240	1.67%	85,562	.256%	8
Sub Total	5.00%	92,732	-.096%	3.30%	89,240	2.00%	102,562	.465%	
QUECHUA	30.37%	563,255	1.195%	33.50%	905,925	34.49%	1,768,673	2.255%	3
AYMARA - QUECHUA	2.00%	37,092	.947%	2.00%	54,085	2.00%	102,562	2.156%	4
AYMARA	23.13%	428,979	1.123%	24.80%	670,655	26.00%	1,333,300	2.317%	2
MESTIZO	26.40%	489,626	.85 %	25.40%	686,880	25.00%	1,282,019	2.102%	5
BLACK	.30%	5,564	-3.475%	.05%	1,352	.01%	513	-3.179%	9
WHITE	12.40%	229,976	.528%	10.50%	283,947	10.00%	512,806	1.99 %	6
FOREIGN	.40%	7,420	1.244%	.45%	12,169	.50%	25,640	2.515%	1
TOTALS	100.00%	1,854,644	.938%	100.00%	2,704,253	100.00%	5,128,075	2.156%	

Source: 1900, 1910, 1950 Census and 1970 Official Estimates.

Figure 10

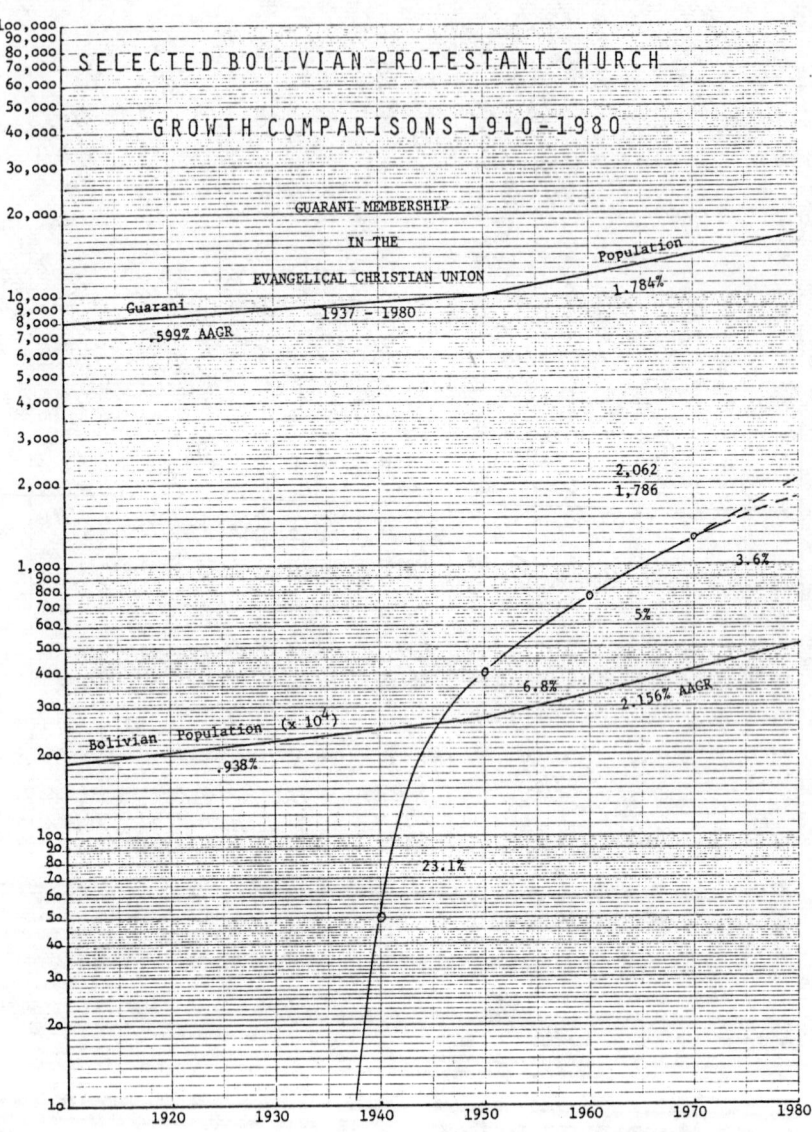

Figure 11

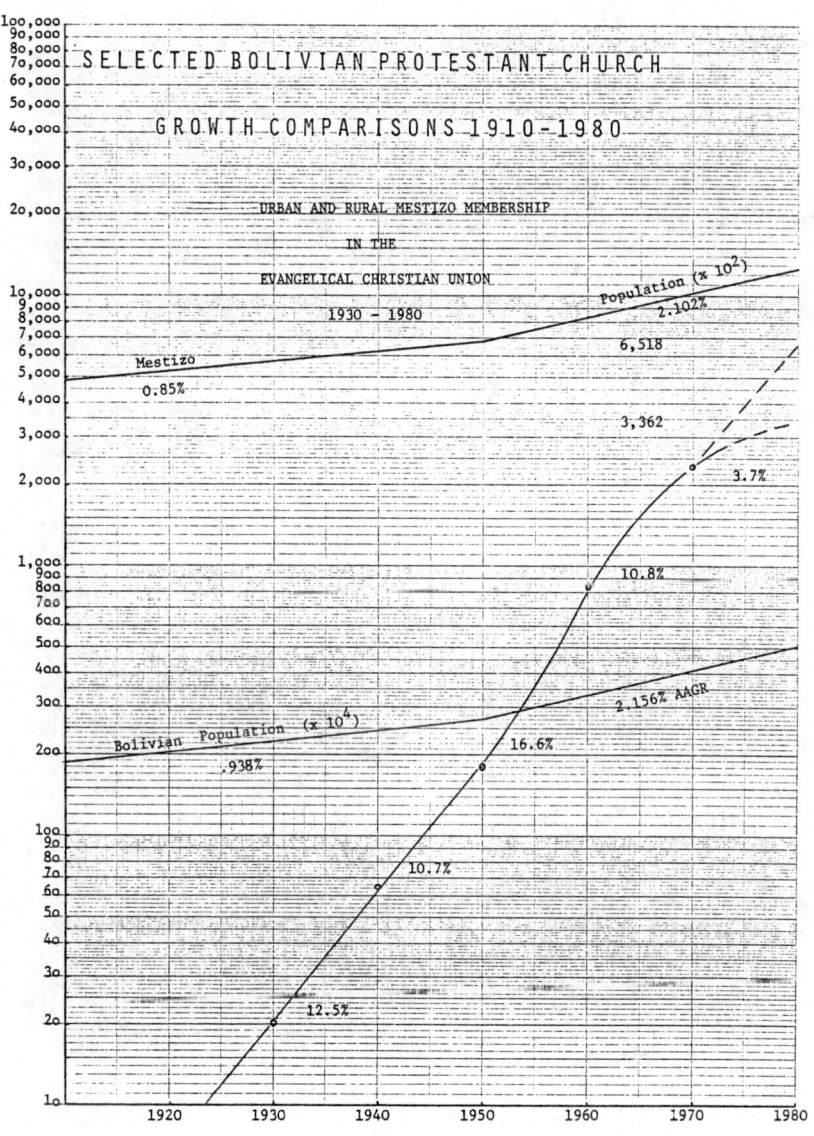

Figure 12

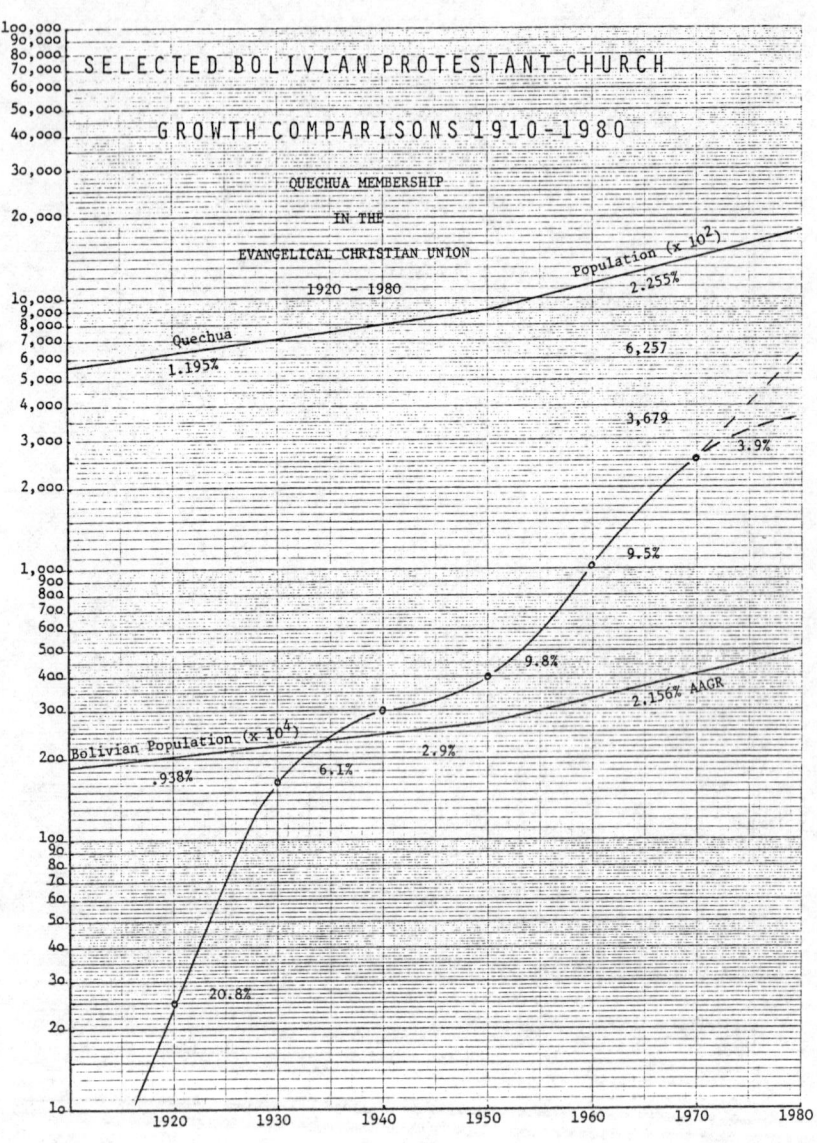

Figure 13

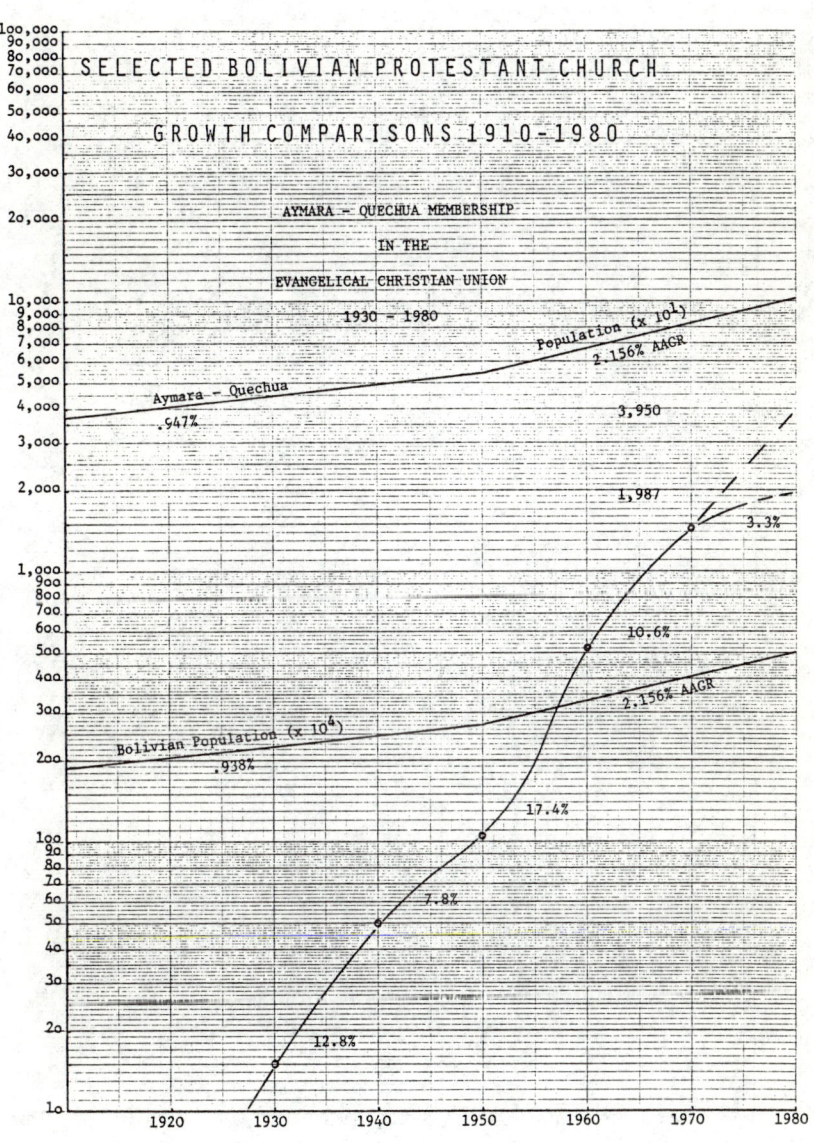

Figure 14

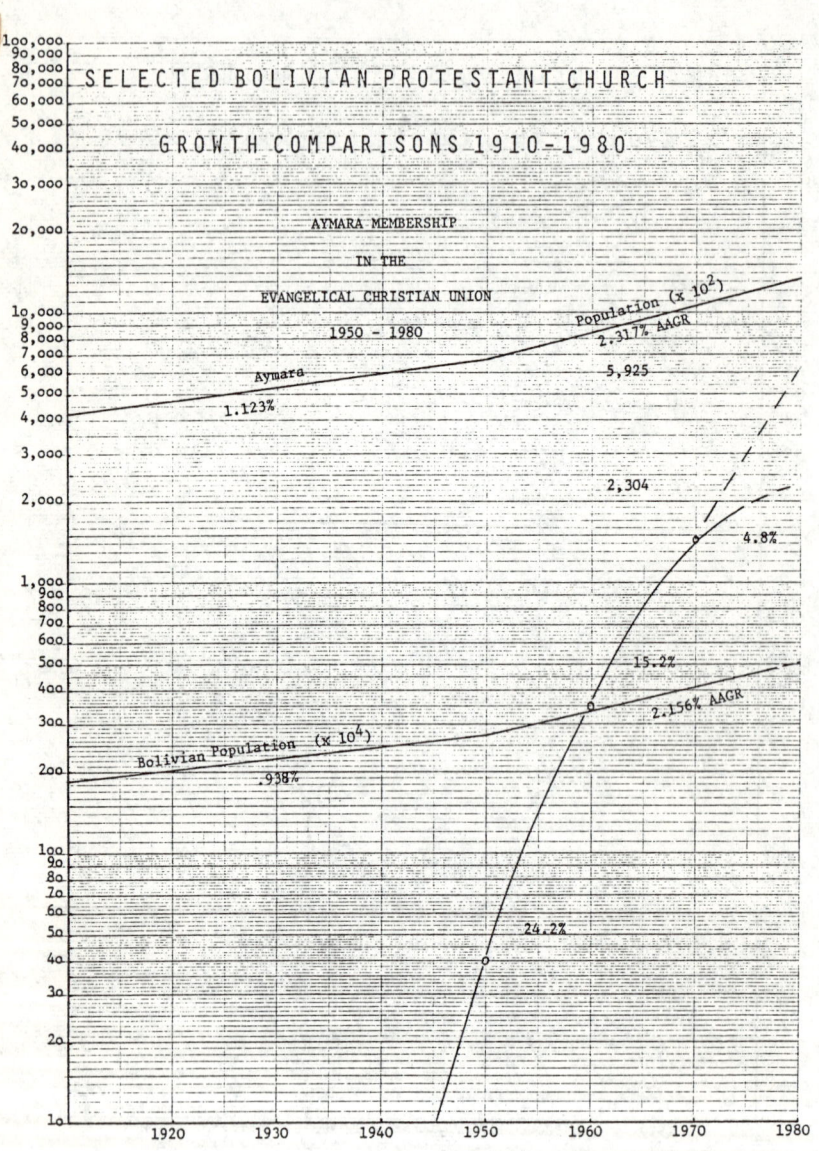

B.

Target Area Maps

TABLE I
NEW ECU AYMARA-QUECHUA CONGREGATIONS

The new Aymara-Quechua congregations formed during the last five years in the target area comprised of five subdirectorates:

a. Challapata, 1st Subdirectorate, Figure 1
```
   Estalza           5    average number of new worshippers
   Avicaya          10
   Totoral          27
   Ticaña            9
   Ckackachaca      21
   Pampa Aullagas   40
   6 Subtotal      112
```

b. Pocoata, 2nd Subdirectorate, Figure 2
```
   Pairumani        10  ⎫
   Ocuri            10  ⎪
   Maragua          10  ⎬  all east of the target area, but
   Kheya-Kheya      10  ⎭  applicable. See Figure 17 under
   4 Subtotal       40     Chapter Three.
```

c. Cochabamba, 6th Subdirectorate, Figure 3
```
   Payuta           30
   Ichukawa         23
   Kaluyo           10
   Challa           60
   Pachateri        20
   Parani           10
   Wilayaque       100
   7 Subtotal      253
```

d. Oruro, 7th Subdirectorate, Figure 4
```
   Chuachuani       24
   Popo             10
   Bombo            40
   Challacollo      30      west of target area, but applicable.
   4 Subtotal      104
```

e. Potosí, 12th Subdirectorate, Figure 5
```
   Belén Pampa      25      Chiacoro              4
   Cutiri           40      Kilpani               4
   Urmiri           80      Kuchawa               4
   Agua Castilla    30      Salinas de Yochalla  30
   Paco Chico      150      Kayara               20
   Ingenio Callada  20      Carlos Machicado     40
   Mojona           20      Caracota             25
                            14 Subtotal         492

         Grand Total        36 churches    1,001 New Worshippers
```

Figure 1

CHALLAPATA, 1st SUBDIRECTORATE

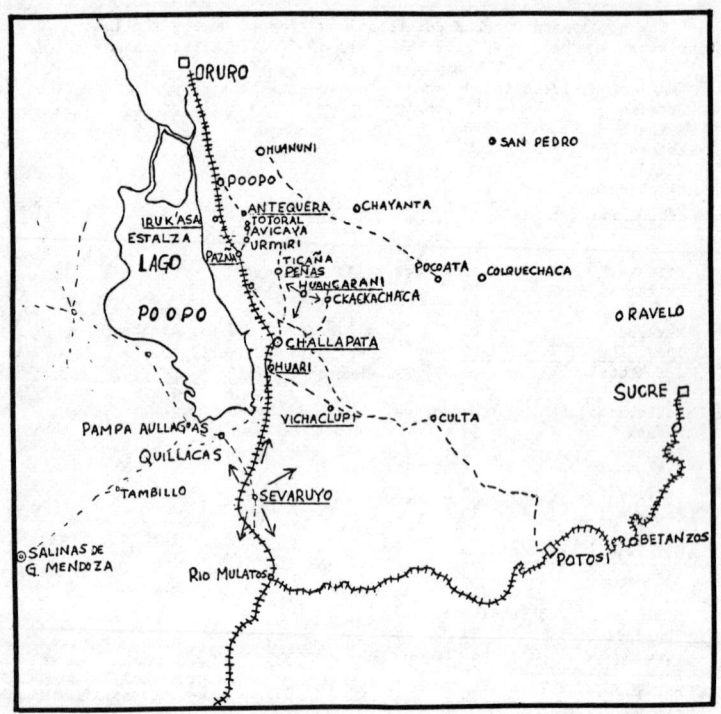

Figure 2

POCOATA, 2nd SUBDIRECTORATE

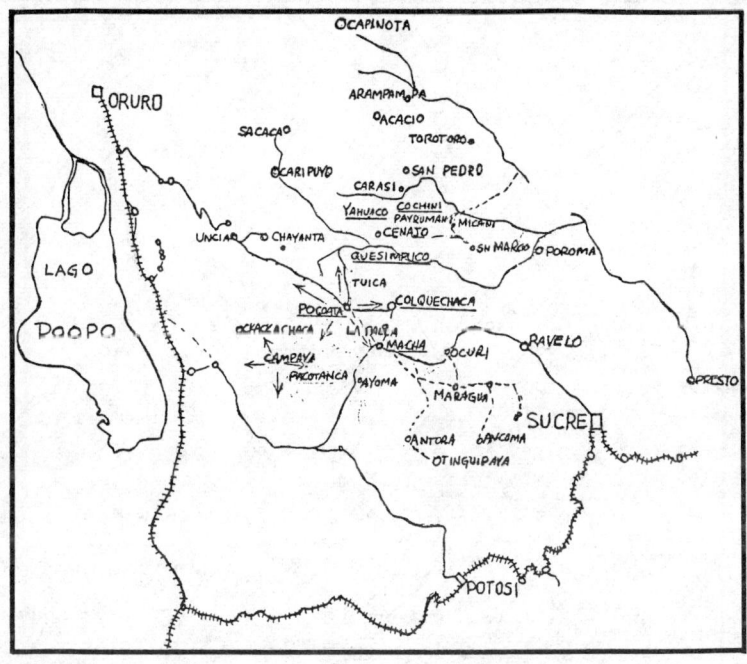

Figure 3

COCHABAMBA, 6th SUBDIRECTORATE

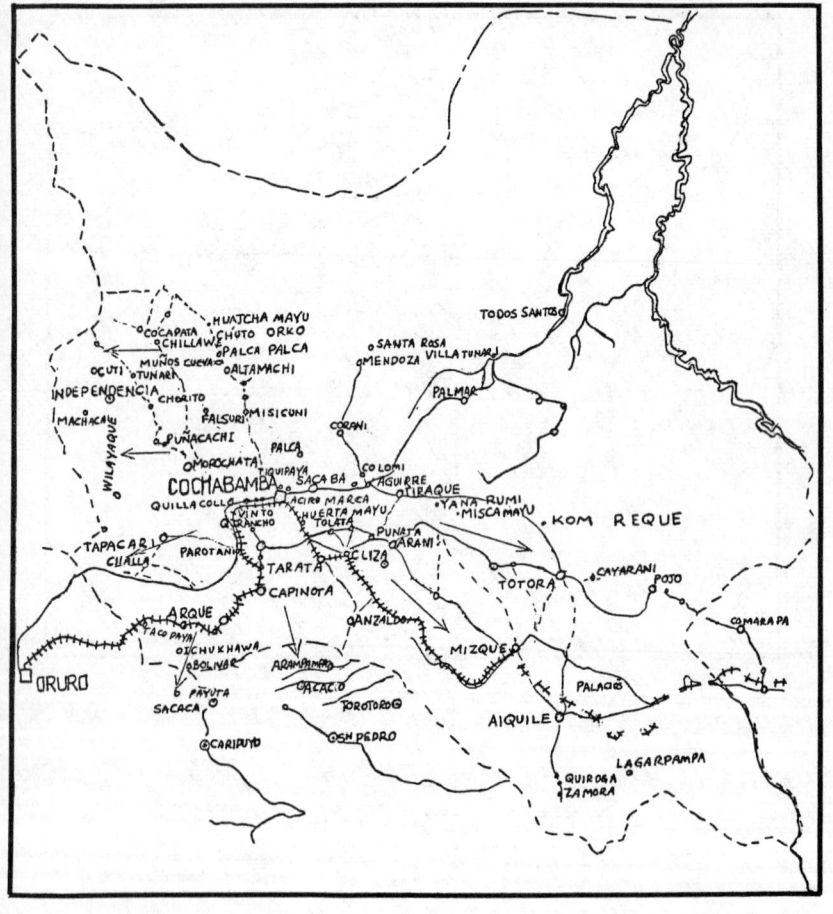

Figure 4

ORURO, 7th SUBDIRECTORATE

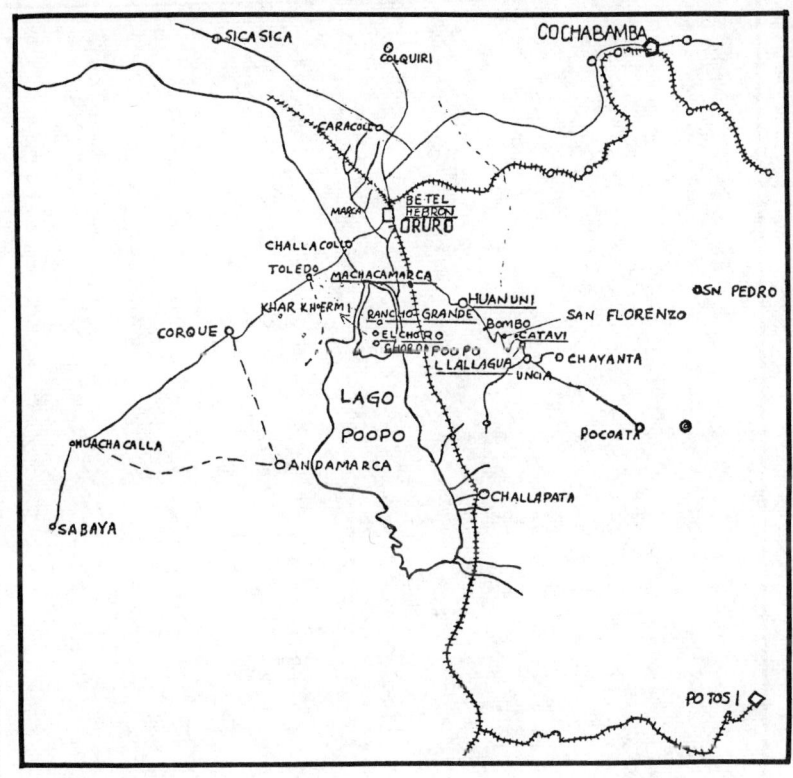

Figure 5

POTOSI, 12th SUBDIRECTORATE

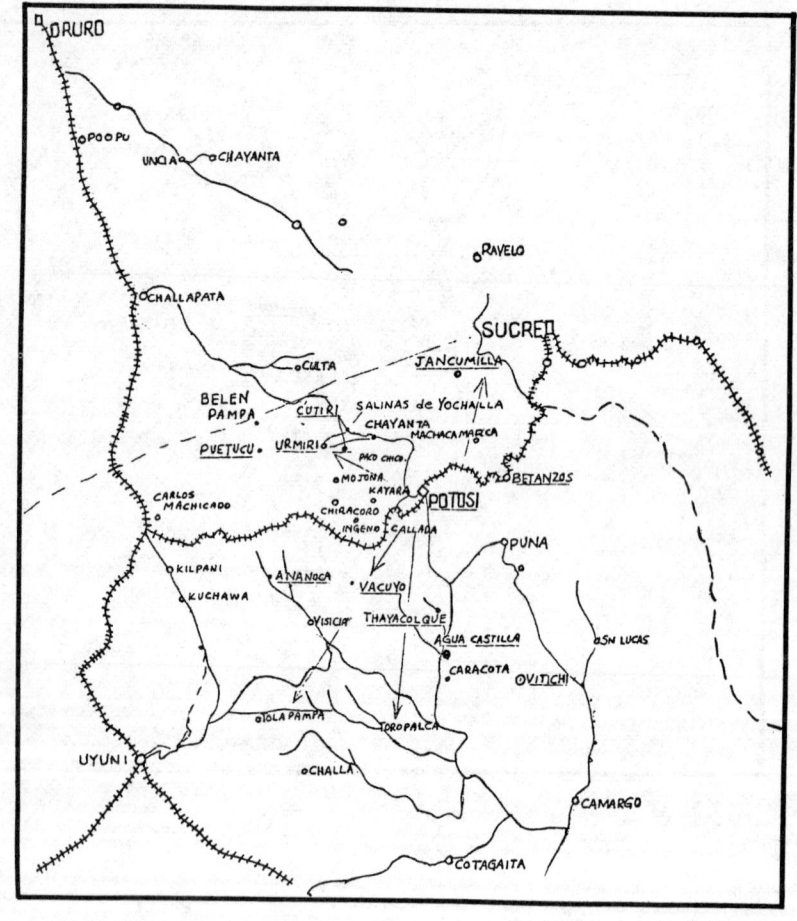

Bibliography

ADAMS, Richard N.
    1962   "Ethnohistoric Research Methods: Some Latin American Features." *Ethnohistory*, 9:179-205.

ALONSO, Isidoro, ed.
    1961   *La Iglesia en Peru y Bolivia*. Madrid, Ochha.

ARISTOTLE
    1953   *Problems*. XVI.10, (Translated by W.S. Hett), Cambridge, Harvard University Press.

AYRES, Francis O.
    1962   *The Ministry of the Laity*. Philadelphia, Westminster.

BAINTON, Roland H.
    1960   *Early Christianity*. Princeton, N.J., Van Nostrand.

BLAUW, Johannes
    1962   *The Missionary Nature of the Church*. Grand Rapids, Eerdmans.

    1974   *The Missionary Nature of the Church*. Grand Rapids, Eerdmans.

BOCKING, Ronald A.H.
    1961   "Has the Day of the Missionary Passed?." London, London Missionary Society.

BONHOEFFER, Dietrich
    1949   *Life Together*. London, SCM Press.

BOSCH, David J.
    1975   "Missiological Developments in South Africa." *Missionalia*. 3:1, April.

BREESE, Gerald, ed.
    1969   *The City in Newly Developing Countries*. Englewood Cliffs, New Jersey, Prentice Hall.

BRIGHT, John
    1953   *The Kingdom of God*. Nashville, Abingdon.

    1967   *The Authority of the Old Testament*. London, SCM Press.

"Bolivia."
    1910   *Encyclopedia Britannica*. Vol. IV:171, Cambridge.

    1959   *Encyclopedia Britannica*. Vol. III:818-19, Chicago.

BROCKHAUS, Der Grosse
    1953   *Bolivien*. Wiesbaden, Eberhard Brockhaus.

BROEK, Jan O.M. and John W. Webb
    1968   *A Geography of Mankind*. New York, McGraw Hill, (Second edition)

BRUNER, Edward M.
    1973   "Kin and Non-Kin." *Urban Anthropology*. Aidan Southall, ed. New York, Oxford University Press.

BUECHLER, Hans C. and Judith Maria Buechler
    1971   *The Bolivian Aymara*. New York, Holt, Rinehart and Winston.

CAREY, William
    1792   *An Enquiry into the Obligations to Use Means for the Conversion of the Hearhens*. London, Carey Kingsgate Press. (New facsimile edition)

CARTER, William E.
    1964   *Aymara Communities and the Bolivian Agrarian Reform*. Gainesville, University of Florida Press.

    1971   *Bolivia. A Profile*. New York, Praeger Publications.

COLE, H.S.D. and Christopher Freeman, Marie Jahoda, K.L.R. Pavitt,
    1973   eds.
             Models of Doom. New York, Universe Books.

COLEMAN, Robert
    1969   *The Master Plan of Evangelism*. Huntington Valley, Pa., Christian Outreach.

COMAS, Juan
    1962   "Bolivia," *Indianist Yearbook*. Mexico, Inter-American Indian Institute.

COOK, Harold R.
    1975   "Who Really Sent the First Missionaries?" *Evangelical Missions Quarterly*. Vol. II, No. 4, 233-240.

COSTAS, Orlando E.
    1974   *The Church and its Mission: A Shattering Critique from the Third World*. Wheaton, Tyndale.

    1976a   "Church Growth and Human Liberation." Mimeographed notes of joint symposium sponsored by the Inter Instrumentality Staff Team on Evangelism of the United Church of Christ and the Latin America Office of the United Church Board for World Ministries, 7 Nov., 1975, New York, Interchurch Center, 475 Riverside Drive, Jan.

    1976b   *Theology of the Crossroads in Contemporary Latin America*. Amsterdam, Rodopi.

DAANE, James
    1973   *The Freedom of God*. Grand Rapids, Eerdmans.

DABBS, Norman H.
    1952   *Dawn Over the Bolivian Hills*. Toronto, Canadian Baptist Foreign Mission Board.

DARK, Philip
    1957   "Methods of Synthesis in Ethnohistory." *Ethnohistory*. 4; 3:231-278.

DAVIES, Howell
    1955   *The South American Handbook*. London, Trade and Travel Publications, Ltd.

DAYTON, Edward R., ed.
    1973   *Mission Handbook: North American Protestant Ministries Overseas*. Monrovia, Missionary Advanced Research and Communications Center (MARC).

    1974   *God's Purpose/Man's Plans, A Workbook*. Monrovia, World Vision International, (MARC)

    1975   *Planning Strategies for Evangelism, A Workbook*. Monrovia, World Vision International, (MARC)

    1976   and Ted Engstrom
              Strategy for Living. Glendale, G/L Regal.

    1977   *Planning Strategies for Evangelism, A Workbook*. Monrovia, World Vision International, (MARC), Second edition.

DELURY, George E., ed.
   1977   *World Almanac and Book of Facts*. New York Newspaper Assn., Inc.

DE RIDDER, Richard R.
   1975   *Discipling the Nations*. Grand Rapids, Baker.

DODD, C.H.
   1936   *The Apostolic Preaching and its Developments*. London, Holder and Stoughton, Ltd.

DOSTAL, W., ed.
   1972   *The Situation of the Indian in South America*. Geneva, World Council of Churches.

EHRLICH, Paul R. and Anne H. Ehrlick
   1970   *Population Resources Environment*. San Francisco, W. H. Freeman and Co.

ELLISON, Craig W.
   1974   *The Urban Mission*. Grand Rapids, Eerdmans.

ENGEL, James F.
   1973   "Accountability for World Evangelization." *Church Growth Bulletin* IX 6:331-4, July.

          and H. Wilbert Norton
   1975   *What's Gone Wrong with the Harvest?* Grand Rapids, Zondervan.

EUROPA
   1975   *Year Book, A World Survey II*. London, Europa Publications, Ltd.

FENTON, William
   1962   "Ethnohistory and its Problems." *Ethnohistory*. 9:1-23.

FEUCHT, Oscar E.
   1974   *Everyone a Minister*. St. Louis, Concordia.

FIFER, J. Valerie
   1972   *Bolivia: Land, Location and Politics since 1825*. Cambridge Latin American Studies, No. 13, Cambridge, University Press.

FORELL, George Wolfgang
   1954   *Faith Active in Love*. Minneapolis, Augsburg.

FOX, Richard G.
   1977   *Urban Anthropology*. Englewood Cliffs, N.J., Prentice Hall.

Bibliography

FREYTAG, Walter
    1957   *The Gospel and the Religions*. London, SCM Press.

FRIGOLI, Bruno
    1975   "In Bolivia: An Evangelistic Movement that Doubles Every Year!" *Today's Christian*. Pasadena, Fuller Evangelistic Association, Sept.

FULLER, W. Harold
    1971   "'Creative Tension' The Church Mission Controversy." *Christianity Today*. 22 Oct.

FURTH, Hans G. and Harry Wachs
    1975   *Thinking Goes to School*. New York, Oxford University Press.

GEE, Donald
    1963   *Spiritual Gifts in the Work of the Ministry Today*. Springfield, Mo., Gospel Publishing House.

GERBER, Vergil
    1973   *God's Way to Keep a Church Going and Growing*. South Pasadena, William Carey Library.

    1976   "Let's Anticipate the Harvest", *Church Growth Bulletin* XII; 4:516-19, Donald A. McGavran, ed., Pasadena, Institute of Church Growth, Fuller Theological Seminary, March.

GETZ, Gene A.
    1974   *Sharpening the Focus of the Church*. Chicago, Moody Press.

GLASSER, A.F.
    1976   "Theology of Mission". SWM Course M610 notes, Winter Quarter, Jan.-Mar., Pasadena, Fuller Theological Seminary.

    1977   "Culture, the Powers and the Spirit." *Missiology* V; 2: 135, April.

GLEN, J. Stanley
    1960   *The Recovery of the Teaching Ministry*. Philadelphia, Westminster.

GLOVER, Robert Hall
    1953   *The Process of World-Wide Missions*. New York, Harper and Bros, (Fourth edition)

GOBLE, Frank G.
    1970   *The Third Force*. New York, Grossman.

GOTHARD, Bill
   1971   "Advanced Seminar in Institute of Basic Youth Conflicts."
            Oak Brook, Ill., Institute of Basic Youth Conflicts.

GREEN, Michael
   1970   *Evangelism in the Early Church*. Grand Rapids, Eerdmans.

GREENWAY, Roger S.
   1973   *An Urban Strategy for Latin America*. Grand Rapids, Baker.

        ed.
   1976   *Guidelines for Urban Church Planting*. Grand Rapids, Baker.

GRUBB, Kenneth G.
   1938   *The West Coast Republics of South America, Review of Ten Years of Evangelical Progress to 1938*. London, World Dominion Press.

GRUBER, Howard E.
   1973   "Courage and Cognitive Growth in Children and Scientists." *Piaget in the Classroom*. Milton Schwebel and Jane Raph, eds., New York, Basic Books.

GULICK, John
   1973   "Urban Anthropology." *Handbook of Social and Cultural Anthropology*. Honigmann, ed., Chicago, Rand McNally.

HAHN, Ferdinand
   1967   "Pre-Easter Discipleship." *The Beginnings of the Church in the New Testament*. Eduard Schweizer, ed., Edinburgh, St. Andrew Press.

HAMILTON, Donald, ed.
   1976   "Just How Healthy is Western Missions? Who Knows?" *ACMC: in Focus*. Vol. I:3, Pasadena, Association of Church Missions Committees, Sept.

HAMILTON, Keith E.
   1962   *Church Growth in the High Andes*. Lucknow, India, University Press.

HANKS, Tom
   1973   "Would Jesus Stoop to Canned Evangelism?" *Eternity*. Sept.

HAUSER, Philip M.
   1965   "Observations on the Urban-Folk and Urban-Rural Dichotomies as Forms of Western Ethnocentrism." *The Study of Urbanization*. Hauser and Schnore, eds., New York, Wiley.

HEATH, Dwight B. and Richard M. Adams
   1965   *Contemporary Cultures and Societies of Latin America*. New York, Random House.

HERODOTUS
   1921   *Herodotus*. I:131, London, Heinemann (Loeb Classical Library).

HODGE, Charles
   1965   *Systematic Theology*. I, Grand Rapids, Eerdmans.

HOLSTEN, W.
   1971   "Warneck, Gustav (1834-1910)," *Concise Dictionary of the Christian World Mission*. Stephen Neill, Gerald H. Anderson and John Goodwin, eds., Nashville, Abingdon.

HOWARD, David M.
   1969   *Hammered as Gold*. New York, Harper and Row.

   1977   *Declare His Glory among the Nations*. Downers Grove, Ill., Inter Varsity Press, (editor).

HUDSPITH, Margarita A.
   1958   *Ripening Fruit*. Harrington Park, N.J., Harrington Press.

JONES, Ezra Earl
   1976   *Strategies for New Churches*. New York, Harper and Row.

JUDGE, E.A.
   1960   *The Social Pattern of the Christian Groups in the First Century*. London, Tyndale Press.

KENNEDY, D. James
   1970   *Evangelism Explosion*. Wheaton, Ill., Tyndale House.

KILINSKI, Kenneth K. and Jerry C. Wofford
   1973   *Organization and Leadership in the Local Church*. Grand Rapids, Zondervan.

KLASSEN, Jacob Peter
   1975   *Fire on the Paramo*. Unpublished M.A. research project submitted to Fuller Theological Seminary, School of World Mission, Pasadena, Fuller Theological Seminary.

KLEIN, Herbert S.
   1969   *Parties and Political Change in Bolivia 1880-1952*. Cambridge, University Press.

KRAFT, C.H.
   1973   "Toward a Christian Ethnotheology." *God, Man and Church Growth*. A.R. Tippett, ed., Grand Rapids, Eerdmans.

KUHNE, Gary
   1976   *The Dynamics of Personal Follow-Up*. Grand Rapids, Zondervan.

LA BARRE, Weston
   1911   *The Aymara Indians of the Lake Titicaca Plateau, Bolivia.*
          J. Alden Mason and Mrs. Dorothy C. Donath, eds., Menasha,
          Wisconsin, American Anthropological Association.

LADD, George Eldon
   1974   *A Theology of the New Testament.* Grand Rapids, Eerdmans.

LATOURETTE, Kenneth Scott
   1938   *A History of Christianity.* II, New York, Harper.

LEWIS, C.S.
   1959   *Mere Christianity.* London, Fontana, (Sixth edition).

LEWIS, Oscar
   1965   "Further Observations on the Folk-Urban Continuum and
          Urbanization with Special Reference to Mexico City."
          The Study of Urbanization. P.M. Hauser and L.F. Schnore,
          eds., New York, Wiley.

LLOYD, John R.
   1973   "Quechua Church Growth." Unpublished paper presented to
          Dr. Kwast for Sociology 405, Granada Heights, Biola, Jan.

   1976a "How You Helped." *Today's Christian.* Pasadena, Fuller
          Evangelistic Association, March, 5,6.

   1976b "Quechua Evangelism." Unpublished project submitted to
          the Fuller Evangelistic Association, Pasadena, Dec., 1-5.

MARTIN, Alvin, ed.
   1974   *The Means of World Evangelization.* South Pasadena,
          William Carey Library.

MARTIN, Ralph
   1964   *Worship in the Early Church.* London, Marshall, Morgan
          and Scott.

MASLOW, Abraham H.
   1964   *Religions, Values and Peak Experiences.* New York, Viking.

MCGAVRAN, Donald A.
   1955   *The Bridges of God.* New York, Friendship Press.

   1970   *Understanding Church Growth.* Grand Rapids, Eerdmans.

   1973   *How to Grow a Church.* Glendale, Regal.

   1976   "Worldwide, Hundreds of Such Movements Occur." *Church
          Growth Bulletin.* Donald A. McGavran, ed., Pasadena,
          Institute of Church Growth, May.

MCGAVRAN, Donald A.
  1977a "The Homogeneous Unit in Mission Theory." Mimeographed article presented to Advanced Church Growth M760 class, Pasadena, Fuller Theological Seminary, School of World Mission, 1 Feb.

  1977b "Healing and the Evangelization of the World." Mimeographed article presented to Advanced Church Growth M760 class, Pasadena, Fuller Theological Seminary, School of World Mission, 8 Mar.

  1977c "Turn Over, Go on Twenty Miles, and Do it Again." Mimeographed paper given in M760 Advanced Church Growth Class, Pasadena, Fuller Theological Seminary, School of World Mission, Winter Quarter, Jan.-Mar.

MCINTOSH, Stewart
  1971 "Ratio of Neglect." *Regions Beyond*. First Quarter, XXII; I:6,7, Philadelphia, Regions Beyond Missionary Union

MCNEE, Peter
  1976 *Crucial Issues in Bangladesh*. South Pasadena, William Carey Library.

MCQUILKIN, J. Robertson
  1974 *Measuring the Church Growth Movement*. Chicago, Moody Press.

MAGBANUA, Fred M.
  1971 "Effective Evangelism through LEGS." Lay Evangelistic Group Studies, Evangelical Missions Information Service, II:4, Nov.

MEADOWS, Donella H., Dennis L. Meadows, Jorgen Randers, William W. Behrens III
  1972 *The Limits to Growth*. New York, Universe Books.

MESAROVIC, Mihajlo and Eduard Pestel
  1974 *Mankind at the Turning Point*. New York, E.P. Dutton and Co., Inc.

MINER, Horace
  1965 *The Primitive City of Timbuctu*. New York, Doubleday.

MITCHELL, J. Clyde, ed.
  1969 *Social Networks in Urban Situation*. Manchester, University Press.

MONTGOMERY, J.W.
    1966   "The Theologian's Craft." *Concordia Theological Monthly.* XXXVII., Feb.

MORRIS, Leon
    1960   *The Spirit of the Living God.* Chicago, Inter Varsity Press.

MOTT, John R.
    1900   *The Evangelization of the World in this Generation.* Chicago, Missionary Campaign Library.

MOULE, C.F.D.
    1961   *Worship in the New Testament.* London, Lutterworth.

MURDOCK, George P.
    1961   *Outline of Cultural Materials.* New Haven Human Relations Area Files, Inc.

MURPHY, Edward F.
    1975   *Spiritual Gifts and the Great Commission.* South Pasadena, Mandate Press.

    1976   "The Missionary Society as an Apostolic Team." *An International Review.* IV:1, Jan., 103-118.

MYERS, Paul F.
    1975   "1975 World Population Data Sheet." Washington, D.C., Population Reference Bureau, Inc.

    1977   "1977 World Population Data Sheet." Washington, D.C., Population Reference Bureau, Inc., Personal telephone conversation, 7 Feb.

NEE, Watchman
    1961   *What Shall This Man Do?* London, Victory Press.

NORDYKE, Quentin
    1972   *Animistic Aymaras and Church Growth.* Newberg, Oregon, Barclay Press.

OLIVER, Dennis Mackintosh
    1973   *Make Disciples.* Unpublished dissertation, Pasadena, Fuller Theological Seminary, School of World Mission.

ORR, J. Edwin
    1973   *The Flaming Tongue: Evangelical Awakenings, 1900.* Chicago, Moody Press.

Bibliography

ORTIZ, Juan Carlos
   1975   *Call to Discipleship*. Plainfield, N.J., Logos International.

ORTLUND, Ray
   1974   *Lord, Make My Life a Miracle*. Glendale, Regal.

OSBORNE, Harold
   1952   *Indians of the Andes, Aymaras and Quechuas*. London, Routledge and Paul.

   1964   *Bolivia, a Land Divided*. New York, Oxford University Press, (Third edition).

PALMER, Bernard
   1976   *Peoples Church on the Go*. Wheaton, Victor Books, a division of Scripture Press Publications, Inc.

PAYNE, Will and Charles T.W. Wilson
   1904   *Missionary Pioneering in Bolivia with Some Account of Work in Argentina*. London, H.A. Raymond.

PETERS, George W.
   1970   *Saturation Evangelism*. Grand Rapids, Zondervan.

PHILLIPS, David B.
   1968   *Protestantism in Bolivia to 1952*. Unpublished M.A. thesis submitted to the Department of History, Calvary, Alberta, University of Calgary.

PONCE, Garcia, Jaime y Oscar Uzin Fernandez
   1968   *El Clero en Bolivia. Sondeos, No. 59, 1970*. Cuernavaca, Mexico, Centro Intercultural de Documentación (CIDOC).

PRIMOV, George
   1974   "Aymara-Quechua Relations in Puno." *Class and Ethnicity in Perú*. Pierre Van Den Berghe, ed., Leiden, E.J. Brill.

READ, William R., V.M. Monterroso and Harmon A. Johnson
   1969   *Latin American Church Growth*. Grand Rapids, Eerdmans.

REDFIELD, Robert
   1941   *The Folk Culture of Yucatán*. Chicago, University of Chicago Press.

   1947   "The Folk Society." *American Journal of Sociology*. 52:293-308.

RENGSTORF, Karl Heinrich
   1964   "*Apostolos.*" *Theological Dictionary of the New Testament.* I, Gerhard Kittel, ed., Grand Rapids, Eerdmans, 398-447.

RICHARDSON, Don
   1974   *Peace Child.* Glendale, Regal.

RICHARDSON, Miles and Barbara Bode
   1969   *Urban and Societal Features of Popular Medicine in Puntarenas, Costa Rica.* Working paper No. 3, Ser. 1, Latin American Studies Institute, Lousiana State University.

SAPIR, Edward
   1958   "Time Perspective in Aboriginal American Culture." *Selected Writings of Edward Sapir.* D.G. Mandelbaum, ed., Berkeley, University of California Press.

SCHAEFFER, Francis A.
   1969   *Death in the City.* Chicago, Inter Varsity Press.

SCHULLER, Robert H.
   1967   *Move Ahead with Possibility Thinking.* Old Tappan, N.J., Revell Spire Books

   1974   *Your Church Has Real Possibilities.* Glendale, Regal.

SCHULZE, Gunter
   1976   "Quechuas on the March in Ecuador." *Church Growth Bulletin* XII:5, Donald A. McGavran, ed., Pasadena, Institute of Church Growth, Fuller Theological Seminary, May, 529-531.

SEATON, Ronald S. and Edith B.
   1976   *Here's How: Health Education by Extension.* South Pasadena, William Carey Library.

SILVOSO, Edgardo
   1974   "The Naranjo People Movement in Argentina." *Church Growth Bulletin.* XI:4, Institute of Church Growth, Pasadena, Fuller Theological Seminary, 399-407.

   1977   "Rosario Plan." Prayer letter of Luis Palau Evangelistic Team, Santa Clara, California, Overseas Crusades, 15 Mar.

SMALLEY, William A.
   1967   "Cultural Implications of an Indigenous Church." *Readings in Missionary Anthropology.* South Pasadena, William Carey Library.

SMALLEY, William A., ed.
1974   *Readings in Missionary Anthropology.* South Pasadena, William Carey Library.

SMITH, Ebbie C.
1976   *A Manual for Church Growth Surveys.* South Pasadena, William Carey Library, Preliminary edition.

SMITH, James C.
1976   *Without Crossing Barriers, The Homogeneous Unit Concept in the Writings of Donald Anderson McGavran.* A dissertation presented to the faculty of the School of World Mission, Fuller Theological Seminary, Pasadena.

SMITH, Mont W.
1976   *Homogeneity and American Church Growth: A Case Study.* Unpublished dissertation, Pasadena, Fuller Theological Seminary, School of World Mission.

SMITH, W. Douglas, Jr.
1969   *Grace and Law from Adam to Moses in Pauline Thought.* An unpublished thesis submitted in partial fulfillment of the requirements for a M.A. in Biblical Studies at Trinity Evangelical Divinity School, Deerfield, Ill., June.

1972   "Where Are We Going in the Seventies?" A mimeographed paper given to the 34th Field Conference of the Andes Evangelical Mission, Cochabamba, Bolivia, Aug.

1973   "El Primer Informe del Departamento de Datos Historicos." A mimeographed statistical report of the churches, pastors and membership comprising the Evangelical Christian Union, Cochabamba, Bolivia, 18 Aug.

1974a   "Status of Christianity, Country Profile: Bolivia." Monrovia, World Vision International, (MARC), July.

1974b   "¿Empieza Recién la Cruzada 74 Palau?" *El Faro.* Cochabamba, Bolivia (la quincena de noviembre).

1975   "Full Circle Evangelism Process." *Power Pack Bible Study.* Fuller Evangelistic Association, Dec.

1976a   "The Major Differences between the Old Testament and the New Testament Are Cultural not Theological." Joint paper with Robert C. Douglas written for M730 Christianity and Culture I, Dr. C.H. Kraft, Pasadena, Fuller Theological Seminary, School of World Mission, Feb.

SMITH, W. Douglas, Jr.
   1976b "The Apostolic Band and the Local Church in the Spiral Evangelism Process." Unpublished paper submitted to Professor Arthur Glasser for Theology of Mission, M610, Pasadena, Fuller Theological Seminary, School of World Mission, Mar.

   1976c "Church Growth Masterplanning." Pasadena, Fuller Evangelistic Association, Department of Church Growth, Sept.

   1976d "Paul's Use of *Stoicheia Tou Kosmou* for Culture." A xeroxed study submitted to Dr. E.F. Harrison for Reading and Conference Course M791, Fall Quarter, Pasadena, Fuller Theological Seminary, School of World Mission, Dec

SNYDER, Howard A.
   1975 *The Problem of Wine Skins*. Downers Grove, Ill., Inter Varsity Press.

SPEER, Robert E.
   1902 *Missionary Principles and Practice*. New York, Revell.

   1912 *South American Problems*. New York, Student Volunteer Movement for Foreign Missions.

STEDMAN, Ray C.
   1972 *Body Life*. Glendale, Regal.

   1974 *Birth of the Body*. Santa Ana, Vision House.

   1975 *Authentic Christianity*. Waco, Texas, Word Books.

STOTT, John R.W.
   1975 *Christian Mission in the Modern World*. Downers Grove, Ill., Inter Varsity Press.

STURTEVANT, Wm.C.
   1966 "Anthropology, History and Ethnohistory." *Ethnohistory*. 13:1-51.

SUNDKLER, Bengt
   1960 *The Christian Ministry in Africa*. London, SCM Press.

TIPPETT, A.R.
   1965 "Biblical Basis of Church Growth." *Church Growth Bulletin*. I; 3:28,29.

   1967 *Solomon Islands Christianity*. South Pasadena, William Carey Library.

TIPPETT, A.R.
　1970　*Church Growth and the Word of God.* Grand Rapids, Eerdmans.

　1973a　*Aspects of Pacific Ethnohistory.* South Pasadena, William Carey Library.

　1973b　*Verdict Theology in Missionary Theory.* South Pasadena, William Carey Library.

　1974　"Missiology, a New Discipline." *The Means of World Evangelization.* Alvin Martin, ed., South Pasadena, William Carey Library.

　1975　"The Evangelization of Animists." *Let the Earth Hear His Voice.* J.D. Douglas, ed., Lausanne, ICOWE, 16-20 July, 1974, Minneapolis, World Wide Publications.

TOWNS, Elmer L.
　1973　*Is the Day of the Denomination Dead?* Nashville, Thomas Nelson, Inc.

TSCHOPIK, Harry, Jr.
　1951　*The Aymara of Chucuito Peru.* Anthropological papers of the American Museum of Natural History, Vol. 44, Part 2: Vol. 1, *Magic.* New York, The American Museum of Natural History.

UDA, Susumu
　1974　"Biblical Authority and Evangelism." ICOWE, *Let the Earth Hear His Voice.* J.D. Douglas, ed., 1975, 88-93, Minneapolis, World Wide Publishers.

VAN GENNEP, Arnold
　1961　*The Rites of Passage.* Chicago, Chicago University Press.

VAN LEEUWEN, Arend Th.
　1964　*Christianity in World History.* New York, Scribner's Sons.

WAGNER, C. Peter
　1967　*Defeat of the Bird God.* South Pasadena, William Carey Library.

　1970　*The Protestant Movement in Bolivia.* South Pasadena, William Carey Library.

　1971a　*Frontiers in Missionary Strategy.* Chicago, Moody Press.

　1971b　"Training in the Streets." *Christianity Today.* 6 Aug., 5-8.

WAGNER, C. Peter
  1972   "Fierce Pragmatism in Missions - Carnal or Consecrated."
         Christianity Today. 8 Dec., 13-18.

  1973a "The Babylonian Captivity of the Christian Mission."
         Unpublished paper presented to EFMA-IFMA AERM Study Conference, Nov. 26-30, Overland Park, Kansas.

  1973b *Look Out! The Pentecostals Are Coming.* Carol Stream,
         Ill., Creation House.

  1974a "Sharpening Issues in Church Growth." Mimeographed paper
         circulated at Evangelical Foreign Missions Association
         Mission Executives Retreat, Winona Lake, Indiana,
         30 Sept.-3 Oct.

  1974b *Stop the World I Want to Get On.* Glendale, Regal.

  1976a *Your Church Can Grow.* Glendale, Regal.

  1976b "Guidelines for Making Church Growth Calculation."
         Four mimeographed sheets for students, Pasadena, Fuller
         Theological Seminary, School of World Mission and Fuller
         Evangelistic Association.

  1976c "How I See It." *Today's Christian.* Pasadena, Fuller
         Evangelistic Association, Mar.

  1977   *Culturally Homogeneous Churches and American Social
         Pluralism: Some Religious and Ethical Implications.*
         Unpublished Ph D. dissertation presented to the faculty
         of the Graduate School of the University of Southern
         California, Los Angeles.

WEIL, Thomas E.
  1974   *Area Handbook for Bolivia.* Washington, D.C., U.S.
         Government Printing Office, U.S. Department of the Army.

WHITTAKER, Alfred A.
  1977   "Saying 'God Loves You' to a Starving Man." *Christianity
         Today.* April 1, XXI;13:17-21.

WILKERSON, David
  1974   *The Vision.* Dallas, Pyramid.

WINTER, Ralph D.
  1966   "Gimmickitis." *Church Growth Bulletin.* II;3:126-8,
         Institute of Church Growth, Fuller Theological Seminary,
         Jan.

WINTER, Ralph D.
- 1970a "The New Missions and the Mission of the Church." *The Warp and the Woof, Organizing for Mission.* Ralph D. Winter and R. Pierce Beaver, eds., South Pasadena, William Carey Library, Jan.

- 1970b "The Fate of Missions." *The Twenty Five Unbelievable Years 1945-1969.* South Pasadena, William Carey Library, 4:47-73.

- 1972a "Quality or Quantity?" *Crucial Issues in Missions Tomorrow.* Donald A. McGavran, ed., Chicago, Moody Press.

- 1972b "The Planting of Younger Missions." *Church/Mission Tensions Today.* C. Peter Wagner, ed., Chicago, Moody Press.

- 1973 "The Two Structures of God's Redemptive Mission." Address to All-Asia Mission Consultation, Seoul, Korea, 27 Aug. - 1 Sept. *Missiology.* II:1, Jan., 1974, 121-139.

- 1974a "Seeing the Task Graphically." *Evangelical Missions Quarterly.* X;1:11-24, Wheaton, Evangelical Missions Information Service.

- 1974b "The Two Structures of God's Redemptive Mission." *Missiology.* II;1:121-139.

- 1975a "The Highest Priority: Cross-Cultural Evangelism." *Let the Earth Hear His Voice.* J.D. Douglas, ed., ICOWE, 16-20 July, 1974, 225-232, Minneapolis, World Wide Publications.

- 1975b "The Historical Development of the Christian Movement." Course 651, History I, Fall Quarter, Fuller Theological Seminary, School of World Mission, Sept.-Dec.

- 1977 "The Grounds for a New Thrust in World Mission." Opening Address at Oct., 1976 IFMA/EFMA Executive Retreat and Chapter 1 in new book: *Evangelical Missions Tomorrow.* Pasadena, William Carey Library.

WRIGHT, G. Ernest
- 1950 *The Old Testament Against its Environment.* London, SCM Press.

- 1952 *God Who Acts, Biblical Theology as Recital.* London, SCM Press.

- 1954 "The Old Testament: a Bulwark of the Church against Paganism." *Occasional Bulletin.* New York, Missionary Research Library.

Index

Acculturation, 33, 84
Adventist, Seventh Day (SDA), 52-53
Age Sex Pyramid, 10-11; frequency distribution, 28
Allan, George and Mary, 115
ALFALIT (Latin American Literacy and Literature Movement), 112, 135, 137
Altiplano (highland), 110
America, North and South, 34
Andean Communications Center, 112
Andes Evangelical Mission (AEM), 3, 28, 30, 45-49, 52-53, 59, 62, 99-100, 102, 105-107, 111, 134, 136, 138
Animism, animistic background, 65, 98
Animists, Ripe, 55-57, 105
Apostoloi, apostolic bands, 82, 84, 88, 90
Aristotle, 24
Asians, 52, 56
Assemblies of God, 24, 26-27, 52
Association of Church Missions Committees (ACMC), 5
Average Annual Growth Rate (AAGR), 7, 16-20, 23-24, 31, 33, 35, 45, 53
AAGR Time Graph, 20-21, 99, 110, 112-114, 117, 126, 133
Aymara-Quechua, 37-38, 41-42, 44-45, 53-55, 97-101, 104-106, 112, 114-115
Aymara(s), speaking, 6, 31, 37-38, 41-42, 44-45, 52-55, 97-100, 102, 113, 122
Ayore, 71

Baptists, Canadian, 10, 52-53, 99, 112
Black, 37-38
Blauw, Johannes, 77, 80, 167
Bolivia, 3-5, 10-11, 16, 22, 30-31, 39, 43-46, 50-52, 56, 58, 62, 98-100, 102-103, 114-115, 126
Bolivian Indian Mission, 3
Bonhoeffer, D., 86, 167
Boundaries, ally; Demographic, 100, 126; Ethnic, 101, 126; Geographic, ally, 100-101, 126
Brazil, 33

Campesino, peasant, 31-32, 120
Carey, William, 58, 67, 74, 82, 168
Carangas, 112-113

Census, 30
Chaco War, 31, 53
Charisma, 86
Chile, 25, 33
Cholo, 121, 126, 129-130
Christians, total, 56-57;
   Catholic, 56; Committed,
   56; Nominal, 56-57, 62;
   Protestant, 56; Spanish
   Catholicism, 98, 104
Christian Nationals' Evangelism Commission (CNEC), 112,
   135, 137
Church, health clues, 9, 20,
   22
Church, indigenous, 52;
   Modality, 81, 89-91, 93;
   Sodality, 87, 89-91, 93
Church, national, 4, 56, 58,
   62, 77
Cities, nine capital, 20, 31,
   33, 38, 54-55; Cobija, 103;
   Cochabamba, 100, 103, 116;
   La Paz, 103, 116; Oruro,
   100, 103, 116; Potosi, 99-
   100, 104; Large, 31; Santa
   Cruz, 31, 33, 103; Sucre,
   100, 103-104; Tarija, 103;
   Trinidad, 31, 103
COMBASE, Bolivian Evangelical
   Social Action Commission,
   112, 135, 137
Communicators, maximum, 57,
   60
Contextualize, 9, 58, 73, 100
Cook, Harold R., 76, 81, 89,
   169
Costas, Orlando, 58, 105, 169
Culture(s), 65-66, 68-69, 72
Czechoslovakia, 31

Daane, James, 69, 169
Dayton, Edward A., 65, 97
Demographers, 28, 100, 117
Demographic, ally, data, 29
Departments (States), Nine;
   Beni, Cochabamba,
   Chuquisaca, La Paz, Oruro,
   Pando, Potosi, Santa Cruz,
   Tarija, 31, 33

Diakonia, 8
Directorate, Regional;
   Challapata, Pocoala,
   Andamarca, Camiri, Aiquile,
   Cochabamba, Oruro,
   Magdalena, Chuquisaca, La
   Paz, Santa Ana, Potosi,
   Chapare, Corque, Camargo,
   Santa Cruz, 43
Disciple, Disciples, 82-83;
   Discipling (perfecting),
   84, 85; Discipleship, 86,
   88
Distribution(s), 25-26, 100
Doubling Time Strategy, 18,
   58, 97, 107, 111, 115, 132

Ecuador, Orian, 99, 112-114
Engel, James F., 73, 84, 105,
   170
Equipping, 85-89, 106-108,
   110-111
Ethnic Group(s), 23, 30;
   Subtotals and trends, 34-
   44
Ethnohistorical, 29
Ethno-Linguistic(ly), grid
   divisions, 35, 44, 54-55,
   100
Europe, 31
Evangelical Christian Union
   (ECU), 3, 5, 10, 17, 23-
   28, 30, 39-43, 45-46, 49,
   52-53, 59, 62, 99-102, 105,
   111-112, 115, 132-136, 138,
   156-161
Evangelical Union of South
   America (EUSA), 3, 43, 49,
   100
Evangelism, four types
   defined, 10-13; E_0 internal
   conversion and nurture, 10,
   51, 105; E_1 expansion conversion near neighbors, 51,
   105, 110; extension in
   church planting, 12; E_2
   bridging conversion of
   similar, 51, 56-57, 105,
   120; E_3 bridging conversion
   of unsimilar, 12, 51, 56-

57, 105, 110; effective follow up, 84; 3-P, presence, proclamation, persuasion, 83, 85, 87, 89, 108
Every Home Literature Crusade, 112, 137

Foreign, 37-38, 54-55; Missions, missionaries, 52, 57
Frigoli, Bruno, 110, 122, 171
Fuller, W. Harold, 76, 171

Gerber, Vergil, 116, 126, 171
Germany, 16, 32
Glasser, Arthur F., 66, 70, 88, 171
Glover, Robert Hall, 67, 171
Gothard, Bill, 76, 172
Graphs, 14, 22
Great Commission, 8
Green Lake, 76
Greenway, Roger S., 117, 130, 172
Growth, biological, 9, 16, 18, 20, 23-24, 26
Growth, comparisons, 20
Growth, conversion, 9, 18; external, 84; internal, 84
Growth, negative, 9
Growth, net, 10
Growth, population, 24
Growth, quantitative, qualitative, and organic, 8-9, 13, 84
Growth, transfer, 9-10
Growth, various types: single-congregational, 10; denominational, 10; cross-cultural, 10
Guarani, 37-38, 41-42, 44-45, 53-55

Hanks, Tom, 86, 172
Hamilton, Keith, 6, 50, 97, 172
Heterogeneous, -eity, 34, 125
Highlands, Andean, 31

Hinge Year, 33
Homogeneous, groups, units (HU), 3, 14, 28, 30, 34-36, 39, 58, 101, 114
Howard, Dave, 88, 105, 173
Hudspith, Margarita A., 50, 173

Identity, Six Self, 87
Iglesia Nacional Evangelica Latino Americana (INELA), 24, 26-27, 52-53
Indian population, 31
Indio, Indian, 120
Independence, 18, 25, 98
Infantile mortality, 31
Institution, life cycle, 60
International Congress on World Evangelization (ICOWE), 35

Jerusalem, 88
Jews, 52
Judson, Adoniram, 82

Klassen, Jacob Peter, 45, 173
Kraft, Charles, 65, 68-69, 73, 77

Latin America, 34
Latourette, Kenneth Scott, 90, 174
Lausanne, Int'l Congress on World Evangelization, 35, 74
Leaders, -ship, five classes, 25, 28, 86, 87
Lewis, C. S., 68, 174
Lloyd, John, 5, 100, 109-111, 136
Luther, Martin, 69, 90

McGavran, Donald A., 5, 7, 14, 25, 33-34, 39, 59, 81, 84, 86, 91-92, 122-123
McIntosh, Stewart, 45, 175

Index

McNee, Peter, 51, 176
Maslow, Abraham H., 66, 174
Melting Pot, model, 34
Mestizo, 31-32, 37-38, 41-42, 45, 53-55, 58, 98, 116, 120-122, 124, 126-127, 129-131
Methodists, 10, 52-53
Methodology, church growth, 31; diachronic, 30; synchronic, 31; upstreaming, 29
Missions Advanced Research and Communication Center (MARC), 35, 52, 61, 125
Mission(s), 57, 123; agency, 91; apparatus, 62; body, 84; foreign, 77; paternalism, 76; protestant, 67; own new national, third world, 77, 92, 106; sodality, -ies, 87, 90-91; strategy, 97
Missionary, -ies, 76, 89
Modality, church, 87, 89-90
Montero, Tito, 111, 136
Mott, John R., 77, 176
Murphy, Ed, 76, 81-82, 88, 176

Nee, Watchmen, 70-71, 176
Neesima, 71
Non-Christians (unreached), 57; animists, 57; syncretists, 57
Nordyke, Quentin, 101, 105, 110, 176
Nurture, Christian, 45, 47-48, 57

Oil money, 34
Oliver, Dennis, 80, 176
Omnipotence, 68
Ortlund, Raymond, 80, 177
Ortiz, Juan Carlos, 86, 177
Orientation, rural, 38; urban, 54-55
Orr, J. Edwin, 57, 122, 176

Palau, Luis, 116, 123, 126, 136
Park Street Congregational Church, 77
Paternalism, 76
Pencille, Bill, 71, 74
Pentecostals, Assemblies of God, 10, 24, 26-27, 52
Peters, George, 86, 177
Percentages, 25
Perfecting, 84
Phillips, David B., 50, 177
Physician, skilled, 30
Plymouth Brethren, 3
Population, Bolivian, 7, 16, 30-31, 35, 44, 52, 57-58, 65; density, rural, 100-101; urban, 31
Population Reference Bureau, 7, 16
Portuguese neighbors, 31
Primov, George, 98, 100, 177
Priorities, establish, 30, 65, 75, 91, 97
Projection(s), faith, 112-114
Protestant, movement, 30, 52-56, 58, 60, 67, 98

Quechua(s), speaking, 6, 31, 37-38, 41-42, 45, 53-55, 98-102, 109, 115

Radio Station, *Cruz del Sur*, 111
Rate, birth, 31; death, 31
Rate of Change (slope), 9, 15, 22
Ratios, 25; Ratios for correction of data, 33
Read, William, 5, 50
Receptivity, 4, 30
Renewal, revival, 57
Research, -ing, and Training Center, 29, 60
Resistance, 30; receptivity axis, trends, 33, 45
Resettlements, lowland, 20, 33
Resources, 4

Revolution, Bolivia's 1952, 99
Richardson, Don, 73, 84, 178
Roman Catholic, 20, 52, 55-56, 98
Ruival, Julio Cesar, 121, 123, 125

Schaeffer, Francis, 69, 178
Schuller, Robert, 58
Semi-Logarithmic Graph, 22-24, 112
Shaliach, 80
Silvoso, Ed, 84, 116, 178
Smith, Dr. Paul, 135
Smith, Ebbie, 14-15, 20
Smith, W. D., Jr., 35, 39, 56, 66, 76-77, 100, 116, 121, 179-180
Sodalities, voluntary second commitment, 13
Sodality, missionary structure, 82, 87
Sogaard, Viggo, 73
Spanish conquerors, 31
Statistics, irregular, 7; lumping, 10; problems, 17; sample size, 17; probability, 17; frequency of observation, 17; expansion growth, 17
Stedman, Ray, 81-82, 84, 86, 180
Stew Pot model, 35
Stoicheia, 66
Stott, John, 74, 77, 84, 88, 105, 180
Synchronization, growing, 115
Syndrome, St. John's, 23
Syncretists, -tism (Christo-pagans), 55-57, 98, 100, 105-106

Taylor, Hudson, 82
Theological Education by Extension (TEE), 111

Theology, monocultural, 65
Three Billion, 67, 75
Tippett, Alan R., 9, 13, 30, 50, 61, 84, 87
Towns, Elmer, 60, 181
Trend(s), 1, 4, 20, 22, 30; population totals and trends, 31; to 1980 and beyond, 52
Tschopik, Harry, Jr., 104, 181

United States, 31
Uda, Susumu, 69, 181
Unreached, 65%, 55, 57, 59, 65, 74, 115, 122, 124, 139
Upstreaming, 29

Van Gennep, rites of passage, 84, 181
Van Leeuwen, Arend Th., 66, 181

Wagner, C. Peter, 5, 13, 22-23, 34-36, 50, 59, 71, 76-77, 84, 86, 88, 90-91, 97, 105, 121
Weil, Thomas E., 120, 126, 130, 182
White population, 31, 37-38
Wiebe, Ron, 111, 136
Winter, Ralph D., 13, 20-21, 35, 45, 51, 56, 67, 75, 77, 82, 90, 92, 135
Workers, class two, 25, 28; class four ECU, 53
Workshop(s), 3, 14, 58, 62, 111
World, Western, 51

YMCA, 90